HOLLYWOOD
·AND THE·
SUPERNATURAL

HOLLYWOOD
• AND THE •
SUPERNATURAL

BRAD STEIGER AND
SHERRY HANSEN-STEIGER

ST. MARTIN'S PRESS
NEW YORK

DESIGN BY BARBARA M. BACHMAN

Library of Congress Cataloging-in-Publication Data
Steiger, Sherry Hansen.
    Hollywood and the supernatural / Sherry Hansen-Steiger and Brad Steiger.
        p. cm.
    ISBN 0-312-05099-2
    1. Motion picture industry—California—Los Angeles. 2. Motion picture actors and actresses—California—Los Angeles—Biography.
    3. Hollywood (Los Angeles, Calif.)—Social life and customs.
    4. Supernatural. I. Steiger, Brad. II. Title.
    PN1993.5.U65S74   1990
    384'.8'0979494—dc20   90-36133
                                                                CIP
FIRST EDITION: NOVEMBER 1990
10   9   8   7   6   5   4   3   2   1

A NOTE OF CAUTION TO THE READER

Some of the scenes and supernatural encounters described herein may be considered frightening or unsettling by certain readers. The contents of this book are intended to be precautionary as well as informative, inspirational, and entertaining. There is no intent to promulgate any particular belief structure or philosophy. The authors ask the reader to proceed with a sense of exploration and the responsibility of discernment.

CONTENTS

ACKNOWLEDGMENTS

A book of this scope could not succeed without the help of the talented men and women who shared their experiences, their expertise, and their insights. So many gave generously of their time and encouragement, yet the following list cannot hope to name them all. We must apologize to whomever may have been inadvertently omitted. However, we wish to thank: Paul Andrews, Dr. Maxine Asher, Paul Bannister, Timothy Green Beckley, Clarisa Bernhardt, Dr. Earlyne Chaney, Linda Claire, Christina Crawford, Dr. Patricia Rochelle Diegel, Siri Dharma Galliano, Angela Louise Gallo, John William Galt, Mary Ann Halpin, John Harricharan, Lisa Hart, Dr. Stephen Kaplan, Kenny Kingston, J. Z. Knight, Lar Park Lincoln, Ann Miller, Dr. Ernesto Montgomery, John Newland, Molli Nickell, Nick Nocerino, Charles Pelton, Ry Redd, Dr. Franklin R. Ruehl, Kevin Ryerson, Bob Slatzer, Carol Spilman, Dick Sutphen, Barry Taff, Alan Vaughan, Clint Walker, and Peter Weber.

We would like to give special thanks to our agent, Agnes Birnbaum, for her unfailing encouragement and support, and to our editor, Bob Weil, for his patience and guidance.

HOLLYWOOD
•AND THE•
SUPERNATURAL

INTRODUCTION: SUPERNATURAL PROJECTIONS FROM BEHIND THE MAGIC LANTERN

Darkness has always brought us the supernatural. Ghostly forms, eternally restless, move across the face of the earth. Images undefined lurk in the thick fog that swirls around naked trees stretching their bare limbs toward the October moon. A bat, its leathery wings briefly disturbing the awful quiet of the night, swoops low over the prowling form of a wolf, its hungry eyes glowing. That terrible scraping noise coming from the graveyard is the sound of one of the loathsome undead pushing back the lid of his coffin as he prepares to rise in search of human blood to feed his life force. It is night, and the hours before dawn are filled with the strange and the unknown. We can only pray for the light.

Although we have always been frightened by the unknown—terrified by tales of "ghoulies and ghosties and long-leggety beasties and things that go bump in the night,"—the fear of the supernatural achieved an even greater grip on our collective unconscious when, in 1900, it gained a powerful new ally in the nascent art of motion pictures. Georges Méliès, a French pioneer of film, brought audiences into the darkness of theaters and gave them flickering light from a magic lantern that had been blended with the horrors of the Grand Guignol, a small theater in 1908 Montmartre, Paris, specializing in dramatic entertainment featuring the gruesome or horrible. In 1919, when the German producer Erich Pommer used his camera to peer inside *The Cabinet of Dr. Caligari*, he opened a line of direct access to fears that had been hiding in the human subconscious since Eden.

Despite the fact that one will discover *Frankenstein* listed in film catalogues of 1908, the motion picture community in the United States found its first forays into the supernatural scorned by the public, refused by the exhibitors, and reviled from the pulpit. However, with

1

the impetus provided by the arrival of German directors and their sophisticated treatment of preternatural themes, such film masters as Rex Ingram, James Whale, and Tod Browning established the communion between Hollywood and the supernatural that has only grown stronger with time.

The essence of our dread of the supernatural lies in our fear of death. For human mortals, with ''our threescore years and ten,'' death has always been too final, too great a change. In this ominous decade of the 1990s, we who live in our condominiums with our shining technology feel a great frustration that we should still share this same fear as that of our primitive ancestors who huddled around the flickering light of an open fire to keep back the darkness.

It is no wonder that those who direct the flickering light of Hollywood's magic lanterns should so often concern themselves with presentations that argue against the pessimistic attitude that death is the end, that a brief strut across the stage of life is all there is to existence. Even the most elementary ghost story is a statement that we have within us a nonphysical element that survives the grave; even the most simplistic of supernatural tales provides the actors with an everlasting life on film that can long survive their own mortality.

From those early efforts to film the unknown and hold it captive to the most sophisticated methods of contemporary cinematography, Hollywood has expressed a deep interest in the supernatural—both in its celluloid creations and in the private lives of its stars, writers, directors, and producers.

Spirit guides, Ascended Masters, secret doctrines, past-life explorations, astrological charts, and haunted houses were as much a part of Hollywood in the twenties as they are in the nineties and may even become more pronounced as the millennium imminently approaches. Mediumship, arcane teachings, tarot cards, and visionary experiences have always been fashionable among the citizens of the Hollywood hills. As incredible as it may seem, the supernatural happenings that have occurred to certain celebrities off-camera, in real life, can more than equal the on-camera fantasies of their reel-life characterizations.

*   *   *

In the 1920s, such figures as Rudolph Valentino and his wife Natacha Rambova made mediumship and spirit teachers chic. When the Great Lover died in 1926, Natacha continued to channel messages from her dearly departed husband, thus establishing a precedent for those who wish to make direct communication with the celestial soundstages. Today's mediums and channels contact the spirits of Rock Hudson and Sal Mineo for the gay community, John Wayne for the conservatives, John Lennon for the maturing flower children, and Elvis Presley for those who want that old-time rock and roll. The spirits of Elvis and Princess Grace of Monaco have even been credited with a number of miracle healings.

The spirit form of Marilyn Monroe has been seen in many of her favorite Hollywood places. Bob Slatzer, a former husband, has not only felt her ghostly presence on several occasions but he told us that she materialized physically to him and other witnesses on the anniversary of her death.

Many stars have themselves displayed mediumistic talents. Mae West wrote many scripts directed by spirit control while in a trance, and we learned from medium Clarisa Bernhardt that today, on the Other Side, Mae is a member of "the Crossover Club," a group of benevolent spirits that assists newcomers to adjust to life beyond the grave.

Comedic genius Peter Sellers was one of the most outspoken advocates of spirit guidance. Among other stars who have displayed an interest in the psychic world are Lee Marvin, Susan Strasberg, John Travolta, Linda Evans, Elke Sommer, Clint Walker, Lindsay Wagner, and, of course, Shirley MacLaine.

It is still difficult for some to accept Shirley MacLaine, the freewheeling mascot of Frank Sinatra's old Rat Pack, as the reigning Hollywood High Priestess of Metaphysics, but there seems no reason to doubt the sincerity of her beliefs.

In retrospect, it is interesting to go back to 1972, when she starred in *The Possession of Joel Delaney,* a supernatural thriller that dealt with a form of witchcraft known as *Espiritismo,* in which the spirit of a dead person takes control of a living human. She played the older sister of Perry King, who made his debut as the possessed youth.

At that time, the actress said that she had come to view her life as having constituted a continual rebellion against the "white Southern-

Christian'' ethic that had governed her Virginia childhood. ''My home is inside my head,'' she said. ''The most intelligent manner of crusading is to work at expanding human consciousness.''

Shirley MacLaine has most certainly expanded the consciousness of millions. As an avowed advocate of the philosophy of reincarnation, she is by no means alone among those in Hollywood who express a belief that they have lived previous existences. Among the stars who agree that they, too, have ''been here before'' are such individuals as Sylvester Stallone, Ernest Borgnine, Loretta Lynn, Juliette Greco, Willie Nelson, David Carradine, Ann Miller, Richard Conte, Rose Marie, Glenn Ford, John Travolta, and Tina Turner.

Channeling, which might be defined as spirit mediumship gone Hollywood, was introduced to mid-America primarily through Shirley MacLaine's 1987 television movie, *Out on a Limb*. Although the Los Angeles area has boasted a spirit medium on every block for decades, the two-part movie of her best-selling book set in motion a channeling craze that has many stars swearing by the guidance received from their favorite channels. In certain instances, the celebrities insist that messages are being beamed directly to them from a multidimensional entity of their own.

Kevin Ryerson, the articulate channel who appeared in *Out on a Limb* playing himself, has granted a lengthy interview for this book that very ably defines the process of spirit communication from the perspective of a professional medium. J. Z. Knight, who channels the remarkable entity ''Ramtha'' and who advises such Hollywood luminaries as Linda Evans and Richard Chamberlain, was also generous with her time and appreciative of the opportunity to present her work in a manner with which she felt comfortable.

While many stars find themselves at peace with their channels and guides and their own personal ''spooks,'' the Hollywood hills also appear to be haunted by a great number of American Indian ghosts who are not altogether pleased with the current occupants of their sacred ground. Then there are those, such as Elke Sommer, Donald Pleasence, Susannah York, Mitzi Gaynor, Ann Miller, and Susan Strasberg, who moved into homes that contained very eerie—and sometimes nasty—ghostly occupants. Of course, ghosts of the stars also haunt houses.

Columnist Joyce Haber and her husband, producer Douglas Cramer, bought the sumptuous Beverly Hills mansion that had previously been owned by singer Grace Moore and actor Clifton Webb. Soon after they had taken possession of the home, Joyce began finding her cigarettes ripped to shreds wherever she might leave them. At the same time, doors began opening and closing of their own volition.

She finally caught the ghost of Webb, a militant antismoker, who, according to psychic Kenny Kingston, destroyed the pack of cigarettes that she had left in a bathroom.

A dentist and his wife moved into the former residence of Jean Harlow and Paul Bern without any knowledge of its history of haunting. They had not lived there long before they were awakened one night by the sound of a feminine voice crying for help. Next, they heard the sound of blows landing and felt chilling drafts around them before they were startled by the sensation of something heavy—like a human body—being thrown across their bed. A few nights later, they heard sobs issuing from a corner of their bedroom.

It was not long before they could take no more of the haunting and moved out—but before they did, the wife investigated and discovered that Bern and Harlow, in some dimension of reality, continued to relive that terrible night of beating and sexual humiliation before Bern took his own life.

Christina Crawford told us of the bizarre haunting phenomenon and the spontaneous fires that break out on the walls of the home that she once shared as a child with her mother, Joan Crawford.

Hollywood has been described by some as a vortex of energy where multiple learning opportunities present themselves. In many ways,

Hollywood is a mirror for our culture, projecting both our physical and nonphysical attitudes toward ourselves on the silver screens of the darkened theaters.

The great numbers of ghosts and those who perceive them may be due in large part to the high population of sensitive, creative men and women in the Hollywood area. Indeed, there may be a very thin line between the creative person who becomes a painter, a poet, a screenwriter, or an actor and the sensitive individual who becomes a spirit medium.

On the other side of that assumption, however, is the extensive research of parapsychologist Frank R. ("Nick") Nocerino, who states that while there are more haunted houses in the San Francisco area of California, there are more homes in the Hollywood area that are afflicted with negative or demonic activity.

Not surprisingly, witchcraft, satanism, and the black arts have fascinated the citizens of Hollywood since the days of silent films. In 1926, for example, Rex Ingram, the director of such major films as the 1921 version of *The Four Horsemen of the Apocalypse* starring Valentino, became fascinated with and filmed W. Somerset Maugham's early novel, *The Magician,* which had been inspired by the notorious Aleister Crowley, the devil-worshiping Englishman who had once dubbed himself "the wickedest man in the world."

During the 1950s, rumors buzzed in Southern California that Crowley had lived in Pasadena long enough in the 1920s to have founded a black magic coven, whose membership had remained active and had steadily recruited new followers. There is strong evidence that Crowley sowed the seeds that would mature into the bitter fruit that nurtured the likes of Charles Manson, Sirhan Bishara Sirhan, and Richard Ramirez, the Night Stalker.

The murders of the prominent members of the Sharon Tate circle by the Manson family in August 1969 cast an unprecedented malaise over Hollywood. Never before had the stars felt so threatened in their own homes. Graphic news stories of the horrible carnage and photographs of the words "Death to the Pigs" scrawled in human blood on the walls of the Polanski home burned indelible images of fear into the psyches of Hollywood royalty who had previously held themselves inviolable.

Incredibly, Sharon Tate had had a visionary preview of her murder nearly two years before the actual event, and psychic Ernesto Montgomery had tried months in advance to warn the residents of the neighborhood where the assassins struck that prominent Hollywood figures would be slain there.

There seems little question that the inquiring but sometimes jaded minds of far too many stars have become ensnared in the more sinister webs of the supernatural. Jayne Mansfield's flirtation with satanism, as you will read later on, may have brought upon her the malediction that left her decapitated in an automobile accident.

We will delineate the perverse manifestation of destructive energy that culminated in the tragic deaths of Sharon Tate and her friends, and we will present our findings in a manner that will expose the maddeningly seductive devil's dance for the distortion of the Light that it truly represents.

Amidst the tales of ghosts and haunted mansions, spirit séances, bizarre cult activity, and the rampages of occult-inspired assassins, there are numerous Hollywood stars who are engaged in a serious examination of the higher levels of spiritual experience. Sincere men and women are seeking to explore those aspects of human activity currently deemed supernatural and are attempting to define the future in ways that will benefit the entire planet and usher in a new age of peace and hope.

As Hollywood so often leads and inspires, rather than simply reflects our culture at large, there may well be the elements of a new and worthwhile understanding of what is truly human and what is divinely supernatural evolving somewhere in those glittering Hollywood hills.

1 • HOLLYWOOD STARS WHO HAVE MET THE SUPERNATURAL

It has often been observed that the Los Angeles area offers the seeker an entire "supernatural supermarket" from which to choose the form of spiritual expression that most suits his or her individual taste.

While the citizens of Hollywood may select from all the representative churches and synagogues of orthodox America, there are also far more metaphysical, occult, Eastern, experimental, and New Age faiths than one would find in either Dubuque or Dallas.

In the 1930s, Guy and Edna Ballard brought the I Am movement with its "unveiled mysteries" to Los Angeles. The Ballards claimed to communicate with the Ascended Masters—cosmic beings of great wisdom, power, and love—and with Count St. Germain, a French aristocrat of the eighteenth century who walks eternally through time and space. The Count and the other Masters live on today in the work of Elizabeth Clare Prophet and the Summit Lighthouse.

In 1951, Earlyne Chaney, who had been a fast-rising starlet, appearing in such films as *Kiss and Tell* (1945) with Shirley Temple, discovered that she could speak to entities on higher levels of consciousness and formed Astara with Robert, her spiritualist minister husband. Dr. Earlyne's messages from Koot Hoomi, Rama, and Zoser have brought several Hollywood stars to speak from the Astara pulpit.

L. Ron Hubbard, best known for his tales in such magazines as *Astounding Science Fiction,* wrote the classic book *Dianetics* in 1950 and created the movement of Scientology, which prospers today with such devotees as John Travolta, Karen Black, and Sonny Bono.

The "mystic with the mostest," Krishna Venta, was murdered in 1958 at his Fountain of the World headquarters in Box Canyon, California, when some very disgruntled followers with some very material dynamite decided to transform Krishna Venta into a wholly immaterial substance.

8

In the 1960s, the Maharishi Mahesh Yogi made Transcendental Meditation a household word not only in Hollywood but throughout the world. Of course, he did have a little help from some very important friends, namely, the Beatles and Mia Farrow.

The Maharishi opened the golden gates of Hollywood to other Indian-oriented mystical movements, such as Swami A. C. Bhaktivedanta's International Society for Krishna Consciousness, Paul Twitchell's Eckankar, Sai Baba, and Baba Ram Das, who, in an earlier incarnation during the Harvard LSD/drug days, had been Timothy Leary's associate, Richard Alpert.

Desi Arnaz, Jr., is the national spokesperson for the reality that mystic Vernon Howard offers to people. Ally Sheedy assists Brother Charles in moving his Synchronicity Meditation tapes. There seems little question that in such a heady spiritual environment the citizens of Hollywood would have to be acutely aware of their own spontaneous interactions with the supernatural.

When Academy Award–nominee Gary Busey (*The Buddy Holly Story,* 1978) suffered a near-fatal motorcycle accident on December 4, 1988, it seemed as though the actor's career was finished. However, two weeks later, according to Busey, a supernatural being appeared in the corner of his room at Daniel Freeman Hospital and informed him that it was not yet his time to pass over, that the actor still had gifts that he must share. It was such "positive reinforcement" that enabled Gary Busey to stay on the road to recovery.

Another Oscar nominee, Sigourney Weaver, said that she had been aware of the spirit presence of naturalist Dian Fossey protecting her while she was in Africa filming *Gorillas in the Mist* (1988).

Comedian Robin Williams has left his "Mork and Mindy" days far behind with such box-office hits as *Good Morning, Vietnam* (1988) and *Dead Poets Society* (1989) to his credit. Williams has said that he has experienced several accurate prophetic glimpses into his future and states that he also meditates, uses creative visualization, and believes in past lives. One of his own, he says, was as a Shakespearean actor.

Jack Scalia, the television star of "Wolf," stood on a windowsill of a hotel in Munich, totally burned out on drugs and alcohol. He was about to jump when he had a spiritual experience that turned his life around. God revealed that he had more in store for the actor.

Because actors are first of all human beings, we should expect them to have at least as many spiritual experiences as the public at large, if not more because of their public celebrity. In the January/February 1987 issue of *American Health,* well-known priest, author, and sociologist Father Andrew Greeley, together with colleagues at the University of Chicago and the University of Arizona in Tucson, revealed that nearly half of American adults—forty-two percent—believe they have been in contact with someone who has died, usually a deceased spouse or a sibling. More statistics from Father Greeley's national survey noted that twenty-nine percent of the adult population in the United States admit to having had visions, thirty-one percent claim to have experienced clairvoyance, and seventy-three percent believe in life after death.

The fact that the citizens of Hollywood percentagewise appear to have more supernatural encounters than the general adult population may be due in large part to the fact that the kind of sensitivity that it takes to be a successful actor, screenwriter, director, and so forth, may be very much akin to the kind of sensitivity necessary to tune into the unseen world of the supernatural.

In this section, we shall examine the experiences of Hollywood stars who have encountered the supernatural in their own lives, whether it was a premonition of one's own death or a spiritual rebirth.

VALENTINO SPEAKS FROM THE SPIRIT WORLD

In 1923, a moviegoers' poll listed Rudolph Valentino as the most popular motion picture star in the United States. Trailing the dark-eyed Latin lover were Wallace Reid, the all-American type; Douglas Fairbanks, an athletic swashbuckler; Tom Mix, a roughriding cowboy; and two comedians, Harold Lloyd and Charlie Chaplin.

Valentino had upset the early conventional Hollywood image of the blue-eyed, Anglo leading man and had managed to stir the hearts of millions of women who sat in darkened theaters, suffering from unrequited love. It is unlikely that more than a scant handful of those legions of women who fantasized about being taken in the passionate sheik's arms were aware that the decisive and commanding screen hero in real life followed the dictates of "Meselope," his spirit guide.

The Great Lover Was Guided by an Ancient Egyptian

Sid George Ullman, Valentino's agent, was annoyed with Rudy's and his wife's obsession with spirit writing and their complete reliance on the "old Egyptian" to guide and direct them.

"They never made a move without consulting this power," Ullman said. "They were never surprised by the unexpected."

Rudy's wife, Natacha Rambova, claimed powerful mediumistic abilities, and she communicated with Meselope through light trance states or through the Ouija board. The couple attended séances in every city where they played on a dancing tour of the country.

Valentino had always considered himself mildly psychic, but Natacha was convinced that he could become a great spirit medium. She became very excited with the prospect of more completely developing his latent extrasensory talents and tutored him in the occult with great enthusiasm.

Yeats Visits Hollywood with His Spirit Guide

It is interesting to speculate whether Natacha and Rudy might have been influenced by the experiments in spirit contact that had been conducted by another glamorous couple who had visited the Hollywood hills only a few years before their own interaction with Meselope. The brilliant Irish poet, William Butler Yeats, who won the Nobel Prize for Literature in 1923, had discovered that his wife was extremely successful in the esoteric realm of spirit communication; it was while they were on a lecture tour in the Los Angeles area that Yeats determined that their guide could answer questions put to it while his wife lay entranced.

Yeats identified his spirit guide as Leo Africanus, who was actually a sixteenth-century traveler, poet, and geographer. His spiritual instructions were often accompanied by strange sounds and peculiar, unexplainable odors. Yeats's verse most certainly was affected by his dabbling in the occult, and the imagery of his poetry is strongly influenced by the experiences he shared with the remarkable world of the paranormal.

The Mass Hysteria Surrounding Valentino's Funeral

When Valentino died—supposedly of a burst appendix, though a few theories differ from that—on August 24, 1926, the New York City police were confronted with the worst display of mass hysteria and unrestrained anarchy since the bloody Civil War draft riots of 1863. The death of America's so-called love god at the youthful age of thirty-one set loose unruly mobs in the heart of metropolitan New York City. An estimated 80,000 people were caught up in the emotional frenzy of mourning the Great Lover, hundreds of whom were trampled under foot by maniacal legions.

Valentino had come to New York City to premiere his latest film, *Son of the Sheik* (1926), and gossip columnists had teased readers with accounts of how the handsome actor was eager to return to the arms of his latest love, Pola Negri. Natacha Rambova, who had recently divorced Valentino, was in Europe at the time of his death.

Natacha Channels Rudy

Upon her return to the States, Natacha quickly established herself as the high priestess of the Cult of Valentino. It was only natural, she explained in front-page newspaper stories, that Rudy should choose her as the instrument by which to communicate messages of spiritual comfort to his devoted fans. After all, Natacha boldly asserted, their psyches had been the most dynamically intermeshed on the earth plane.

Valentino's first spirit communication had come three days after his death while she was in southern Europe. With the aid of George B. Wehner, a trance medium, she had managed to conduct lengthy discussions with her former husband, and she shared highlights of those messages in numerous interviews that appeared in newspapers and magazines. The following questions were answered by Natacha:

What was Valentino's reaction to his funeral?
Great happiness. As he watched the mobs fighting for a view of his body, he realized his great popularity as he never had before. He also then knew what he had lost by being taken to the Other Side. To him, it was wonderful but cruel.
What was Rudy's immediate reaction after his death?

He was lonely. He could not reach his friends. He could not touch their sorrow. He tried to talk to them, but they could not hear. Of course, he also felt the loss of adulation. Soon, however, the interests of the astral world began to hold him. Now he is radiantly happy, anxious to begin his work there.

Has he met any fellow movie stars on the Other Side?

He has named Wally Reid, Barbara La Marr, and Olive Thomas. He has been most interested in meeting and talking with Enrico Caruso, who was, of course, the idol of so many young Italians. Rudy has also met the personal friends with whom we used to communicate by means of automatic writing. They have explained the astral world to him, and he is slowly coming to comprehend the sublime qualities of the new life about him.

Does Valentino know of the great sorrow that swept the world at his death?

Naturally he was conscious of the world's sorrow. It was visible all about him. It tortured him in those earthbound days.

What earthly successes does Valentino remember?

He remembered all at first. Rudy wandered the film theaters where his last film, *Son of the Sheik,* was being shown to sorrowing audiences. He walked his old haunts on Broadway, particularly around 47th Street, where he used to spend many hours of his earlier penniless dancing days. He suffered because his old friends used to pass him by unknowing. He tried to speak to them, but to no avail. He shouted, "I am Rudolph Valentino!" but they did not hear. It was hard for him to understand. He was just as alive but in a different vibration. As Rudy has grown in astral knowledge, however, these earthly recollections have lost their appeal. The old glamour of earth people is passing. Our world is growing fainter.

Has Valentino any message for his old host of worshipers?

Yes, he has a message for everybody. He wants earth people to know and to realize that there is no death and no separation. He wants them to accept and believe in the beauty and perfection of the afterlife.

If he were to be born again, would he attempt another motion picture career?

He would attempt whatever circumstances permitted. He would have to meet the problems and challenges of that earth life.

How do you know that it is really Rudy who is speaking to you and not some other spirit?

When we receive a telephone call from another city, how do we know who is speaking? From mannerisms, from thoughts, from topics of conversation. Every message from Rudy undeniably has carried authentic earmarks.

What is the meaning of marriage on the astral plane?

Marriage is physical and of the earth. If, however, this union is sincere and real, the spiritual contacts remain the same after one's passing. It is my spiritual closeness with Rudy that enables me to receive his messages.

Encounters with the Spirit of Rudolph Valentino

As might have been expected of such a passionate entity as Valentino, his ghost could not be satisfied with mere communication through his former wife. It was not long after the great screen lover's untimely death that stories began to circulate about Rudy's spirit form having been seen at certain of his favorite locales. Falcon Lair, the dream home that he had built for Natacha, became the most frequently reported place for a ghostly manifestation of Rudolph Valentino.

Although the number of fans who trespassed on the grounds in the hope of seeing Rudy's ghost became a security problem, a fortunate few managed to beg or bribe their way into Valentino's own bedroom to spend the night in the mansion. Accounts of ''spirit kisses'' and impassioned messages abounded among the faithful.

One of the most popular of the Valentino spirit legends tells of the stabler who left the grounds without bothering to collect his belongings when he saw the ghost of the master petting his favorite horse at sunset one evening. Another account has a caretaker running down the canyon in the middle of the night screaming that he had encountered Rudy's ghost face-to-face. A woman from Seattle, who was a friend of the caretakers of Falcon Lair, claimed that she had been alone in the mansion writing a letter when she heard footsteps and saw doors open and close. Her only companions at the time had been Rudy and Brownie, Valentino's two favorite Great Dane watchdogs trained to bark and to snap at everyone—except their master.

The Great Lover's ghost continues to be sighted in the shadows of the city that made him an international legend. In April of 1989, a young actress said that she encountered the amorous spirit as she lay in bed. According to her account, she felt a heavy weight press down on the edge of her bed as she was drifting off to sleep one night in the old apartment building known as Valentino Place, which, according to Hollywood tradition, was once an elegant party site favored by the sheik and his intimates. For several minutes, the twenty-eight-year-old actress was too paralyzed by fear to move.

The body of what she assumed to be a man then stretched out beside her, she who was covered only by a thin sheet. As he pressed up to her and began breathing heavily, she at last had the courage to open her eyes.

"I saw the handsome face of Valentino lying on my pillow," she said. "I was so terrified that the 'man' was actually Valentino's ghost that I fainted."

When she recovered, she was relieved to see that although the ghost had left the bedsheets and pillow in complete disarray, it had returned to whatever dimension of reality it now called home.

JOHN BARRYMORE'S MYSTICAL QUEST FOR REGENERATION

In his youth and growing maturity, John Barrymore established an immortal niche in Hollywood's Hall of Fame. The youngest of "the Fabulous Barrymores"—which included his sister Ethel and brother Lionel—the handsome Jack, who became known as "the Great Profile," had tremendous talent and an enthusiastic following.

Tragically, the sterling quality of his work in such films as *Beau Brummell* (1924) and *The Sea Beast* and *Don Juan* (both in 1926) became overshadowed by his later dissolutions. Toward the end of his career, his once-fabled memory had deteriorated to such an extent that he could no longer remember the lines in *Hamlet* long enough to make a film of the Shakespearean classic.

The root of Barrymore's problem lay in alcohol. His legendary drinking bouts at times earned him the nickname of "the Monster" from even his closest friends. As his dependency upon his firewater grew and incidents of his outrageous behavior increased, his popularity decreased and he became a caricature of his former self.

One of his early successes in film had been in the dual title role of *Dr. Jekyll and Mr. Hyde* (1920) in which he had managed to distort his handsome, classic features into the grotesque Hyde without the assistance of makeup. The sad reality that life was imitating art in his own life was not lost upon Barrymore. He was rapidly becoming "Mr. Hyde."

In 1934, his marriage to the prominent thirties actress Dolores Costello on the rocks, Barrymore was informed by his doctors that unless he stopped drinking immediately, he would very shortly die. Such an announcement set him off on a desperate quest for mystical regeneration.

A Retreat to Mother India

John Barrymore had heard of the Ayurvedic treatment offered in India. Hoping that it would cure him, he determined to leave both Hollywood and Broadway behind, stating that he was rejecting wives, lovers, and false friends to spend the rest of his life in quiet study and meditation in Mother India.

When he arrived, he contacted Dr. Shrinivasa Murti, who disappointed him because he appeared as a brisk, middle-aged man dressed in Western-style clothes. Barrymore had been expecting a bearded, robed guru.

Dr. Murti described the Ayurvedic treatment as consisting of a combination of spiritual factors and medical applications, with the regimen including a vegetarian diet and the use of certain special herbs, essences, and leaves from the Himalaya Mountains. The treatment would take six weeks and required no hospitalization.

Barrymore was told that the decision to stop drinking would have to be a personal one. Dr. Murti stressed that he could make the actor no promises and added that he had reason to doubt that the American had the necessary discipline to undergo the Ayurvedic process.

Barrymore assured the doctor that he had faith in the method and the philosophy of Ayurvedic medicine and that he would make a commitment to the treatment. After three weeks, the change in the actor was obvious. His memory had improved, his headaches were gone, his interest in art and music had revived, and he felt wonderful. Dr. Murti admonished him that he must continue with the Ayurvedic treatment until it became automatic. Barrymore saw no reason why he could not.

The Yogi's Tragic Prophecy

A few days later, while Barrymore was sitting in his car, an elderly yogi came up to him and offered to read his palm. After several minutes of silent examination, the old man told Barrymore that it would be good for him to stay in India because the land harmonized with him.

"That is exactly what I intend to do, sir," Barrymore replied.

The yogi sighed, shook his head sadly, and told the actor that he would not do as he now intended. "You will return to your native land. Your life will be shortened by too much drink."

Barrymore tried to laugh away the malediction, declaring loudly that he loved India and had no intention of returning to America or to his firewater. He offered the old man a rupee for his fortune-telling, but the yogi turned and walked away, refusing to accept the coin. It was not long after this strange encounter that Barrymore disappeared from his hotel and was not seen for a week. When he returned, it was readily apparent that the preceding weeks of treatment had been for nothing.

Although he confessed to seven days of nonstop drinking and carousing, he called upon his persuasive powers as an actor to convince Dr. Murti that he had learned his lesson and that he would now be unceasingly faithful to the treatment. The doctor again accepted Barrymore as a patient, but when the actor pulled another disappearing act two days later and embarked on another week of revelry, Dr. Murti washed his hands of John Barrymore.

At the age of fifty-three, the actor returned to California. In the remaining seven years of his life, he fulfilled the prophecy that had so saddened the old yogi in India. On May 29, 1942, John Barrymore died of cirrhosis of the liver.

The Hands of the Clock Foretold the Hour of Death

There is a curious footnote to the story of this troubled man who so deliberately drove himself to destruction. Barrymore had died at 10:20 P.M. on the night of May 29. A few days before the actor's death, his close friend, Gene Fowler, commissioned John Decker to make a deathbed sketch of Barrymore to be hung on the wall of Fowler's den next to the Richard III sword that the actor had presented to him.

When Decker delivered the sketch the day before Barrymore's death, he told Fowler that the sword looked out of place next to an old cuckoo clock and suggested that the clock be removed.

Fowler refused, explaining that even though the old timepiece had not run for years, it had been a favorite of Barrymore's. It was the friend's intention to set the hands at the hour of Barrymore's death so the clock would serve as a memorial to the actor.

The morning following John Barrymore's death, Fowler was astounded when he went into the den. When the clock had stopped, two years earlier, the hands had frozen into the exact moment of Barrymore's passing: 10:20 P.M.

PREMONITIONS OF DEATH MAKE FOR DRAMATIC EXITS

The colorful citizens of Hollywood are famous for recognizing a good exit line and for knowing how best to dramatize it for maximum effect. Show business annals are filled with enigmatic departing statements, some delivered to packed houses while others were made privately before close friends.

In some cases, the interpretation runs fifty-fifty. Was it just an off-hand remark that a quirk of fate immortalized or did the person truly have a premonition of death?

"I Don't Think You'll See Me Here Again"

Warner Oland, the Swedish-born actor who became typecast as an Oriental, enacted the inimitable detective Charlie Chan on the screen with conviction. True to his inscrutable guise, his quiet knowledge masked his acceptance of death.

When *Charlie Chan at Monte Carlo* (1937) was being planned, it was suddenly discovered that Oland was nowhere to be found. He was eventually located sunning himself on the sandy beaches of Honolulu. Approached by studio representatives, he strenuously insisted that he would not appear in another Charlie Chan film. The studio prevailed as he gave in with, ''All right. I guess I can do one more for you.''

At the completion of the film, Oland was again approached by the directors with the script for the next Chan. Amid blandishments and pleas, they reminded the actor that the series had been successful for more than ten years and that they certainly did not wish it to end.

Oland listened patiently. He was not difficult. He did not make impossible demands. He simply told them that it would not be wise to count on him. "I don't think you'll see me here again," he said softly. The studio confidently went ahead with its plans, convinced that they could again persuade Oland to come through once more as Charlie Chan.

He confounded them all. A few days later, Warner Oland quietly passed away of natural causes. It was obvious that he had felt no need to argue with the directors and producers. He knew that the studio would have no choice other than to bow to his demise.

"If I [Fly Without Liz,] It Will Be All Over for Me"

When producer-promoter-movie mogul Mike Todd married superstar Elizabeth Taylor in 1957, he announced that he would never again travel alone. He named his private airplane *The Liz* and said that he would never be separated from his bride. They would always travel together.

"If I break that vow," he told his friends, "I know it will be all over for me."

And it was. The first time in their marriage that Todd ever flew alone was also his final flight.

In March 1958, while he was flying to New York to attend a dinner of the National Association of Theater Owners, at which he was to be acknowledged Showman of the Year, *The Liz* plummeted through the sky to break up on the unyielding slopes of the Rockies.

Was it coincidence or had the producer of *Around the World in Eighty Days* (1956) and the creator of the 65 mm, wide-screen process known as Todd-AO had a true premonition of his death?

"I'll Never Sing Julie Again. I Just Won't Be Here"

One of the most dramatic exits from the world of entertainment was that of Helen Morgan, the original torch singer, who collapsed onstage. In this way, the curtain could, with true double entendre, end the act.

It was an uncomfortably known fact that Helen, the manager of several speakeasies during the Prohibition era, had a drinking problem, yet her doctors all insisted that, organically, Helen, the star of *Glorifying the American Girl* (1929) and *Frankie and Johnnie* (1936), was "strong enough to throw off even a protracted bender." The woman who became famous for portraying fallen women had a remarkably robust constitution.

Helen had made the role of the tragic Julie in the musical *Showboat*, originally based on the best-selling novel by Edna Ferber, her very own. She had created the role in the original Broadway production, had starred in the 1929 part-talking film version, and had repeated her Broadway triumph in James Whale's 1936 remake of the classic musical production. Helen Morgan was the only Julie.

When word got around in 1941 that an all-star revival of the stage version was being planned for Los Angeles and San Francisco, there could be no speculation as to the cast: Norma Terris would be Magnolia; Howard Marshe would play Gaylord Ravenol; Paul Robeson would re-create Joe; and, of course, Helen Morgan would do Julie.

Then rumors began to drift down from the producers that the exception would be Helen, who was too unstable and could not be relied upon. Her many friends on both sides of the footlights refused to allow this injustice and stories spread via the grapevine that the other stars would not fulfill their contracts unless Helen Morgan played Julie. The furor finally resolved in a compromise in which Helen would be allowed to play Julie in Los Angeles while another actress-singer would perform in San Francisco. With some trepidation, her agent broke the news but was surprised to learn that Helen was already at peace about the matter.

"It's all right." She smiled, looking a little tired. "Don't worry about it. I'll play Los Angeles like I want to, and we won't make a fuss. Just take the money. I'll accept whatever the others are getting."

Then with a bit more of the old spark in her eyes, she stated clearly, "Los Angeles will be the last time that I'll ever do Julie. I'll never sing Julie again. I just won't be here." As surely as if she had been receiving her lines from a higher source, the words she spoke to her agent proved to be prophetic. Helen Morgan sang Julie in Los Angeles to thunderous applause, but she never sang the role again.

"Helen knew the role of Julie was the high point of her entire career," a friend said. "It was the apex. She knew she could climb no higher. After Los Angeles, she knew that she had lost the ball game, and she simply up and quit. Everyone in Hollywood knew her to be a warm, generous person, but she could not bear the thought of anyone else playing Julie.''

A few weeks later, Helen Morgan collapsed onstage while singing in an old vaudeville theater in Chicago. She died in 1941 at the age of forty-one.

Did each of these sensitive performers know in some way that their final exit was near? It would appear that they all followed the advice of the Ultimate Director and allowed the final curtain to become the veil between this world and the next.

MAKING CONTACT WITH THE SPIRIT OF WILLIAM HOLDEN

As the appealing young boxer-violinist Joe Bonaparte in *Golden Boy* (1939), William Holden became a star with his first real screen role. His all-American, boy-next-door good looks kept him busy in a string of action-adventure films that included a number of Westerns, such as *Arizona* (1940) and *Texas* (1941).

With his service as a U.S. Army lieutenant in World War II behind him, Holden returned and began to shape a new screen persona that found dramatic expression in his Academy Award–winning performance as the tough, cynical antihero in *Stalag 17* (1953). He remained a rugged leading man in such classic films as *The Bridge on the River Kwai* (1957), *The Wild Bunch* (1969), and *Network* (1976) until his unfortunate death on November 16, 1981.

In January 1983, a team of four psychic investigators from the Extension of Life Foundation in Durham, North Carolina, led by the foundation's president, Patricia Hayes, made a pilgrimage to Hollywood to gather in a television studio with the agreed upon goal of communicating with William Holden's spirit by way of séance. Throughout the experiment, the investigators were in telephone contact with Hal Cope, a longtime friend of Holden's who was in Honolulu.

In life, the actor had been no stranger to tales supernatural. In the fantasy film *The Remarkable Andrew* (1942), he appeared as Andrew

Long, who receives a visit from the ghosts of such historical figures as Andrew Jackson; with their help, he cleans up corruption in a small town. In 1964, he made a brief appearance as a vampire in *Paris When It Sizzles,* and in *Damien: Omen II* (1978), he played Richard Thorn, the ill-fated and unsuspecting uncle of the Antichrist.

"A Tingling Sensation, as of Electricity Flowing Through Us"

Patricia Hayes told Dr. Franklin R. Ruehl how the séance was conducted:

> We sat in a circle with our hands joined. Each of us breathed deeply and concentrated on sending energy down our right arm and into the left hand of the person beside us. Within just a couple of minutes, we all felt a warmth in our hands.
>
> There was nothing illusory about this experience. In addition to the heat, we all felt a tingling sensation, as of electricity flowing through us. We then concentrated on forming a column of light with our minds in the center of the circle. This served as a focal point by which we could concentrate our energies.
>
> Each of us concentrated on the name of William Holden. Simultaneously, Hal Cope, his good friend in Hawaii, was concentrating on a significant episode in life that they had shared. Within seven minutes of beginning the experiment, we had received our first telepathic communication from Holden!

Patricia Hayes assessed the results of the séance in positive terms: "Remarkably, William Holden made contact with our group from beyond the grave!"

Although the ghost of Holden did not materialize or make any utterances, the participants felt that the actor's spirit did communicate physically with each of them during the one-hour session. The circle stated that they had received confidential tidbits of information about Holden's life that only Cope could verify.

To one member of the séance circle, researcher Cheryl Burns, the spirit of Holden related a confrontation that he had had with African natives over bird poaching and described an elephant hair bracelet that he had received.

For investigator Janice Hayes, the entity depicted a turbulent plane ride that Holden had once experienced over the African bush. His spirit essence also confirmed through psychic William Clema that the actor's death had been completely accidental.

"Most assuredly, we were in psychic communication with a spirit identifying itself as William Holden," Clema stated. "The entity acknowledged that he had too much to drink on the night of his passing and that his death was completely accidental."

A Spirit Free of Time and Space

Dr. Ruehl was told that Holden's spirit appeared to be darting back and forth between the séance circle in Hollywood and Hal Cope in Honolulu, delivering messages transoceanically to both locations.

According to Cope, he was ". . . absolutely certain that Bill Holden's spirit was present" that night in January 1983. To the late actor's old friend, the session was "truly proof of life after death."

Continuing his observations, Cope said that he had immediately felt a presence in his room in Honolulu when Patricia Hayes first began to report telepathic communication from Holden. "It was analogous," he explained, "to the feeling of a sunburn on your face and hands. At one point during the session, I felt a presence on my right shoulder, as though Bill were standing right beside me with his hand on my shoulder."

Patricia insists that the physical manifestations and the psychic perceptions sensed by the investigators could not have been transmitted telepathically by Cope. "They originated from William Holden's spirit!"

THE MYSTICAL SIDE OF LEE MARVIN

"I don't want to go out like Duke [John] Wayne, having to be helped up on his horse," rugged actor Lee Marvin said emphatically just a few months before his death in 1987. "Menahem Golan has got me talked into filming a sequel to *Delta Force* [1985]. It seems that he has decided that my character has a daughter that has to be rescued by Chuck Norris. That will be my last action-adventure film."

In response to protests that he was too young to retire from films at the age of sixty-three, Marvin laughed. "I didn't say anything about retiring. I'm just going to leave the derring-do to the young guys like Norris and [Sylvester] Stallone. I want to do comedy roles now."

Such as his dual role in *Cat Ballou* (1965), for which he had won the Academy Award for Best Actor?

"Naw," came the actor's husky-voiced reply. "Sophisticated comedy. Drawing-room comedy."

Marvin was unable to surprise his fans with a new career as a comic actor, however, nor was he able to complete Golan's sequel to *Delta Force*. The white-haired, craggy-featured tough guy of countless action movies passed on in 1987.

Few people knew that the tall, rough-hewn star of such films as *The Wild One* (1954), *Bad Day at Black Rock* (1954), *The Man Who Shot Liberty Valance* (1962), and *The Dirty Dozen* (1967) also had a very mystical side to his complex personality.

The Vision of Death That Saved His Father's Life

Lee grimly related the story of how his father, Lamont, a sergeant in World War II, had narrowly escaped death in one of the war's worst Nazi V-2 weapon attacks by paying heed to a vision.

Lamont Marvin, a veteran of World War I, was forty-six years old when the United States entered World War II. Since his two sons were serving in the armed forces, Lamont decided to enlist again. He was in Antwerp, Belgium, when his near miss with death occurred. It was 1944, and the Germans had just evacuated. As the Allies moved in to occupy the territory, the Nazis bombarded them with heavy artillery and V-2 rocket-propelled bombs. On this particular day, however, there had been a lull in the blitzkrieg. Lamont happened to be walking the streets of downtown Antwerp when he came upon the Rex Theater and decided to take a few moments to look at the pictures out front.

As he stood there, he heard an inner voice urging, "Hurry! Hurry!" but he ignored it. Then, as he continued to study the pictures, he suddenly saw the image of a telegram addressed to his wife superimposed over one of them. "We regret to inform you . . ."

Lamont did not need to read anymore. Convinced that he was seeing a vision revealing the death of either Lee or his other son, he let out an anguished cry and ran blindly down the street. After he had run some distance, he felt impelled to duck into a concrete doorway where he stood, panting for breath and holding his arm over his eyes filled with stinging tears. Just at that moment, a buzz bomb, one of the V-2 rockets, dropped squarely on top of the theater.

The blast of the explosion brought searing pain to Lamont's ears. Slowly, he turned his horrified eyes to behold the flaming Rex Theater disaster, where 567 persons were killed and 291 wounded, many of whom died later from their injuries. The carnage was so terrible that the July 21, 1945, *Saturday Evening Post* called it "the war's worst V-weapon disaster."

According to the magazine article, "Two days after the bomb hit, many of the dead were still in their seats. The theater was like a grisly wax museum. . . ."

It was from this horror that Lamont Marvin had been saved.

"Dad ignored his inner voice," Lee pointed out, "so his guardian angel—or whatever—had to give him a visual signal. When the image of the telegram materialized, he was actually seeing a notice of his own death, and he would have assuredly died if he had not run as fast as he did."

The Wound Felt Around the World

Lee Marvin had many other stories to substantiate his firm belief in ESP, most of them concerning his family.

During World War II, Lee had been a Marine stationed in the Pacific. When he was shot in the back by a Japanese soldier, the psychic signals went out to members of his family circle. As he was recuperating in the States, Lee learned that both his mother in America and his father in Europe had sensed that someone had wounded their son the minute that it had happened.

According to Lamont, he awakened in the middle of the night with a terrible fear that Lee had been shot. He immediately looked at his clock and took note of the time. On the same night, Lee's mother opened the front door to their home and saw her son standing before her, his uniform in rags, bandages around his head. She, too, checked the time. When the three of them were reunited, they did some careful figuring of time distances and determined that at the exact instant of

Lamont's dream and his wife's vision, Lee had been shot in the back somewhere in the Pacific.

"There's only one thing wrong, Ma," Lee had said to his mother after they had discussed the telepathic transfer. "You were mistaken about the bandages on my head. It was in the back that I was shot."

"But where did it hurt the most?" his mother wanted to know. Lee had to admit that the pain was most severe in his head, strange as it seemed.

Experiences such as these had long ago convinced Lee Marvin of the reality of extrasensory perception. To him, the power within had become an integral and vital facet of life.

A Psychic Healer's Accurate Diagnosis

In August 1986, while visiting with Marvin in the actor's comfortable home in Tucson, Arizona, we learned of his experiences with a mutual friend, Colin Lambert, a remarkable healer from New Zealand.

Lee had first met Colin at a friend's house in Malibu in 1983. "He was doing some work on some people there, so I jumped up on a table and submitted myself to his procedure of healing. Lambert doesn't place his hands on the body but keeps them just above it."

Colin said that he detected a medical problem in Marvin's lungs.

"I wasn't feeling sick at the time," Marvin said, "but Colin kept saying that I had a lung problem. He couldn't precisely state what was wrong, but he sensed that I would experience difficulties in that area." Shortly after, Marvin flew to Europe to make a film and arrived feeling ill. "X rays indicated that I had contracted pneumonia, and I received medical treatment, but some months later, when I returned to the United States and still hadn't fully recovered, I had additional tests. This time X rays revealed that I had 'valley fever,' which is often mistaken for pneumonia."

Residents of Arizona and other southwestern states are well aware of "valley fever," a rare fungal disease that can trigger meningitis. Once contracted, it takes its victims a long time to accomplish a full recovery.

"It took me a full year to recover from it," Marvin stated, "but Colin Lambert was right on the spot in his diagnosis long before I was aware of any health problem and long before it was confirmed by a physician.''

To Lee Marvin, the psychic diagnosis of Colin Lambert was yet another proof of the inner powers that belong to each of us. As the actor phrased it for our colleague, Dr. Franklin R. Ruehl: ''I am now convinced that there is no limit to the power of the mind to heal the body.''

CORINNE CALVET'S REBIRTH AS "CORONA"

Corinne Calvet made her American debut opposite Burt Lancaster in *Rope of Sand* (1949), and most movie buffs will remember her as the pre-Bardot French sex kitten who was imported by Hollywood to add Gallic sultriness and allure to more than a dozen movies in the 1950s.

Although critics generally said that the shapely actress handled her roles quite well in such motion pictures as *What Price Glory?* (1952) and *Thunder in the East* (1953), Corinne's memories contain little affectionate nostalgia for her past cinematic accomplishments.

''They kept me in those insipid movies and tried to type me. I had about eighty-six words of dialogue in seventeen pictures. I said the same thing all the time.''

Then, in about 1972, Corinne Calvet was reborn as ''Corona.''

Sitting cross-legged on a thick pillow on the wooden floor of her apartment, she explained, ''I think the best way to describe what has happened to me is to say that Corona's soul was living in Corinne Calvet's body. A part of my ego wanted all those things that Corinne Calvet was able to obtain—like fame and luxury and position and admiration and recognition and all those ego trips that we all go through. In the attempt for me to obtain those things, I pushed back the stronger force within me, which I knew was present and of which I was constantly aware.''

With the apartment heavy with the scent of incense and sitar music issuing from a stereo set connected to a series of flashing lights, Corona spoke of how she had constantly attended to the ''stronger force'' within her by first examining dogmatic religions and then by studying at the Self-Realization Center in Los Angeles. ''I received the understanding of the science of Yoga as taught by Paramahansa Yogananda, and I eventually received the blessing that made me Corona, which means 'compassion.' "

The actress had undergone her first mystical experience in early childhood. "I think my first manifestation on that level was the night before my first communion, when I had a dramatic vision of the Last Supper. I walked out of my bed as if I were a sleepwalker to behold it. As far as I am concerned, I was there; and *they* were there, as much as you are here now."

Corona stated that the only plan she now made for the future was simply to be of service. "If I had a plan, I would not be available for the work that is coming, so I live in the flow, and I know that if I live in the flow, everything that is supposed to come my way will have a chance to appear—then I will do it."

Corona said that she could not remember a time when she did not have visions and revelatory experiences but added that the Corinne ego continually pushed back the stronger force within her, the Corona awareness. When Corona did emerge as a result of the spiritual discipline of Yoga training, she assumed a new name along with her new identity.

Today, in seminars and workshops throughout the country, Corona continues to be of service.

THE PSYCHIC WORLD OF SHIRLEY MACLAINE

No doubt can exist that Academy Award–winning actress Shirley MacLaine has had a remarkable influence upon the current psychic scene in Hollywood—not to mention the rest of the United States and overseas. Although she has never sought the position of High Priestess of Metaphysics, thousands of her admirers have awarded her such an unofficial title with the respect that they pay her. Then there are the facts: More than ten million copies of her books are in print, one of which, *Out on a Limb* (1983), served as the basis for a popular two-part television movie.

In recent interviews, Shirley emphasized that she does not wish to become anyone's "New Age Guru." She has even stopped teaching her seminars in order to correct what had become a widespread misconception that she was organizing her own religion. She insists that her metaphysical books—*Out on a Limb, Dancing in the Light* (1985), *It's All in the Playing* (1987), and *Going Within* (1989)—should be read as the sharing of her personal growth experiences and not as dogmatic teachings to her disciples.

"There's stuff going on in my life, too," she pointed out. "I'm not perfect. I'm very healthy spiritually, but I also have my problems, and when I have a problem, I don't hide it. I let people see that I'm just a human being trying to figure out what's going on."

Granted, she does not desire the position of Great Mother Guru of Hollywood, but there is no denying that Shirley's outspoken propagandizing for past lives, UFOs, soulmates, channeling, and other assorted powers and properties of the mind has made appreciable dents in the barriers that our materialistic society had erected around itself. There can be no question that because of her popularity, vast numbers of men and women who might never have explored the psychic world have now been bold enough to do so.

At the same time, her high profile as an outspoken advocate of the New Age requires that she grow a rather thick skin. A special Fall 1989 issue of *People* featured twenty men and women who defined the decade of the eighties. While the profiles of such "destiny's darlings" as Ronald Reagan, Mikhail Gorbachev, Madonna, Oliver North, Jesse Jackson, and Mike Tyson are presented rather straightforwardly, Shirley had to endure such clever smirkiness as "crystal-packin' mama" and such cracks as "It has been said that she had a mind like an oil drill. What a pity it struck mush."

Shirley MacLaine's interest in the inner world of the psyche has evolved over a lengthy period of time, and she has expended a great deal of effort and energy in seeking her own self-mastery.

A Quest for Inner Peace

"I was longing for an inner peace in a competitively driven and deteriorating world," she has said. "So when I met with [the late Prime Minister of India Jawaharlal] Nehru, which I did, and the Dalai Lama, and other great Eastern masters, I learned that the basic fear in the human race is the fear of death. And if death isn't real, there's nothing to fear. And in their view, it isn't real because no energy ever dies. It just changes form. That had a tremendous effect on my mind and sensibility because if we don't die, what are we afraid of? It changed my life. The sense of peace and the sense of calm it gave me was something I started living with.''

In her 1970 autobiography, *Don't Fall Off the Mountain,* she tells of the night that she lay shivering in a Bhutanese house in the Paro Valley of the Himalayas, her teeth chattering as her insides "tied themselves in knots."

As she wondered how she might survive the terrible cold, Shirley remembered the words of a yoga instructor in Calcutta who had told her that there was a center in her mind that was her nucleus, the center of her universe. Once she had found this nucleus, he said, pain, fear, sorrow—nothing—could touch her.

"It will look like a tiny sun," the yogi had instructed her. "The sun is the center of every solar system and the reason for all life on all planets in all universes. So it is with yours."

Now as she lay freezing, Shirley closed her eyes and searched for the center of her mind. The cold room and the wind outside began to leave her conscious mind. "Slowly, in the center of my mind's eye, a tiny round ball appeared," she wrote. "Then I felt I became the orange ball."

The center, the "sun," began to glow and to generate heat, which spread down through her neck and arms and finally stopped in her stomach. She felt drops of perspiration on her midriff and forehead. The light grew brighter and brighter until she finally sat up on the cot with a start and opened her eyes, expecting to find that someone had entered and turned on a light. She was stunned to find the room dark. As she lay back down, she felt as though she were glowing.

"Still perspiring, I fell asleep," she concluded. "The instructor was right: Hidden beneath the surface there was something greater than my outer self."

Maintaining Mind/Body Balance

Shirley MacLaine has maintained her ability to achieve mind/body balance. She gained thirty pounds for her role in *Madame Sousatzka* (1988), retained them for her role in *Steel Magnolias* (1989), then shed the excess pounds so that she would return to playing roles requiring thinner women.

"I had no trouble taking the weight off," she said. "Since I've created everything in my life, I knew I could create a thin body again, too."

Going Way Out on a Limb

In 1983, with the publication of her best-selling book, *Out on a Limb,* Shirley presented her readers with an extensive sharing of that "something greater" than the outer self that she discovered in the Bhutanese house in the freezing Himalayas. There is scarcely a page of the book that does not offer personal exploration carefully intertwined with an attempt to provide some explanation of humankind's physical and spiritual relationship with the Greater Reality.

Together with a confessional accounting of her love affair with a mystery diplomat of suggested British citizenship, the actress tells us of her own past lives, recounting a seemingly multidimensional existence from beyond the stars to a time in an ancient but advanced civilization 500,000 years old. She recalls a time of terrible existence in the poverty-stricken streets of India and a more exciting lifetime in the dance halls of Paris.

A Memory of Being Beheaded Cured Her Stage Fright

Shirley MacLaine has become one of Hollywood's most outspoken advocates of the exploration of past lives, and she understands that she has lived before as both male and female. "I was definitely a prostitute in some lifetimes," she has commented. "It's no accident that I played all those hookers in the movies."

She further believes that her daughter Sachi was her sister in one life and her mother in another. She has also learned through past-life exploration that she was once a court jester, personally decapitated by Louis XV for impertinence. According to Shirley, the recollection of having been beheaded actually cured her of stage fright: "I watched my head rolling on the floor. It landed face up and a big tear came out of one eye."

The New Age Seeker

"It took me so long before I had the courage to say these kinds of things," she admitted. "My friends told me that I would be killing my career if I spoke out on these subjects. Only lately has it become pragmatic to believe in New Age ideas."

During the 1987 filming of the television movie of *Out on a Limb,* Shirley stated that "entities" came through and assisted the producers, the directors, and certain members of the crew. She expressed her delight that so many men and women were being exposed to the "unseen reality."

If we were to distill the essential elements in the psychic world of Shirley MacLaine from her books, her interviews, and her seminars, we would find that her life-style is a virtual prototype for the New Age Seeker:

- She practices daily meditation.
- She communicates with her spirit guides.
- She uses the power of crystals in her life.
- She believes in reincarnation and explores her past lives.
- She is an empath, picking up on the thoughts and emotions of others.
- She accepts the value of holistic and alternative health techniques.
- She seeks to remain in touch with her Higher Self.

The Real Power Is Inside

There was a time, just a few years ago, when the talented actress/dancer/writer/metaphysician admitted to a dream of building a spiritual city with pyramidal architecture and crystal fountains. She also envisioned ". . . a large courtyard, where people can come and collectively meditate, get spiritually nourished, and then go back to life." The place would be, she stated, "a kind of spiritual spa."

By 1989, such plans were abandoned—or at least put on the shelf for the foreseeable future. As Shirley has confessed:

I am basically a recluse. I'm happiest when I am up in the forest with the fire going and my dogs beside me and either a tape recorder or a notebook and a pen handy—preferably raining outside, a little wind blowing, some lightning. No telephone. A television, but only for the evening news and "Entertainment Tonight." Nothing else. And I could stay that way for six months and never leave except to go for a walk and do exercise. That's my natural personality.

Each person's real talent is inside, not outside. Inside is where the real power and energy are, where the spiritual connection is made.

How on earth can we touch that talent and that power without going within to touch it? That means taking as much time to go within yourself as you can. It means finding a silent environment and some music and something pretty to look at.

I've been a seeker and a searcher all my life. All my traveling was about trying to find myself. And that's what the New Age is— looking into yourself to discover who you are.

PETER SELLERS'S GUIDANCE FROM THE SPIRIT WORLD

It was while they were filming *Being There* (1979) that Shirley MacLaine and Peter Sellers discussed the eternality of the soul. As the innocent "Chance the Gardener" (Chauncey Gardiner), the brilliant British actor's last film role was a work of genius. Sellers, however, confided in his friend and costar that he knew his motion picture characters better than he knew himself. In fact, he continued, he felt that he had been each of the characters he had played at one time or another in a past life.

Sellers, at that time, was wearing a pacemaker, a "toy contraption" the doctors had left in his heart after crucial surgery in which the actor had a near-death experience.

"I saw myself leave the body," he told Shirley. "I just floated out of my physical form . . . I wasn't frightened or anything like that because I was fine; it was my body that was in trouble." Sellers watched the doctors open his chest and massage his heart, then he looked around and saw "an incredibly beautiful bright loving white light" above him.

"I wanted to go into that white light more than anything," he said. "I knew that there was love, real love, on the other side of the light." Sellers told Shirley that he was bitterly disappointed when the doctors brought him back into his body, but a voice had told him that it was not yet his time. He had to go back to finish his life properly.

"I know I have lived many times before," Sellers said, "and that experience confirmed it to me because in this lifetime I felt what it was for my soul to actually be out of my body, but ever since I came back, I don't know why, I don't know what it was that I'm supposed to do or what I came back for."

We can only pray along with Shirley MacLaine that the gifted actor felt that he had fulfilled his mission when he died a year and a half later in 1980.

Guided by Past-Life Memories and a Spirit Guide

Whether he was portraying a bumbling French detective with an un-draped Elke Sommer clutching his trench coat (*A Shot in the Dark,* 1964), a timid librarian contemplating an extramarital affair (*Only Two Can Play,* 1962), or the dual roles of a power-mad German scientist and a harried American president fretting about how to "stop worrying and love the bomb" (*Dr. Strangelove,* 1963), Peter Sellers constructed nearly flawless tragicomic masks that enabled him to impersonate an enormously wide variety of characters down to the most subtle nuances.

Not only did he draw upon past-life memories to achieve masterful portrayals, but he also was a clairaudient channel who was able to hear the spirit voice that guided him. British medium Estelle Roberts identified the spirit entity that spoke to Sellers as Dan Leno, a comedian who had died around the turn of the century.

In April 1959, Sellers was accompanied to a séance by fellow comic Spike Milligan, an old friend who had starred with him on the BBC's (British Broadcasting Corporation) popular "Goon" shows. Milligan testified that Mrs. Roberts immediately brought forward the spirit of a man whom they both recognized as Larry Stevens, a talented young writer who had died on the threshold of fame.

Sellers was convinced that Mrs. Roberts was relaying messages that dealt with information about which she could have known nothing. The spirit entity used words and whole phrases that only Milligan, Stevens, and Sellers had used together.

Sellers recalled that he had a strange feeling all of his life that some person on the Other Side was taking a special interest in him and guarding him against danger. Mrs. Roberts informed him that he could just as well have become a great medium as a great actor.

Sellers Preferred Spirits to Stanislavski or Strasberg

Although Peter Sellers protested such a change in careers, he did admit to employing a "mediumistic method" of opening himself up to his characterizations. Other actors might employ the Stanislavski or Strasberg methods, he said, smiling, but he wanted the character to inhabit his body. "I want a spirit to take charge of me so that I can produce what I hope to produce."

Sellers confessed to close friends that he was aware of a "whole new thing" that occurred to him when he made such invocations to the spirits. "I think that in there somewhere is the beginning of the advanced form of mediumship, although I must think at that point that you must start thinking in terms of spirit guides because if you didn't know your way around in that area, you could get taken over by all kinds of wrong things."

In his 1969 biography, *Peter Sellers: The Mask Behind the Mask,* author Peter Evans made note of the fact that the actor discussed spiritualism with a respect that fell short of unction and with an authority that, while not dogmatic, spoke with care about a subject that was of extreme importance to him.

Before Sellers met Mrs. Roberts, he had been a regular client of the British clairvoyant Maurice Woodruff, who had informed Peter that he would meet and marry someone with the initials "B. E."

Sellers, already married at the time, made the gossip columns on both sides of the Atlantic when he met the Swedish starlet Britt Ekland and began an almost classic Hollywood-type courtship of the young beauty.

In 1964, shortly after their marriage, Sellers suffered an attack of coronary thrombosis that stopped his heart eight times. "I knew that I would not die," Sellers said. "I have long held in mind a premonition that I shall live until I am seventy-five and will die in my sleep shortly after that."

Sellers passed away at the age of fifty-five, but regardless of his errant power of prophecy, he felt that his clairaudience guided him in his day-to-day existence as well as assisting in the development of his film characterizations.

The Spirits Warned of an Accident for His Son

Once when Peter Sellers and his thirteen-year-old son Michael were staying at the actor's country place, the teenager asked permission to go horseback riding with a friend. Suddenly, the spirit voice inside his head warned Sellers: "Don't let Michael go! He'll have a bad accident."

Sellers felt paralyzed, helpless. He did not want his son to go riding but neither did he wish to spoil the lad's fun. He admonished Michael to be especially careful and then prayed. The two boys had not gone more than one hundred yards from the stable when a dog ran barking across the road and startled the horses. Both Michael and his friend were thrown.

"Michael, very fortunately, was guided down and fell correctly," Sellers said, "but his friend was kicked and quite badly hurt. I felt terrible."

An Overwhelming Faith in Spiritualism and Reincarnation

In 1967, Sellers told the *London Sunday News* columnist Roderick Mann that he had spoken with the spirit of his mother in a séance with Mrs. Roberts. "My mother even knew that I had her ring in my pocket," Sellers said, "and she thanked me for some flowers that I had sent to Golders Green on Mother's Day."

The actor told journalist Kenneth Tynan that his sittings with Mrs. Roberts had given him an "overwhelming faith in spiritualism and reincarnation." Mrs. Roberts commented, "Peter is working out his salvation in his own way. It is the naturalness of spirit communication that has made Peter so enthusiastic about his spiritualism."

Sellers had been pleased when he discovered a kindred spirit in Shirley MacLaine while they were filming *Being There* because he had always been aware that many people dismissed the spirit voice inside his head as a bit of "dottiness."

Although Peter Sellers may have expressed anxiety over fulfilling his true mission on earth, the multitalented actor continued to assert with calm assurance that he had received the answers to questions that had enabled him to resolve his religious desperation. He had also, at the same time, received the inspiration that had aided him in developing one of the world's most successful and highly respected screen careers.

HOLLYWOOD STARS WHO HAVE MET THE SUPERNATURAL IN FILMS

Although this book concerns itself with the actual, real-life psychic, metaphysical, and spiritual experiences of the citizens of Hollywood, it is certainly relevant to our theme to take note of the motion picture industry's penchant for depicting tales of the supernatural and to point out how many major actors and actresses have appeared in at least one film that dealt with alien life-forms, multidimensional beings, the ghostly, and the paranormal.

Dr. Franklin R. Ruehl, host of the cable television series "Beyond the Other Dominion," assisted us in compiling the following roster of stars who contributed to making Hollywood the world's most extensive purveyor of the supernatural.

Alan Alda: In *The Mephisto Waltz* (1971), Alda, better known for comedy roles, such as his characterization of Hawkeye Pierce on the television series "M*A*S*H," is very effective as a musical journalist who becomes possessed through the satanic incantations of a moribund concert pianist (Curt Jurgens).

Dana Andrews: A handsome minister's son, Andrews starred in such Hollywood classics as *The Ox-Bow Incident* (1943), *Laura* (1944), and *The Best Years of Our Lives* (1946). Then, in *Curse of the Demon* (1957; originally titled *Night of the Demon),* he battled a group of devil-worshipers in London who paid obeisance to a hideous ancient demon.

James Arness: Before he became television's invincible Matt Dillon in the long-running series "Gunsmoke," Arness played an alien being, a giant, carnivorous humanoid vegetable who terrified a group of scientists at an isolated Arctic research station in *The Thing* (1951). In

Them! (1954), he was a government agent trying to subdue giant ants that had taken over the Los Angeles sewer system.

Fred Astaire: The recipient of a special Academy Award in 1949 for his contribution to motion pictures, Astaire, the master of the Hollywood musical, appeared in *Ghost Story* (1981) as one of a group of men being stalked by a vengeful female spirit.

Gene Barry: In *The War of the Worlds* (1953), Barry was a scientist attempting to thwart a Martian invasion of earth. He also starred in *The Devil and Miss Sarah* (1971), an offbeat Western about a satanic outlaw taking possession of his tormentor's wife.

Ernest Borgnine: An Academy Award winner for Best Actor in *Marty* (1955), this stocky, compelling actor was the leader of a devil-worshiping coven in *The Devil's Rain* (1975). In 1978, he was the ghost of an airline navigator who warns of potential crashes in *The Ghost of Flight 401.*

Raymond Burr: Television's masterful attorney in the ''Perry Mason'' series was not quite so smooth in *Bride of the Gorilla* (1951). Burr portrayed a scheming murderer who was transformed into a human gorilla by a witch, the mother of a native girl he had betrayed. In the classic *Godzilla* (1956), he was an American newsman in Tokyo covering the story of a radioactive, prehistoric monster's devastation of Japan's capital. Burr's scenes were deftly spliced into the original Japanese footage.

Joan Collins: In *The Devil Within Her* (1975), the manipulative Alexis of ''Dynasty'' had the role of a nightclub entertainer whose baby had been cursed by an evil dwarf. She fared little better in *Empire of the Ants* (1977), when Collins portrayed a real estate broker who, through a transformation machine, became a slave to intelligent, human-sized ants.

Bette Davis: In *Hush . . . Hush, Sweet Charlotte* (1965), the dynamic actress turned down some of her wattage in order to play the role of an heiress who is deceived into believing she is seeing ghosts so she can be committed to an insane asylum by unscrupulous relatives.

Nancy Davis (Mrs. Ronald Reagan): In *Donovan's Brain* (1953), she was the girlfriend of a scientist who falls under the telepathic control of the rich man's brain that he is keeping alive.

Kirk Douglas: The star of such motion picture masterpieces as *Champion* (1949), *Lust for Life* (1956), and *Spartacus* (1960), Douglas had his opportunity to face the supernatural in two films. In *The Chosen* (1978), he played a nuclear power industrialist whose son, actor Simon Ward, turned out to be the Antichrist. In *The Fury* (1978), he fathered a young man, actor Andrew Stevens, who developed incredible psychokinetic powers.

Clint Eastwood: Although he handily and forcefully dealt with thugs and criminals later in his career, in his cinematic green years, Eastwood was put up against bizarre monsters that were too large for even Dirty Harry to punch out. In *Revenge of the Creature* (1955), he played a laboratory assistant to John Agar, a scientist who was involved in putting the Creature from the Black Lagoon on exhibit at a Florida aquarium. That same year, Clint was a jet pilot trying to kill a giant tarantula that had been created in a laboratory experiment in *Tarantula*.

Glenn Ford: In *The Disappearance of Flight 412* (1974), Ford, the star of such memorable films as *Gilda* (1946), *The Big Heat* (1953), and countless classic Westerns, was an Air Force officer investigating the abduction of an aircraft by a UFO.

Peter Graves: There is something about Graves that simply makes him appear authoritative—maybe even scientifically authoritative. As a scientist in *Red Planet Mars* (1952), he established radio contact with Martians. Courageously, Graves attempted to thwart the takeover of earth by a Venusian creature in *It Conquered the World* (1956), and in *The Beginning of the End* (1957), he battled aliens and their underground menagerie of huge creatures.

George Hamilton: In *The Power* (1968), Hamilton played a man gifted with supernatural powers that had been imparted to him at birth by extraterrestrials. He is forced to battle another powerful but evil mind similarly endowed. In *Love at First Bite* (1979), he brought back his career from limbo with his portrayal of a comedic vampire.

Charlton Heston: In 1968, Heston, the heroic star of *The Ten Commandments* (1956) and *Ben Hur* (1959), for which he won an Oscar, appeared in *Planet of the Apes* as an astronaut who arrived in earth's future to discover that intelligent apes were ruling the planet. He continued his role as an astronaut displaced by time in *Beneath the Planet of the Apes* in 1970. In the grimly futuristic *The Omega Man* (1971), Heston is the single human immune to a terrible virus that is decimating earth's population after the radiation effects of a nuclear war.

John Houseman: In *The Fog* (1980), the distinguished actor is a fisherman who recounts a tale of ghostly pirates who, cloaked in fog, return for vengeance on a town that had wronged them. In *Ghost Story* (1981), Houseman is on the receiving end of ghostly pursuit as a lady spirit seeking revenge stalks a quartet of elderly men.

Deborah Kerr: This elegant British actress, the star of such films as *King Solomon's Mines* (1950), *Quo Vadis* (1951), and *The King and I* (1956), played a governess to two children possessed by ghosts in *The Innocents,* the 1961 film adaptation of Henry James's classic *The Turn of the Screw.* In *Eye of the Devil* (1967), Miss Kerr was the wife of a wealthy man, actor David Niven, who had to become a human sacrifice so that his ancestral lands could once again be fertile.

Cheryl Ladd: Under her original name of Cheryl Jean Stoppelmoor, she joined Kate Jackson in *Satan's School for Girls* (1973). Surely, attendance at such a school was not considered a prerequisite for being one of ''Charlie's Angels.''

Michael Landon: Before there was Little Joe on television's longrunning Western series ''Bonanza''—and long before he was an angel on ''Highway to Heaven''—there was *I Was a Teenage Werewolf* (1957). Landon was a troubled high school youth who was transformed into a werewolf by a scientist who was endeavoring to improve the human race.

Roger Moore: Just before he took over the James Bond role from

Sean Connery, Moore starred in *The Man Who Haunted Himself* (1970). This was the intriguing role of a man whose doppelgänger—spirit double—emerged while he was on the operating table and attempted to displace him in all aspects of his life.

Patricia Neal: This actress established a solid reputation in Hollywood when she starred with Gary Cooper in *The Fountainhead* (1949). Miss Neal would go on to appear in such memorable films as *A Face in the Crowd* (1957), and *Hud* (1963), for which she won an Oscar, but in *The Day the Earth Stood Still* (1951), she played the mother of a youngster befriended by an alien, actor Michael Rennie, who landed his spaceship near the White House. She also got to say those immortal words to the alien's giant robot: *Klaatu barada nikto!*

Jack Nicholson: The winner of the Best Actor Oscar in 1975 for *One Flew Over the Cuckoo's Nest* and again as Supporting Actor in 1983 for *Terms of Endearment,* Nicholson squared off against two masters of the supernatural in *The Raven* (1963) with his portrayal of the son of a man transformed into a large raven, Peter Lorre, by a nasty wizard, Boris Karloff. In *The Terror* (1963), he was a Napoleonic officer who encountered a witch, a mad baron—again Karloff—and the vengeful spirit of a young woman. Nicholson walked the thin line of madness in *The Shining* (1980) and disappointed no one when he erupted on the screen in demonic, axe-wielding fury, goaded to violence by the supernatural forces in a mountain resort. In *The Witches of Eastwick* (1987), Jack got promoted from the demonically insane to Satan himself—or at least a horny little devil.

Leonard Nimoy: It should be noted that Nimoy was playing aliens long before he became Mr. Spock, the "Star Trek" science officer of the *Enterprise*. In *Satan's Satellites* (also known as *Zombies of the Stratosphere;* 1958), he was an alien soldier who was part of a squadron determined to conquer the earth. He also had a small part in *The Brain Eaters* (1958), wherein alien creatures feast on human gray matter.

Jack Palance: In *Torture Garden* (1968), Palance was a devotee of Edgar Allan Poe who sets free the writer's spirit in exchange for the secrets of immortality. He also narrated *Unknown Powers* (1978), which won the Film Advisory Board's Award of Excellence.

Gregory Peck: Peck, the winner of the Best Actor Oscar for *To Kill a Mockingbird* (1962), turned in an excellent performance as the diplomat who learns that his son was actually the offspring of Satan and a nun, the so-called Antichrist in *The Omen* (1976).

William Shatner: A vicious coven of devil-worshipers enslaves Shatner, a decent man, in *The Devil's Rain* (1975), thus making another hitch as Captain Kirk in *Star Trek—The Motion Picture* (1979) seem that much more inviting.

Donald Sutherland: Sutherland pounded a stake into the heart of his beloved bride in *Dr. Terror's House of Horrors* (1965) when he learned that she was a vampire. In *Invasion of the Body Snatchers* (1978), he was a man desperately trying to destroy alien pods that grew into human beings, replacing the originals.

Robert Vaughn: In *Starship Invasions* (1977), Vaughn—"The Man from U.N.C.L.E." star, Napoleon Solo—portrayed a UFO investigator who is enlisted by benign aliens to stop the conquest of Earth by malevolent extraterrestrials. In *Hangar 18* (1980), though, he was the President of the United States attempting to cover up the truth about a crashed UFO.

The above list comprises only a representative number of those stars who have appeared in motion pictures with a touch of the supernatural about them, and it is certain that the list will only get longer as Hollywood continues its fascination with movies that have mystical, metaphysical, or otherworldly overtones.

Consider the highest grossing films of the 1980s. Eight of the top ten deal with "ghoulies and ghosties and long-leggety beasties" from other dimensions:

1. *E.T.—The Extra-Terrestrial* (1982)
2. *Return of the Jedi* (1983)
3. *Batman* (1989)

4. *Raiders of the Lost Ark* (1981)
5. *Beverly Hills Cop* (1984)
6. *The Empire Strikes Back* (1980)
7. *Ghostbusters* (1984)
8. *Back to the Future* (1985)
9. *Indiana Jones and the Last Crusade* (1989)
10. *Tootsie* (1982)

2 · THE ZODIAC, TAROT CARDS, AND NUMEROLOGY

T he stresses of expectancy and hope, the fear of failure, the obsession with writing, directing, or starring in a blockbuster film all make the Hollywood denizens perpetual seekers of reliable means of divining the future.

Astrology remains popular among those stars who are convinced that the signs of the zodiac—Aries the Ram, Taurus the Bull, Gemini the Twins, Cancer the Crab, Leo the Lion, Virgo the Virgin, Libra the Balance, Scorpio the Scorpion, Sagittarius the Archer, Capricorn the Goat, Aquarius the Water Bearer, and Pisces the Fishes—can predict sure pathways to success. As many folks surmised (and Hollywood insiders were aware), former President Ronald Reagan and First Lady Nancy Reagan were devotees of the sun signs long before their tenure in the White House. Reagan was a client of astrologist Carroll Righter when he was an actor attempting to forecast the best career moves.

Righter was famous for his sun sign parties for the Hollywood stars. If it was a Leo shindig, live lions were tethered in the yard. Bulls were haltered and led through the midst of the party-goers if it was a Taurus celebration, and so on.

In addition to Reagan, Marlene Dietrich, Ronald Colman, Tyrone Power, Susan Hayward, and Robert Cummings were frequent celebrants at Righter's parties and were faithful clients of his astrological readings.

PARANORMAL PATHWAYS TO SUCCESS

If Astrology Is Good Enough for Presidents ...

"If Reagan wasn't an astrology freak, why get sworn in at some strange time like six minutes after midnight?" astrologist Linda Goodman asked pointedly.

In her book *My Turn* (1989), Nancy Reagan defended herself against the slings and arrows of her critics by explaining, "Astrology was simply one of the ways I coped with the fear I felt after my husband almost died in the assassination attempt."

Astrologist Joan Quigley provided Mrs. Reagan with the President's "good days" and "bad days." The First Lady said that she saw no harm in receiving such advice. "While astrology was a factor in determining Ronnie's schedule, it was never the only one, and no political decision was ever made based on it."

Growing Evidence for the Validity of Astrology

Skeptics may deride astrology as a psychological crutch for the desperate and the superstitious, but an increasing number of serious scientists are bringing their intellects to bear on the study of the planets and their possible influences upon humankind.

French psychologist and statistician Michel Gauquelin began his investigation of astrology more than thirty years ago. Repeatedly, Gauquelin has verified the importance of the planetary positions at birth.

More recently, Percy Seymour, a British astronomer and Fellow of the Royal Astronomical Society, set forth his theory that astrology is neither mystical nor magical but is magnetic. Seymour theorizes that we may, indeed, be affected by the powerful magnetic activity of the sun, which is stirred up by the movements of the planets, sent earthward on solar winds, and felt by each of us via the magnetic field as we develop inside our mother's womb.

Crystals, Gems of the New Age

The current vogue prescribes crystals for nearly anything that ails you, including removing the clouds that obscure the future. Cybill Shepherd has crystals especially channeled for her family and closest friends. Other crystal enthusiasts include Stepfanie Kramer, George Hamilton, LeVar Burton, Richard Gere, Lisa Bonet, and Bianca Jagger.

Rachel Ward Depends on Her Tarot Cards

Rachel Ward swears by her tarot deck. The star, known to millions for her performance in the 1983 television miniseries *The Thorn Birds,* stated that two of the most important events in her life—success in Hollywood and finding her dream man—were predicted by psychics using tarot cards.

Rachel freely stated that she had been told of major details in her career, including the fact that her costar in a motion picture would be Burt Reynolds. This prediction was realized when she did, indeed, make *Sharky's Machine* (1981) with Reynolds. It was also in a tarot card reading that she was told that she would soon meet her soulmate, who would be a Cancer. This prediction came true when she met the Australian actor Bryan Brown, who starred with her in *The Thorn Birds.* Predictably, the two fell in love and were married.

A Woman with a Surprising Talent for Reading Palms

Some stars do very well reading palms. Writer Tom Calhoun remembers a rainy Sunday morning in 1937 when he and another Harvard chum, Caspar, met Kate from Bennington at a resort in Connecticut. Because Howard, her date, failed to show up, a moody Kate offered to read palms to pass the time. Caspar was first, and she wrinkled her nose in distaste. ''I see something in your future very militaristic,'' she said in a husky voice. ''I simply can't stand the military. I see you with power. Be careful how you use it.''

Tom was told that he would experience a long sea voyage, which certainly proved true since he barely saw land while serving with the U.S. Navy in World War II. His friend Caspar's ambition was to become an attorney like his father, but when Caspar W. Weinberger became Secretary of Defense in 1981, he had to have given Kate credit for a most accurate prophecy.

All things considered, Calhoun muses, it was a most interesting way to meet Katharine Hepburn, and he cannot help wondering what she might have told Howard Hughes if he had kept his date with her that rainy weekend in Connecticut.

Ted Danson has Tried Everything to Woo Lady Luck

Ten Danson, star of the television series "Cheers" and the smash films *Three Men and a Baby* (1987) and *Cousins* (1989), said he has tried palm readers, astrologers, and psychic sensitives—and he loves them all. Mostly, though, he said, he believes in destiny.

"I don't know much about prophecies," Danson said, "but you can certainly observe tendencies and patterns." Ted has been interested in spiritual matters since 1976, when he took a class in EST, the self-motivational group designed by Werner Erhard.

"All that stuff is great," he stated. "It was all part of my growing up—all part of my search."

ANGELA LOUISE GALLO'S GALAXY OF STARS

Angela Louise Gallo's star clientele has been building for forty years, making her one of the most esteemed astrologists in Hollywood. "I came out here in 1948 to be a dress designer," the charming woman said, laughing, "but I went broke. Thank goodness that I had been doing charts for people all along, so when things didn't work out the way I had originally planned them, I began teaching classes in astrology and continued with the charts."

Angela has been the editor of an astrology newspaper and has had her own television show on the zodiac for many years. Speaking in a soft voice that still carries occasional inflections from her native East Coast, she said, "The stars come to see me most often for two basic reasons: Number one, their careers; number two, their health or their love life."

Ed Asner Had to Know If He Would "Make It" in Hollywood

Before Ed Asner had become a success on "The Mary Tyler Moore Show," he came to Angela as a starving actor with only one question: "Will I make it?"

"I was pleased to be able to tell him that he wouldn't have to worry as long as he worked hard," Angela said.

A Shy Burt Reynolds's Main Concern Was His Health

"Burt Reynolds is an Aquarius with Gemini rising," Angela said. "When I saw him, his main concern was his health. He had just received his doctor's report indicating that he was hypoglycemic. He was very polite, and he kept telling me to go on reading his chart. He is very open to astrology."

Angela found Reynolds to be shy, not at all like his more aggressive movie persona. "I outlined his health concerns and told him to be positive. I even said that he would be married in five years."

Though Angela has never met Loni Anderson, Reynolds's wife, she assumes the actress must also be open to such matters as astrology. "I did note that he and Sally Field would never marry," Angela said, chuckling.

Jonathan Winters Does Not Joke About His Investments

Comedian Jonathan Winters, master of mimicry and the star of such films as *It's a Mad Mad Mad Mad World* (1963), was worried about his stock investments.

"I met Jonathan and his wife Eileen in Jamaica," Angela said. "They're both Scorpios and very good for each other. She has had marvelous patience to stay with him! They had me over to dinner, and he expressed how worried he was about his investments. He had just put a lot of money into stocks and into a tax shelter.

"I made out a chart for him, and it became clear that he had no reason to worry. Things worked out fine for him."

Karen Valentine Lost a Man, Gained a Better One

Angela also met actress Karen Valentine while she was visiting in Jamaica. "She was with someone, and she wanted to know if he would marry her.

"I told Karen—she's a Gemini with Pisces rising—that she absolutely should not marry the man. I warned her that he was a manic-depressive."

Concerned, Karen asked, "Will I ever marry?"

"I told her that she would marry someone else before the year was out," Angela said, "and she got married just a few minutes before midnight on New Year's Eve."

The Stars Steered Valerie Bertinelli away from a Potentially Disastrous Romance

Valerie Bertinelli, a Taurus with Scorpio rising, is another member of show business whom Angela found to be very shy. "She had a romance going on behind the scenes," Angela confided. "It could have been unfortunate for her, but her chart guided her through it all. Everything came out exactly as her chart dictated that it would."

Rose Marie: A Performer from Many Lifetimes Past

Rose Marie, one of the stars of the long-running "The Dick Van Dyke Show," was quite skeptical when she first encountered Angela, but now the astrologist declares that she and the multitalented actress-singer are best friends. "Rose Marie is a double Leo," Angela said. "She is aware that it was a past life that put her on the stage at the tender age of three as 'Baby Rose Marie.' She is so talented, but she is a typical actress in that she is nervous about her career and is always wanting to know what is going to happen tomorrow."

Angela told us that it matters not at all whether she knows her subjects personally—or even if she recognizes her famous clientele. "I use pure astrology. Some people have said that I must be truly psychic, but to my knowledge, I am simply using the zodiacal charts. Some stars are very frightened when they first come to see me. Maybe they're between shows or contracts. They feel down and out and very upset."

Barbara Eden Tries an Anonymous Visit

Barbara Eden came at first anonymously to request a chart from Angela. "I sure thought she looked familiar, but she used her maiden name, Huffman. After I got into the chart and was hitting so many things accurately, she interrupted me by laughing and asking me if I didn't recognize her. Here it was Jeannie, the magic genie in "I Dream of Jeannie," asking for her chart to be done. Barbara Eden is very proastrology. She had had a chart done twenty years before that had outlined all the high points of her career.

"What the chart had not done," Angela said, "was to deal accurately with business matters. Barbara had been taken advantage of a great deal. She had made a great deal of money and had it taken from her by listening to the wrong people and by giving them control. The stars were able to help her get back on course."

The Stars Predicted Accurately for Lorne Greene— In Spite of His Skepticism

Lorne Greene, an Aquarius with Libra rising, was a nonbeliever in astrology. At the same time, having just come off "Bonanza," one of the longest-running series in television history, he was understandably a bit restless being between jobs.

"Rose Marie had tried to get him to come to me to have his chart done, but he just scoffed at her," Angela said. "But one night when they were both appearing on a talk show, she just pulled out my chart for him and started reading parts of it right on the air. Rose Marie said that, according to my chart, he was currently working on a series that would fail, but his next series would be a success.

"Lorne Greene snorted that he did not believe it. He was working on a series called 'Griff,' in which he played a detective, and he said that he really liked the idea. He was certain that it would be a success with the viewers. It couldn't flop, he said. He would prove astrology to be bunk." As the stars and the ratings would reveal to Greene, his modern detective series failed, and his next series, "Battlestar Galactica," proved to be much more successful.

John Davidson Loses His Doubts About Astrology

Angela stated that John Davidson, the host of "Hollywood Squares," used to be a very vocal skeptic of astrology. "He became incensed when I told him that he would get divorced. He said that he had a very happy marriage. Rose Marie reminded him of my astrological predictions at the time of his divorce."

Cesar Romero Finds Out That He Is Not Too Old for a Series

Cesar Romero, who was television's Joker on the "Batman" series, as well as the star of films ranging from *The Cisco Kid and the Lady* (1939) to *The Proud and the Damned* (1972), was another actor who was at first skeptical of astrology's ability to pierce the veil of the future.

"I kept telling him that he would play in another long-running television series," Angela said, "but he would just laugh and say, 'Forget it, Angela. I'm in my seventies.' "

Angela recalled how Rose Marie would chide him: "Come on, Cesar. You're a double Aquarius. You have to be open-minded."

"Okay," Romero conceded at last. "I will at least keep an open mind toward astrology."

Now, after several years of a continuing role on "Falcon Crest," Cesar Romero finds it much easier to believe in the power of the stars to impel. "Whenever he runs into Rose Marie, he always says, 'Tell Angela that she was right!' "

Morey Amsterdam Combines Astrology with Prayer and Positive Thinking

Morey Amsterdam, Rose Marie's sidekick on "The Dick Van Dyke Show," is a double Sagittarius "who never stops talking," Angela said. "Morey is a warm and wonderful person, and so is his wife, Kay. He has a mind that never stops working. It just never quits. He writes for other comedians as well as doing his own routines."

Amsterdam is open to all aspects of astrology and psychic phenomena. "His son got off the path a few years ago, and Morey had to work hard on him to get him straightened out. He did it, though, with prayer and positive thinking. Morey is a very positive person."

Actress Julie Parrish, according to Angela, "knows astrology inside out" and has the capability of doing her own charts to keep her balanced and on track with her career.

Tommy Smothers Works with His Destiny

"Tommy Smothers is a good example of someone who is very open and accepting of these things and who has the balance to work with his destiny," Angela said. "Dick is also open, but he follows his brother's direction. It is fascinating how their onstage personalities are just reversed from what they are in real life."

In 1969, members of Tommy's family had been attending Angela's class in astrology, so in March of that year, it did not take the astrologist long to learn that the Smothers Brothers' controversial television series had been canceled. When Angela was told that Tommy wished to consult with her, she immediately agreed to do a chart for him.

"You'll have another series one day," she told him.

"Really?" Smothers questioned. "Another one?"

"Yes," Angela said, "but it won't be for a good number of years."

Tommy sat quietly for a time, contemplating her words—and perhaps all the trials and tribulations they had just endured. "That's fine," he said at last. "I won't push it. I'll develop other interests and pursuits."

Angela reminded us that it was astrology that helped Tommy Smothers stay strong and not become depressed during the long hiatus from television. He may not have realized that it would take nearly twenty years before the Smothers Brothers would get another chance with a network series, but he went on to obtain roles in commercials and feature films and to develop real estate and vineyards.

A Sad Tale of an Aging Star Who Did Not Take Angela's Advice

Of course, the astrologist was quick to point out, not everyone takes her advice. Out of respect for an aging legendary film star who has provided the world with several classic movie roles, we will tell the following story in Angela's voice without using any names.

"In 1975, I received a telephone call from the 'Star's' new girlfriend, who invited me to his house. She was an aspiring actress whom

I knew well. She had come to see me frequently in 1968 and 1969.

"When she met the 'Star,' he had been told by her manager that she came from a very wealthy family and that she wanted to enter show business through the proper connections. Then she told the 'Star' that I had predicted through her chart that she would meet someone famous and marry him."

Angela felt very uncomfortable being put in the middle of such an ill-fated romantic affair, but her integrity and ethics required her to point out to the "Star" that his chart clearly revealed that there would be an early divorce should he decide to marry the starlet.

"I knew that my words would probably fall on deaf ears since he was a Taurus—and so was she. He more than acknowledged his love for her and told me how much he cared for her. She was, of course, very lovely and many years younger than he, and he was flattered by her apparent love and devotion to him."

Angela knew that the "Star" had suffered a number of serious disappointments in matters of the heart, and she did not wish to see him endure another matrimonial shipwreck.

"They married . . . and they soon divorced," Angela said. "Now he is a bit peeved with astrology or psychic readings, feeling that his ex-wife's chart had guaranteed happiness for both of them. He was told what would happen. I tried to warn him, but you know how people are when they are in love."

NUMBERING THE STARS

It was in the mid-1960s that we first heard of a remarkable woman named Marguerite Haymes who had combined the principles of astrology, numerology, yoga, the Indian Vedas, the ancient wisdom of the Egyptians, and the Jewish Kabbala into a science of numbers that she termed Unitology. The mother of Dick Haymes, who had been a popular singer-actor in the forties and fifties—*DuBarry Was a Lady* (1943) and *State Fair* (1945)—Marguerite had also enjoyed a career as a singer as well as being a leader in the world of Paris fashion.

Marguerite spoke often of her teacher in the esoteric mysteries, a master teacher named Athena, who taught her the principle that each individual is equipped with a different assignment. Each individual assignment has been designed to fulfill a destiny, and each of us is created with equal opportunity to direct his or her own fate.

Armed with this philosophy, Marguerite went to Paris to become the first American woman to compete with the French in the world of fashion. Despite warnings from all sides, Marguerite built her Maison de Couture from a small business into a flourishing, million-dollar industry.

She became a well-known Paris figure and made that city her home for twelve years. After such success in the world of fashion, however, she felt a pull back into music. Some intuitive knowing led her straight to Maurice Jacquet, a musical prodigy who had conducted the *Opera Comique* of Paris at the age of thirteen. When Jacquet launched her on a concert tour, Marguerite was soon hailed as the foremost interpreter of Debussy and Ravel.

Jacquet coached her vocally and spiritually. A High Priest of the European Order of Rosicrucians and a mystic, he taught Marguerite the spiritual interpretation of numbers and their mathematical accuracy in relation to music and its interpretation in any form. It was through this man that she began to realize the great necessity for the coordination of mind, body, and spirit.

When she eventually returned to America, Marguerite began to teach modern singing and was soon known as a starmaker, with graduates in every facet of the entertainment field. This section of her life path lasted for more than twenty years. "I loved it," she said. "Being privileged to guide youth through music is a sheer joy. I grew and learned through my students while still doing research in the occult sciences."

It was during this phase of her life that Marguerite was led to her last earthly teacher, Paramahansa Yogananda, a master of Eastern and Western philosophy. It was from this master teacher that she learned all that she was "supposed to know" before he passed on.

According to Marguerite, the great yogi's life-path number was a 9, and thus his destiny was the brotherhood of man. Numbers, she insisted, can assist one in tapping the power within and in planning a successful life, and she set down the principles and mechanics by which she and her students were able to govern their lives.

All that humans are capable of experiencing, Marguerite stated, can be reduced to the digits 1 through 9. These single numbers are derived from the simplification of all combinations of numbers to their basic essence. This essence then vibrates through the single digit.

Beyond the cycle of 9, however, are the two master numbers 11 and 22, which are never reduced to single digits. A personal chart in Unitology will include four major numbers: the life-path number, the day number, the expression number, and the soul-urge number.

The first and most important, the life-path number, is derived from one's birth date. It is one's destiny, which cannot be changed but can be directed. From this number is determined one's potential, hidden aptitudes, talents, and desires. According to Marguerite, the life-path number symbolizes one's personal rate of vibration, one's frequency, one's specific assignment in life.

While the life-path and day numbers are derived from one's birth date, the expression and soul-urge numbers are formulated from one's name. According to the precepts of Unitology, one's name is very important, as it is concerned with sound, a direct manifestation of vibration. Therefore, since each letter of every alphabet has its distinctive sound, it follows that each letter has its own distinctive number. Using the 1 to 9 cycle, it is imperative to establish the essence of the number. The soul-urge number is found by totaling the number of vowels in one's name. By combining all the many metaphysical disciplines mentioned earlier, Marguerite arrived at a particular numerical value for each letter of the alphabet. The letters, translated into numbers, are totaled and simplified into a single digit.

For example, Shirley MacLaine was born Shirley Maclean Beaty on April 24, 1934. According to Marguerite's Unitology, Shirley's given name breaks down to a 9. As a 9 personality, she, like Paramahansa Yogananda, lives in the vibration of the brotherhood of man, a difficult path as it requires complete humanitarianism. Those under this vibration must be prepared to give up all personal desire and ambition. They find their greatest opportunity with emotional, artistic people, as 9 is the highest vibration of the artist. Number 9 operates under the law of fulfillment, and its appeal is to the all-inclusive, to the many.

Shirley MacLaine's soul-urge number is 7, epitomized by wisdom. Seven is a cosmic number, related to the seven planets, seven days of the week, seven colors, seven notes on the musical scale, and so on. Opportunities are brought to her as a 7 person without her actively seeking them. Seven is also the number of the mental analyst. Those under this vibration seek answers, and they use their mental abilities to probe the deep mysteries and the hidden truths of the universe. They are unconcerned with material goods for they know that by applying spiritual laws, they will prosper.

With her soul-urge vibration a 7, Shirley understands that a high-energy personality such as she needs to have time for rest and study.

The entertainer's day number is 6, which in the principles of Unitology signifies that she is capable of devotional, impersonal love toward others. As a 6, Shirley is able to serve cheerfully and efficiently, applying the law of balance in order to adjust to inharmonious conditions.

Tough guy Charles Bronson might surprise you. His birth name of Charles Buchinsky gives him a life expression of 11, a master number, which places him on a high vibrational plane. As a youth, it is likely that he received his ideals on an intuitive level. By changing his name to Bronson, he became a 1, thereby increasing his personal emphasis on individuality. His life-path number—November 3, 1922—is a 2, providing him with the adaptability that is so necessary to one's becoming an effective actor.

Bronson's soul-urge number is a 5, letting us know that his inner self yearns for freedom and the quest for the new and the progressive. Combine all of the above with his day number of 3, self-expression, and we see a pattern profile of adaptability, creativity, and intuition that blends into a sensitive man who just happens to be effective playing action roles.

William Shatner, Captain Kirk of "Star Trek" fame, also has the master number 11 as his life-expression number. According to the numbers, Shatner has it as his destiny to reveal something new and uplifting to the world, thus qualifying him to play roles that have him soaring to cosmic dimensions. His life-expression number is that of the messenger.

Shatner's day number of 4—March 22, 1931—intensifies his leadership qualities. His life-path number of 3, that of self-expression, tells us that he will only be contented when he is seeking fulfillment through his craft of communication. His soul-urge number 8 gives him the inner power to take any opportunity to demonstrate his efficiency and his executive abilities.

When we examine Larry Hagman's numerical scan—September 21,

1931—we can readily see that he is not really as mean and conniving as the tricky J. R. Ewing, whom he has been playing on "Dallas." Since both Hagman's day and soul-urge numbers total 3, the digit of self-expression, we note that he is an artistic sort who enjoys being friendly and sociable.

Hagman's life-expression number is a 1, the numeral of the individual who is always prepared to stand on his own two feet. He has learned, however, to cooperate with others without losing his individuality. His life-path number is an 8, the number of material freedom, the digit of those who love power and success.

Raquel Welch—September 5, 1942—is one whose life-path and soul-urge numbers each break down to a 1. Interestingly, both her professional name, Welch, and her birth name, Tejada, are reduced to the number 1.

Raquel in both her life expression and her soul urge is revealed to be a person who has a great desire to direct her mind, body, and spirit to the utmost efficiency. She is one who must always be independent and be continually seeking to improve herself. Her day number of 5 emphasizes her need for freedom, her desire to travel widely, and her striving to be always adaptable. Raquel's life-path number is a 3, which underlines her need to be a communicator, functioning best in an artistic environment.

"We must obey the laws coming from above us, but on our own plane we must govern and give the orders," Marguerite Haymes once said. "In so doing, we form a part of the whole . . . the oneness. Once we know this teaching, we fall in with the law and operate it—instead of being used by it.

"Everything is accomplished by the power of the mind. We are truly magnetic when we are on our own vibrant mental wavelength. When this is understood, it is easy to see how so-called miracles are performed."

TUNING IN ON THE FUTURE THROUGH ESP

Alan Vaughan, one of the most tested and researched psychics of our time, is himself an investigator of the paranormal. Since he lives in the Hollywood area, it seems obvious that his precognitive abilities have assured him that California is not going to sink into the ocean.

"I have no such fears of my house falling into the ocean," he said. "In fact, it was because of several dreams that I was told to move here. As far as earthquakes go, however, I have received psychic impressions that Southern California will have a big one in 1999."

Vaughan's business card proclaims that he performs "intuitive consultations" for clients who wish to utilize his abilities to peek into the future. He also channels a Chinese entity named "Li Sung," who provides insights into creative and spiritual gifts.

Although Alan said that professional ethics prevented him from giving us the star's name, he told us of an actress who had once enjoyed considerable cinematic success but whose career was on the wane when she came to see him.

"I told her that she should switch to television," Alan said, "and, boy, did I get a lecture about what a big film star she was and how it would be death for a motion picture actress to accept steady television work. I tried to tell her that millions and millions of people would see her in a single evening and that her career in films might be revived. My consultation seemed to have little effect on her attitude, however, and she left in a bit of a huff.

"Some time later," Alan said, "I saw her on Larry King's interview program. She was telling him that she would soon be appearing in a television series and that she would be able to be seen by millions and millions of people in one evening, far more than she would reach in her motion pictures."

Good News for Terry Moore

When Alan Vaughan first met Terry Moore, who starred in *Come Back, Little Sheba* (1952) and *Peyton Place* (1957), the actress was greatly concerned with her efforts to get the Howard Hughes family to recognize the legality of her marriage to the eccentric millionaire.

"When she walked up to me at a party at the home of Dick and Tara Sutphen, I saw neon lights all around her," Alan said, "then I got the number 7 flashing on and off. I told Terry that in seven years she would be recognized by the Hughes estate and receive a financial settlement. I also said that in seven years she would be writing a book and be back in show business. As you know, each of those things have come to pass in her life within the seven-year period.''

Vaughan believes that everyone may obtain his or her own previews of the future. ''Li Sung has told me that more and more people are going to learn to channel so that they might become more receptive to the inner voice within them. The spirit world has a master plan for increased higher consciousness that will spread around the globe. Hollywood is going to play a major part in communicating the higher truths to people throughout the world.''

Doc Anderson Found Oil Wells with His Bleeding Palms

In the late sixties and early seventies, a psychic named Doc Anderson was assisting a number of Texas oilmen and Hollywood stars to find oil by his bleeding palms. The Georgia native would walk around the oil fields until he would have a vision of giant pools of black gold; then his hands would be covered with blood, and the investors would know that Doc had found another place to drill.

George Raft, the star of such films as *Scarface* (1932) and *Nob Hill* (1945), together with screen heavy Mike Mazurki and character actor Denver Pyle, was among the Hollywood set that joined the oilmen in drilling where the psychic dripped his telltale blood.

Doc Anderson died a few years ago when a flash flood claimed his life. Although he had announced his vision of a very hard earthquake striking California, he did not foresee the entire state sinking into the ocean.

''There are volcanic forces building up off the coast of California, beneath the sea,'' he said. ''The start of volcanic activity not too far out at sea is the signal that there will be subterranean disturbances that will cause an earthquake along the fault line in California.''

Dr. Montgomery Believes the Future Can Be Changed

Dr. Ernesto Montgomery moved to Los Angeles in 1961 and organized the Universal Metaphysical Church. Born on the island of Jamaica, Montgomery served in a secret British intelligence agency during World War II. Later, when he visited Dallas, Texas, in 1957, he predicted the death of a U.S. President in that city.

"In October of 1957, I informed Jess Curry, who was then the chief of police of the Dallas Police Department, that within a short span of years there would be a U.S. President murdered in that city," Montgomery said. "A photograph was taken—and published—that shows me pointing out the site to Dallas police officials. It was at Dealy Plaza where President John F. Kennedy was assassinated in 1963."

Montgomery has provided psychic counsel for Winston Churchill, Princess Margaret, police departments around the world, and numerous Hollywood stars and celebrities.

My psychic impressions come to me in two forms. The first form is a vision when I go to sleep. Once I am in slumber, a revelation will be revealed to me. This method is accurate on a statistical basis approximately ninety percent of the time. The other method I use is called "psychic insight." That is, I place myself into what is known as a trance state. I am hypnotized into deep and continuous concentration by focusing upon a particular problem. Consequently, I am able to predict with an accuracy that has been, perhaps, ninety-nine percent effective in the past.

Can the future be changed? That is an interesting question.

I believe that the future can definitely be changed by an individual being warned of a impending tragedy or knowing of something that seems destined to occur. If the individual can be warned—as I tried to warn the victims in the Sharon Tate murders [see Chapter Five: "Unholy Nights: The Dark Side of the Force"]—then they can take appropriate steps to prevent the occurrence.

Now a phenomenon like an earthquake or any other disaster is very difficult to change because there is no individual free will involved. All that can be done by the psychic receiving the impression is to give the warning. So far as I am concerned, I do not have any power to change what God, who has given me this gift, tells me. I do believe seriously that humankind cannot drastically change destiny. What we have is the power to change what may happen to each of us as individuals.

Olof Jonsson Creates a Special Surprise for Glenn Ford

In February 1971, the international news services carried an account of an electrifying ESP experiment, a telepathic communication through space between Apollo 14's astronaut Edgar D. Mitchell on the moon and the psychic engineer Olof Jonsson on earth.

Although Jonsson may have been largely unknown to the world at large before this dramatic entrance into public consciousness, he had been a psychic celebrity for years. Both in his native Sweden and in parapsychology laboratories throughout the United States, Jonsson was famous for his ability to "guess" correctly twenty-five out of twenty-five ESP cards, to levitate objects, to solve crimes clairvoyantly, and to predict the future.

Film star Glenn Ford—*The Blackboard Jungle* (1955) and *The Courtship of Eddie's Father* (1963)—is among those who have witnessed Jonsson score one hundred percent, and Jonsson, along with writer-educator James Hurley and his wife, met with Ford in April 1964 to discuss the actor's interest in starring in a film biography of Jonsson's incredible psychic career.

According to Hurley, even before they met Ford, Jonsson had vividly described some of the more subtle details of the actor's home to Hal Clifton, Ford's personal secretary. The psychic-sensitive had accurately foreseen the oils portraying bullfighting scenes, the layout of various rooms, and even the red-cushioned stools in front of the bar designed by Ford.

Hurley dismissed Jonsson's clairvoyant images of a "little doll, dressed in a cape, standing on the bar" until they arrived at Ford's home and Hurley saw the figure for himself, a memento from the crew of Ford's movie, *The Four Horsemen of the Apocalypse* (1961).

Clifton and Ford's mother were also present. "As the evening progressed," Hurley said, "Olof's faculties became more acute due to either the refined beauty of the house or the comradeship of strangers who had quickly become friends."

An avid souvenir collector, Ford showed the psychic a number of objects that he had obtained while making films in other countries from which Jonsson picked up impressions with great accuracy. He also correctly identified Mrs. Ford's morbid fear of fire. With her permission, he revealed to the others that when she was close to delivering

Glenn, a house fire almost took her life, though she had escaped un-harmed. Capping that evening's demonstration, Olof called twenty-five out of twenty-five ESP cards correctly, having never touched the deck as he remained out of the room until Ford, who controlled the experiment, asked him to enter.

The next night, Olof and his friends were invited to have dinner with Ford only to discover themselves included in a surprise birthday party for the actor. Perhaps as a gift, Olof demonstrated psycho-kinesis—mind over matter—for Ford; while standing by the pool, he moved a glass by mental effort alone.

A Private Demonstration for Morey Amsterdam

Morey Amsterdam, an astute businessman as well as a bright and witty comedian, became so excited and enthusiastic after witnessing an Olof Jonsson display of psychic abilities that he, too, began to talk about a possible film treatment of the Swedish sensitive's life story.

One night at Amsterdam's suite in Chicago's Palmer House, Morey, his wife, a prominent Chicago industrialist, his wife and daughter, and a young singer starring at the Playboy Club asked Olof to give them a private demonstration of his talents. Although Jonsson had never met any of those assembled in the suite before that evening, he told all of them past, present, and future details of their lives. He spoke of the singer's fall from a horse some time before and of the injury that she had suffered. He gave the industrialist the details of a secret business venture that he had masterminded that very day. He also warned the man about an injury that would—and did—take place.

One thing that seems certain about true precognition, whether it comes about through a dream, a vision, or a prophet's prediction, the percipient does not see possibilities but actualities. In view of this, some psychical researchers maintain that the age-old query "Can the future be changed?" has no meaning. The foreknowledge of the fu-ture—of which some level of the subconscious is aware and of which it sometimes flashes a dramatic scene to the conscious in a dream or a trance—is founded on the knowledge of how the individual will use his freedom of choice. The future event conditions the subconscious self. The level of the subconscious that "knows" the future does not con-dition the future event. The transcendent element of self that knows what "will be" blends all time into "what is now and what will always be."

For the conscious self, what is now the past was once the future. We do not look upon past events and feel that we acted without freedom of will. Why then should we look at the future and feel that those events are predetermined? That a subconscious level in the psyche may *know* the future, these psychical researchers insist, does not mean that the conscious self has no freedom of choice.

Simply stated, if the future could be changed, it would not be the future. In a true precognitive experience, when one perceives the future, he or she has glimpsed what will be and what, for a level of subconscious, already exists. Therefore, most readings of the future are really picking up on the possible choices that one has by which to attain a desired goal, and for someone riding the fast-moving Hollywood merry-go-round of success, he or she seeks all the advice that is obtainable in determining which choices are the better ones.

ANTHONY QUINN'S PERSONAL FORTUNE-TELLER

When Anthony Quinn, the Academy Award–winning star of both *Viva Zapata* (1952) and *Lust for Life* (1956), met Iolanda Addolori, he had been told that she was an accomplished costume designer. He could see for himself that she was a lovely blonde with golden brown eyes and an attractive figure. It took him a little longer to realize that he had fallen in love with a seeress.

Iolanda had had her natural psychic abilities developed by her father, Ferruccio Addolori. No member of his family would dream of taking a trip or beginning any important venture without first consulting Papa and having him spread his battered deck of cards. With the blessing of her father and his cards, Iolanda had gone to Rome to study costume design, but first he had taught her how to read the cards for herself. Then, on the night of April 7, 1960, at 7 P.M., she received a call from her family in Venice that Papa was dying of a heart attack. She tried immediately to board a train for home, but none were leaving Rome that night.

As the youngest child, and perhaps the closest to her father, Iolanda returned to her little room, sick with concern. As an attempt to receive some solace, she began to lay out the cards. At every turn, they spelled death. Terribly distraught, she went to bed and finally managed to fall asleep.

At 2 A.M., she was awakened by the sound of her father's voice calling to her. With a chilling sense of dread, she phoned her family in Venice, knowing that they would only confirm her psychic message from her father. Indeed, she learned that Ferruccio Addolori had died at the exact moment she had heard him calling to her.

Her Legacy Was a Worn Deck of Cards

Iolanda inherited her father's battered and worn deck of fortune-telling cards, and they soon predicted that she would be meeting many important people, that she would receive a great deal of notoriety, and that her marriage would be reported in all the newspapers.

A year later, in 1961, she met Anthony Quinn. The dynamic actor was legally separated from his wife and was very lonely on location in Italy, where he was filming *Barabbas* (1962). Iolanda was assigned to the picture as costume designer. Although she tried to keep their relationship on a professional basis, it was not long before Quinn had begun to weave a spell of his own, and she fell in love with him. She bore two out-of-wedlock children to Quinn before his divorce was finalized. True to the prediction of the cards, the scandal wagged tongues on the Continent, and the wagging did not cease until Iolanda and Anthony Quinn were happily joined in marriage.

Quinn, a man with a reputation for being a bit too kind and generous, learned to heed Iolanda's reading of the cards to warn him about those seeming friends who hid ulterior motives behind their smiles. She did not enjoy hurting her husband's feelings by revealing the schemes that certain of his trusted colleagues were hatching behind his back, but Iolanda felt such painful disclosures to be preferable to Quinn's truly being burnt by their chicanery.

Predicting a Film's Box-Office Potential

Iolanda also possessed the ability to predict unfailingly the success potential of the films on which Quinn worked. In this area of her precognitive prowess, the actor always insisted that she keep her impressions to herself. He felt that if he was told in advance that a film would be bad, he would have difficulty keeping his morale up and turning in a good performance.

Iolanda could not restrain herself from predicting the great success of *Zorba the Greek* (1964), however. From the moment she saw the rough cut, she knew that the film would become one of her husband's most popular achievements. Quinn was pleased with his work in the picture, but he wondered how it would stack up against his recent successes in *The Guns of Navarone* (1961) and *Lawrence of Arabia* (1962). They had been action-adventure roles, the kind in which audiences seemed to like him the best. Zorba was quite different from his familiar roles as the gunfighter, the fistfighter, and the soldier of fortune. Iolanda was firm in her interpretation of the cards. *Zorba* would be an international success. In her heart, she knew Anthony deserved another Oscar for his efforts, but something inside advised her that he would not receive the Best Actor award for 1964. On the night of the Academy Awards, she tried to keep encouraging Tony that he would win the coveted award for the third time, but he saw through her facade. The award went to Rex Harrison for *My Fair Lady*.

A Gift with Mixed Blessings

Like so many psychic-sensitives, Iolanda had complained at times that she wished she did not have the abilities that she possesses. Just as quickly, though, she has strongly declared that the gift does have its blessings. At one desperate point in their marriage, Lorenzo, their youngest child, lay in a hospital bed, dying of an infection of unknown origin. In this dark hour, Iolanda went again to her trusty cards. Putting all her faith in their ability to reveal the truth about her son, she laid them out. As card after card overturned, she read with joy that they were undeniably revealing life for the young Lorenzo. Both of the Quinns took strength from the verdict of the cards; in time, the baby of their family was restored, alive and healthy, to his parents' arms.

Saving Quinn from Unnecessary Throat Surgery

At another time, the cards prevented a premeditated tragedy for Anthony Quinn. While Iolanda was in their home in Los Angeles, she received a long-distance call from Tony in New York City. "I have cancer of the throat," he told her. As she listened in horror, he explained that the doctor was in the process of preparing him for surgery. Iolanda refused to accept the diagnosis and begged her husband to wait until she asked the cards if such a terrible thing were true.

Tony grew impatient. This was his life, his career. What was an actor without his voice? He would not delay the doctor's presenting him the only chance he had to continue his life's work. Nevertheless, Iolanda spread the cards and saw that Tony did not have cancer. The cards had never lied to her, and according to their revelations, her husband's trouble was only psychological. He definitely did not require an operation.

She tried in vain to tell Tony not to permit the operation, but he was completely under the influence of the surgeon. Although she normally has a great fear of flying, Iolanda replaced her airplane panic with the greater terror of Tony needlessly destroying his voice. She boarded the first plane leaving for New York City.

When she arrived, she managed to persuade Tony to see an independent X-ray technician at another laboratory. The new tests confirmed what the cards had told her: Tony was perfectly healthy.

Iolanda has learned that her departed father will come to assist her over the rough spots in life. She always made a point to carry his picture with her, and she placed flowers around it daily. When she calls, he comes to her. Iolanda freely revealed her belief that her beloved father continues to oversee her development and still guards his legacy of one deck of well-worn and frayed playing cards.

DICK POWELL'S PREVIEW OF THE FUTURE

Dick Powell began his career as a band vocalist and instrumentalist. He made his film debut in 1932 in *Blessed Event,* played a dozen or more choirboy-type leads, then, as his baby face became ruggedly handsome, switched to tough-guy, private-eye roles, as in *Murder, My Sweet* (1945).

It was in 1925, when he was a twenty-one-year-old saxophone player, that Powell received an astonishing preview of his future from a fascinating seer—Chaw Mank.

Mank, a band leader–musician, met with Powell when he was playing at the Fox Theatre in Saint Louis, Missouri, greeting the young singer-musician with the attention-getting statement that he was even more handsome than Rudolph Valentino. Powell showed genuine surprise, protesting that he was just a plain old country boy from Mountain View, Arkansas. "I know Valentino," Chaw insisted. "The public is getting tired of the Latin-lover types. You are new and different. The fans will go wild over you." Powell managed a sheepish grin. The two men had struck up an instant, easy friendship.

When Mank was only twenty-one, actress Ruth Roland had tried to persuade him to sign a movie contract that would be designed to make him the next Wallace Reid, the all-American actor who had died an early, tragic death. Mank refused the tempting offer and made the decision to continue with his Blue Ribbon Dance Band. In the early 1920s, he had begun a correspondence with Valentino and was assigned the task of organizing the official Valentino fan club. Such an idea was a new concept in 1922, and Mank's bimonthly *Movie Fan's News* soon became an extremely important factor in molding the Valentino image.

Now, Mank found himself receiving psychic impressions about Dick Powell's future. Even as a small boy, Chaw, who was part Cherokee Indian, had given evidence of mediumistic abilities. A medicine woman had told him that an Indian spirit was with him and that whenever Mank faced west, he would receive glimpses of tomorrow.

When Powell saw that his new friend was serious about his seership, he wanted to know what it was that Mank was seeing in his future. Chaw thought a few minutes then answered quietly. "You will gain much fame as a singer and an actor. I see a 'three' in connection with your name, meaning you will have three loves, three marriages. Your greatest love will be an actress in her own right, and I see that her name begins with a 'J.' [Powell was married three times. His second wife was actress Joan Blondell; his widow was actress June Allyson.] As for children, I see but one boy and one girl."

Mank became cautious over his choice of words. "I do not think that you will be around to enjoy the pinnacle of your success. At the height of your career . . . I suddenly see a large blank."

As Chaw spoke, Dick's face paled. "I have felt since high school that I would not live long," he whispered. "It's one of the reasons that I have tried to do something with my voice while I could."

Chaw nodded. "Money will be no object to you, for as the time of your passing approaches, you will become more spiritual in your orientation. A restlessness is going to overtake you and a dreadful disease will follow your footsteps. Until that day, though, there will be nothing at which you will fail. I see only golden success for you, and you will bring happiness to many people." [When Powell died of cancer in 1963, he had successfully progressed from singer to actor to director to producer to part-owner and president of the prosperous Four Star television production company.]

The two men continued to keep in touch. Though twice Mank turned down Powell's offer to become his private secretary, Chaw was always being surprised by short notes and gifts from his friend. When Dick Powell passed on, Mank wondered if he recalled those prophetic words spoken to him when he was but a young man playing the saxophone in Saint Louis.

FREDERICK DAVIES'S STAR SIGNS

The late Frederick Davies was an English astrologer who became famous on both sides of the Atlantic working as a personal astrological consultant to many Hollywood celebrities and writing for national newspapers in both Great Britain and in the United States. He was the television host of the popular "Frederick Davies Star Power Show" in New York and helmed "Star Signs" for BBC television.

A mutual friend, British journalist Paul Bannister, who served as Davies's collaborator on several projects, supplied us with the master astrologer's insights into the star patterns of a number of Hollywood luminaries.

Debbie Reynolds (April 1, 1932, at 5:49 P.M., in El Paso, Texas): "She's happiest when she's working hard."

"Like all Aries," Davies said, "Debbie Reynolds is happiest when she is working hard. If there is one special asset that has made her a star, it is that capacity for effort. It is her Libra rising that gives her that ageless quality. She still looks facially and physically as she did in *Tammy and the Bachelor* (1957).

"The moon, located in Aquarius, gives her that wonderful comedy timing and talent for impersonation. Mars, the planet of action, is in the sign of Pisces, which rules the feet, in the Sixth House of Work, as this is the key to Debbie's dance performances, in which energy and precision are fascinatingly combined."

Candice Bergen (May 9, 1946, at 9:52 P.M., in Los Angeles, California): "She could one day run for political office."

Candice Bergen, according to Davies, is a brilliant combination of the Venus-Mercury-Taurus influence of her birth, but she also has the added talents of her ascendant Sagittarius, which took her into the world of photojournalism. Her moon in Virgo gives her the added talent of the writer: Candice's Part of Fortune is located in her Third House of Writing and Communication, and there is where her great fortune will come.

The sun highlights her Fifth House of Show Business and Love, but it was her ambivalent Saturn in the Seventh House of Marriage that delayed her union with director Louis Malle—a "critical but emotionally balancing Scorpio"—whom she wed in 1980.

The astrologist insisted that Jupiter, the Planet of Greater Good Fortune, high in Bergen's chart in the Tenth House of Career and Fame, destined her to have success in any area she chose.

Jupiter, well-placed in her Tenth House, ruling the government, "could indicate that Candice will be asked to represent the United States in some official capacity, and there is always the chance that she will run for office."

Cher (May 20, 1946, at 7:31 A.M., in El Centro, California): "Her greatest lessons must be learned in the House of Self-Undoing."

Davies reminds us that Sonny and Cher first arrived on the professional scene as Caesar and Cleo, reflecting not only Cher's exotic looks but her fascination with Egypt. Cher's Saturn is in Cancer, directly in opposition to her moon in the House of Marriage.

"Saturn represents all the men in Cher's life and indicates the separation from and loss of the ones that should have meant much to her."

Mercury, the planet of communications, is next to her sun, thus enabling her to write, speak, sing, and express herself with such candor that fans and detractors alike cannot help admiring her.

"She may appear flippant and unreliable at times as she has Venus in Gemini [flirtatious tendencies], Uranus in Gemini [unexpected verbal reactions to situations], and the North Node also in Gemini, showing where her lessons must be learned in this life—all in the Twelfth House of Self-Undoing!"

Sylvester Stallone (July 6, 1946, at 7:20 P.M., New York, New York): "He has transformed violence and terror into visions of beauty."

Frederick Davies admonishes the Italian Stallion to thank his lucky stars that his mother was an astrologer who advised him that he would make it as a writer and an actor if only he would "hang in there."

Impressed by the Cancerian determination exhibited in Sylvester Stallone's film characters of Rocky and Rambo, Davies remarked that both the actor and his cinematic alter egos are like his sign's symbol, the crab, hanging onto its objectives.

"True to his Cancerian tendencies, Stallone's films have most often been about the downtrodden and the underdog. The Rambo pictures reflect the governmental and foreign-affairs aspects of the sign."

Because he has Taurus in the Fifth House of Children, Stallone consulted his astrological charts to be certain that the time of conception would bring him a Taurus child. His son Sage Moonblood was born a Taurean in 1976. He has one other son, Sergio.

Stallone's ascendant, Sagittarius, the archer, aims the arrow at enemy, prey, or target ahead: "With Libra in his mid-heaven, he is an artist; he has transformed violence and terror into visions of great beauty."

Dustin Hoffman (August 8, 1937, at 5:57 P.M., in Los Angeles,

California): "He could only assume a perfectionistic approach to acting."

A Leo with Aquarius ascending, and his moon in the sign of Virgo, Dustin Hoffman could only assume a perfectionistic approach to acting. Davies stated that with Hoffman's Part of Fortune in Pisces in his First House, he received the personality that would attract the right sort of success.

"Venus, the planet that rules music, drama, and the fine arts, is in his Fifth House of Show Business. The Fifth House also represents children. Dustin has two children by his first wife, dancer and actress Ann Bryne, and three by his second wife, lawyer Lisa Gottsegen. With the sun in his Seventh House of Partners, marriage is very important to him." Because of this, it was also a natural choice for Dustin to team up with fellow Leo Robert Redford in *All the President's Men* (1976).

Robert Redford (August 18, 1937, at 8 A.M., in Santa Monica, California): "Frank and outspoken for causes in which he believes."

Robert Redford is a fascinating mixture of his sun sign Leo and his hard-working ascendant Virgo. "These, plus the effect of his moon in Capricorn, give him those wonderful photogenic lines and a grim determination to stick things out," Davies said.

Redford's star pattern makes him basically very honest and frank and often outspoken when it comes to causes in which he believes. "Though he is forceful and can lose his temper, he is easily appeased and very forgiving. He rarely holds a grudge. He is happiest when making others happy—as actor, director, husband, or friend."

His Virgo ascendant "makes him a perfectionist in everything he does and gives him an innate sense of what is right for every occasion— as does the good taste bestowed by the Leo-Virgo combination."

Goldie Hawn (November 21, 1945, at 8:45 A.M., in Washington, D.C.): "Transformed from a ditzy blonde into one of the most powerful women in Hollywood."

While Goldie Hawn's moon in Gemini has been a major influence in her life—for it brings her humor and her good-natured approach to life—it also has a strong effect on romance and marriage.

Uranus, the planet of talents, also in Gemini, allowed her to take her unique comedic style to television. Sagittarius, her ascendant, has permitted the once doll-like and ditzy comedienne to become one of the most powerful women in Hollywood.

"The planet of good fortune, Jupiter, is in her Tenth House of Career, Fame, and Honors, located close to Neptune, the creative planet . . . in the sign of Libra, the sign of those who always look young."

Elizabeth Taylor (February 27, 1932, at 7:56 P.M., in London, England): "A true romantic martyr, ruled by Venus."

Davies characterized Elizabeth Taylor as a true romantic martyr, suffering through one big love affair or marriage after another, devoting herself both to her current mate and his career at the same time that she labors at her own glittering occupation. The astrologist declared that it is the sign of Libra rising in her chart that gave Elizabeth her beauty: "Traditionally ruled by the planet Venus, the goddess of love and beauty, this Libran influence blesses people with a youthful appearance. Unfortunately, the planet of love is conjunct with Uranus, Planet of Unexpected Happenings and Changes, within one degree of each other, thereby creating many sudden changes, losses, and separations from loved ones."

It should hardly be surprising to learn that most of the activity in Elizabeth's chart centers around show business, as well as love affairs and speculation. Jupiter, Davies asserted, helped her to attain many of her life's personal desires, dreams, and wishes, "thus protecting her from some whose thoughts and ambitions may not be as pure and well defined as hers."

A PINCH OF SALT TOSSED OVER THE LEFT SHOULDER CAN'T HURT

Everyone has a pet method of wooing Lady Luck. Some people call them good-luck charms. Others prefer to say that they employ their personal omens. The unsympathetic term them superstitious.

Most experts on such matters agree that no matter how mature we may think we are, we all have a few superstitions, private little rituals in which we engage to make things go our way. As we might suppose, the folks in Hollywood who are subject to the peculiar stresses of show business are certainly no exceptions.

- Lena Horne, the beautiful, ageless singer-actress, says that a hat on the bed means death.
- Karen Black is never without her good-luck scarab.
- Jerry Lewis never used to go on the stage without pictures of all his family in his pocket.
- If you should whisper in Mitzi Gaynor's dressing room, she will make you walk out, turn around, spit, and swear before you can reenter.
- Dick Cavett must touch every eighth parking meter as he walks down the street.
- In order to avoid becoming a "dumb blonde," Charlene Tilton only trims her hair behind drawn shades during the full moon.
- Although Ohio is not her home state, Crystal Gayle always carries a Buckeye charm with her.

On Academy Award nights, someone will always admonish the nominees to be certain that they show enthusiasm at all times. Luise Rainer won two successive Oscars for *The Great Ziegfeld* (1936) and *The Good Earth,* (1937) then watched her career disintegrate into nothingness. Those who know their omens say that it was because she was so unenthusiastic when she accepted the coveted statue.

3 • REINCARNATION: SCENE 5 ... TAKE 28 ... YOU'LL DO IT UNTIL YOU GET IT RIGHT!

Ernest Borgnine has spoken of his memories of having served in the Roman legions as a centurion. No, he doesn't mean in a film—he means in a former lifetime.

Ever since a 1982 Gallup Poll disclosed that twenty-three percent of Americans said that they believed in reincarnation, it has become a bit more respectable for the average person to admit his or her own past-life memories. Of course, a good many individuals, such as Ernest Borgnine, have never been shy about discussing their former life experiences, and it didn't take the Gallup seal of approval to allow a number of motion picture stars to declare that they, too, had lived before.

It is, of course, easy for the skeptical and the cynical to dismiss the account of an actor who claims to remember a past life. Isn't that what acting is all about, after all? Pretending to be someone you aren't is the essence of dramatic characterization. We've all heard about actors who become so lost in their characters that for a time they cannot separate the two personalities.

To those for whom knowledge of previous existences is a serious matter, the memory of the recall is another form of awareness. The devotees of past-life exploration argue that such an extended awareness can bring much more than flashes of an alleged prior existence. By exploring past-life experiences, they affirm, you may truly come to know yourself and to recall physical and mental skills that you may have mastered in other lifetimes. You may rediscover talents that can bring greater creativity to your present life. You may also relearn how to become more efficient in the performance of daily tasks.

Interestingly, the believers claim, the extended awareness that you receive from past-life memories will serve to enhance all the pleasures that you derive through your senses in your present life. Sight, hearing, touch, smell, taste will all become keener.

Since 1976, more than eighty-five thousand people have attended past-life and awareness seminars conducted by Dick Sutphen. There is little question that this man with the persuasive voice has placed himself in the forefront of the reincarnation movement with such works as *You Were Born Again to Be Together, Predestined Love,* and *Past Lives, Future Loves.*

Sutphen stated that he felt the various stars and celebrities from the Hollywood set who attended his seminars were sincere in their interest in reincarnation; he saw no reason to doubt their genuine fascination with the subject.

"It doesn't seem to be anything faddish at all," he said. "Interest in exploring one's past lives is all a part of what is occurring in the New Age."

We have known Dick Sutphen for nearly fifteen years, and we have never observed him taking any other than a practical approach to the whole matter of past lives. "What reincarnation is, or is not, is really not the point," he once commented. "Past-life regressions in themselves, unless used for a purpose, are no more than an amusement. What is important, in my opinion, is: If reincarnation is valid, then what does it mean to me and to humankind? How can such knowledge of *reality* be related to the here and now?"

Sutphen believes that everyone on the planet has past-life memories locked away in the subconscious mind. What is more, he maintains that such memories are affecting each of us right now. We are all the result of our past programming from all of our past lives. Karma, cause and effect, is the supreme universal law, the very basis of reality.

In his *Finding Your Answers Within,* Sutphen stated either we live in a random universe and our lives are soulless and meaningless or there is a plan behind it all, a meaning to life. "And if there is a plan, then it would follow that an intelligence is behind the plan and justice has to be a part of it all. Look around you. Where is the justification for the misery and inequality in the world? How can you justify millions of starving people . . . wars . . . victims of senseless crimes? Reincarnation and karma can explain it all, and there is no other philosophy or religion that can.''

As a metaphysician, Sutphen believes that all of our thoughts and our actions disturb in some way the balanced harmony of the universe. Everything that we do somehow creates vibrations that flow out and return to us until, through our lifetimes, our karma is eventually balanced and we are harmonious once again. Karma reacts upon us with a force equal to the one that we established when we set it in motion.

''Karma is constantly in motion, acting on every level of your body and mind,'' Sutphen said. ''Everything you think, feel, or do creates or erases karma, and this includes the motive, intent, and desire behind every thought and action.''

The good news, Sutphen said, is that the law of grace supersedes the law of karma, and what that means is that if we go about giving love, grace, and mercy to others, we will receive the same in return. All of our positive and loving thoughts and actions go to cancel out our stored-up bad karma.

''Since this is so,'' Sutphen said, ''it is probably time for you to begin to think about how you can be more positive, loving, and compassionate, and how you can support good works and serve this planet—if only to reduce the amount of undesirable karma that you have awaiting you in the future.''

Not long ago, Dick was asked why he, a key New Age communicator, lived in the ''decadent little community of Malibu.'' Sutphen replied that the only thing decadent about Malibu was the way that home values had soared in recent years.

''I don't think Malibu has any special spiritual energy,'' he said, ''but it does seem to attract its share of spiritual people. A Hindu group has built a religious center of beautiful temples in Malibu Canyon. Recently, a large tract of land was given to the Dalai Lama for a center. Several other groups are based here.''

Dick has always kept a sense of humor about himself that has kept his spirits undimmed through the stresses of both the adulation and the condemnation that come with the territory of reincarnation research. ''The challenge to attain what you want should be a joyful journey,'' he said.

ADMITTING PAST-LIFE MEMORIES

Past Lives Aplenty for Loretta Lynn

Country singer Loretta Lynn has recalled three past lives without the assistance of a hypnotic regressionist or anything other than her own memories. Spontaneously, the singer, who was the subject of the movie *Coal Miner's Daughter* (1980), has remembered existences as a Cherokee princess, a rural American housewife, and an Irishwoman.

Although she has expressed her opinion that "one life is enough for anyone," Loretta did undergo a hypnotic session that stimulated the apparent memories of three additional lifetimes: One was as the wife of a bedridden elderly man; another was as a male restaurant employee in the 1920s; and the third was much more colorful for she recalled a time as a maid in the royal household of King George of England.

The September 10, 1984, issue of *Time* magazine quoted Loretta Lynn as stating that she had had an affair with King George that set in motion her own murder: "The King's best friend [a courtier] kept grabbing me behind the King's back, and I was afraid to tell the King about it because they were such buddies. The King died before I did, and his best friend choked me to death."

Stallone Remembers Madame Guillotine

Sylvester Stallone has been open to the concept of reincarnation ever since he was a youth, and he is certain that in one of his previous existences he was guillotined by the Jacobins during the French Revolution. Stallone also believes that his affinity for American Indians and for certain of their dances indicates a past life as a native tribesman.

Robin Williams: Souls Remain in a Holding Pattern Awaiting New Bodies

Caught in a philosophical moment, comic genius Robin Williams admits that he believes "heavily" in reincarnation.

"While I haven't really examined my past lives, I have a feeling that one of them had to be as a Shakespearean actor in the time of Shakespeare. Sometimes I think that if you look, you have an awareness of different civilizations or a tendency toward certain things, and then there is the feeling that you might have been some place before when you know you haven't. A friend has a theory that souls wait in a kind of holding pattern, like that in an airport, and as soon as there's conception, a voice like that on an intercom says, 'Thank you. Next we have a Caucasian male. Thank you.' And down the soul goes."

Willie Nelson's Personal Proof of Reincarnation

Willie Nelson says without hesitation that he has lived several past lives, the most recent probably as an Indian somewhere in Texas. His personal proof of reincarnation comes to him in the form of his own writing.

He was writing poems when he was only four or five years old, and he was writing about subject matter that should have been beyond his knowing. "What does a four-year-old know about love triangles?" he asked. "Yet I was writing about them, and they were my own ideas."

As do so many other believers in reincarnation, Nelson maintains that we are drawn together with people whom we have known before in past lives, and that includes both the folks to whom we are attracted and those with whom we feel uncomfortable.

JOHN TRAVOLTA'S BELIEF IN REINCARNATION FREES HIS SPIRIT

John Travolta, the star of *Saturday Night Fever* (1977), *Look Who's Talking* (1989), and television's "Welcome Back, Kotter," has often expressed his belief in reincarnation, telling writer Henry Schipper that he was a firm believer that "we live forever" and that "we go into other lifetimes."

Because of this belief, Travolta explained, he was not so worried and desperate about his present life experience:

A few times early in my life, life started to be suffocating to me. I thought, "If I die, that's it. I'm in the ground." And that's when

I found out that I . . . was a spirit! A spirit in a body. And it had nothing to do with earthly considerations. I was so freed by that realization.

I have the distinct feeling that I chose my family. It was a very loving, attractive situation, so I felt fairly causative about the last lifetime, but in the next one, I may be even more causative. Who knows what I'll be if I clear up the junk that's in the way this time?

When you come into a lifetime, you're not only dealing with your own complexities, but you're dealing with those of everyone around you—friends, family, business associates. If I had to live here with the mundaneness of just the physical universe, then I honestly wouldn't really want to be here.

The actual pleasure in life, to me, is heart-to-heart affection, affinity with other people. That's what I live for, whether it's my family or my friends. I look for these connections. If I can't have that in my life, then I'm not interested.

JULIETTE GRECO REMEMBERS BEING BURNED AT THE STAKE AS A WITCH

The French actress-singer Juliette Greco is delighted that more people are placing serious credence in the paranormal and in those who give evidence of psychic abilities. It was not too long ago, she said, that channels and mediums were labeled as witches. "And that's exactly what happened to me," she said. "Four hundred years ago, I was burned at the stake as a witch."

Juliette cares little if anyone else believes her allegation or not. "But I believe that in a former lifetime, I was a sorceress. For my activities, I was tried and convicted of practicing black magic, for which I was duly punished according to the laws of the day and burned at the stake."

She cannot remember any further details about that past life nor does she see much difference between her sorcery of a prior existence and her psychic abilities of the present.

A successful recording star in Europe, one wonders if she can also recall a past life as a chanteuse. Juliette will be remembered by American audiences for her appearance in *The Sun Also Rises* (1957) with

Tyrone Power and for sharing the billing with Errol Flynn in *The Roots of Heaven* (1958). Her major psychic talent is precognition, the ability to glimpse the future. The first manifestation of this talent came at the age of four when she astonished her parents by correctly calling out who was ringing the doorbell or who was calling on the telephone—before either the door was opened or the telephone was picked up.

During the Nazi occupation of France, her mother and older sister Charlotte were deported to concentration camps in Germany. Young Juliette was left behind with relatives, and for almost three years, the two women were presumed dead. Then one morning Juliette awoke with tears of joy. She knew that her mother and sister were coming home that very day. Trembling with excitement, she left her relatives' house and rushed to her old home. Two hours later her mother and Charlotte walked through the door and into her waiting arms.

The multifaceted Frenchwoman shares such a powerful psychic bond with her older sister that should Charlotte suffer a headache or a more serious malady, Juliette will experience the same pains and give evidence of the same symptoms. Her gift has frightened her at times in the past—and still has the power to do so. For protection, she wears a heavy gold cross and a medal made of heavy silver. On her finger, though, she wears as a wedding band what the French call a sorceress ring, with three thin intertwining bands of gold.

"I am glad that my kind of sorcery goes by a different name today," Juliette said. "Perhaps this time it can do me more good than the last memory I have of it."

PATRICIA ROCHELLE DIEGEL'S PAST-LIFE READINGS FOR THE STARS

For the past twenty-five years, Patricia Rochelle Diegel has divided her time between Hollywood, Hawaii, and Sedona, Arizona, giving lectures on reincarnation and providing past-life readings for more than forty-five thousand men and women.

Patricia has developed a system of doing past-life readings that permits her to enter a slight altered state of consciousness and yet remain awake. "I prefer to be called a reincarnationist. I term the kind of consultation that I do an 'immortality consultation,' so that I am able to trace the person as an immortal being, using his entire time track.''

She asked us to visualize a figure eight lying on its side as a continuous strip. ''This is the 'Möbius strip,' and it is the symbol that I use to show people that they have had more than one incarnation, that they have worn many suits of clothes, and that the body that they are now using is just one of several suits which they have worn.''

The reincarnationist stated that the advantage of such awareness of past lives for her clientele was in the fact that they could bring talents, knowledge, and abilities that they had before into their present body and mind and glean the benefit of all those past lives. During a two-hour consultation, Patricia Rochelle Diegel gives her clients the information that they need at the present time in their lives.

''I usually identify the potentials that they brought into this lifetime—that is, the creative, psychic, and other types of knowledge that they need to know in order to fulfill the mission for which they came into this life. I tell them what they have already accomplished, materially and spiritually, so that they know what is left for them to do.''

The second part of Patricia's reading includes six of her clients' most important past lives and the connections that they might have with people currently around them to those previous lives. We asked Patricia to run a number of Hollywood stars around the Möbius strip of time and to share some of her thoughts concerning their past lives.

"Dr. Livingstone, I Presume?"

''Years ago, long before he came out so strongly as a conservationist for African wildlife, I wondered why it was that whenever I would run into William Holden I would keep getting images of Africa,'' Patricia said. ''I spoke to one of his managers, William Hickok, and asked him if he knew of Holden's special interest in the so-called 'Dark Continent.' At that time, even his own managers could not foresee Holden's eventual obsession with that country.''

Patricia did a past-life reading on Holden and learned that in a prior incarnation, he had been the Scottish missionary and explorer Dr. David Livingstone, 1813–1873. ''That would certainly explain his growing interest in Africa,'' she said. ''I have yet to find out who Stanley is in his present life.''

Jane Fonda, Suffragette

Patricia met Jane and Peter Fonda at a party when they were in the midst of their Vietnam protest period. As she listened to Jane's rhetoric that evening, she immediately picked up the name "Angeline" in connection with the volatile young actress.

"I saw images around her that made me think of suffragettes and abolitionists," she said, "but I could not receive more than that first name connected with Jane."

Some time later, Patricia was giving consultations to two of Gloria Steinem's close friends when she suddenly saw Gloria, herself, as Sarah Grimke, an abolitionist who also fought for women's rights. "At the same time," she said, "I saw the image of Jane Fonda and knew that she had been Angeline Grimke, sister of Sarah, and I saw clearly the association with their present life experience. Before the Civil War, Angeline/Jane had sought to free the slaves. In Jane's present incarnation, she had envisioned the soldiers fighting in Vietnam as 'slaves' to the military, and she was seeking to free them."

Mel Gibson Had to Find Fame in Australia

When Patricia was watching one of Mel Gibson's films, she saw clearly why the American-born actor had to move to Australia to become famous. "Mel Gibson had been one of the leaders of a group of men who escaped to the outback from the British penal colony at Botany Bay. He needed to return to Australia in his present life to emerge again as a leader."

Patricia also picked up on another of Gibson's past lives: "He was Mike Fink, the rugged riverboat man."

Tom Cruise's Deja Vu in *Top Gun*

Tom Cruise, she says, served as a member of the Lafayette Escadrille, the French-sponsored group of mercenary fighter pilots of World War I. "*Top Gun* [1985] was déjà vu for Tom, and I heard that he said that he had never been happier than he was while making that picture."

Tracy and Hepburn—A Love Affair That Stretched Across Time

Spencer Tracy's love affair with Katharine Hepburn was no secret to anyone in Hollywood. When Patricia met Tracy at a party, she instantly tuned in on his previous life in the France of the 1600s as the Count Francoise de La Fayette. In that lifetime, he was married to Katharine, who was Madame de La Fayette, the author of three books. They had an intensely happy relationship.

"I also picked up on another lifetime that they had shared," Patricia said. "This was in the Napoleonic era. Katharine was his mistress this time, not his wife. Spencer was a clerk of court who gave speeches for those who could not make their own pleas. It was this lifetime in particular that prepared him to be an actor in his present life experience."

Stephen King Has Come Back to Scare Us Again

Patricia stated that in one past-life reading she had seen horror novelist Stephen King as Bram Stoker, the author of *Dracula*.

Vincent Price, Forever on the Stage

Vincent Price wrote and produced plays in the ancient Greek theater, Patricia perceived during a scan of the lives of this versatile actor. He was also a Shakespearean actor named Edmund who lived at the time of Shakespeare and who was a friend of Bill's (as in William S.).

Kathryn Grayson Could Have Been a Great Medium

Kathryn Grayson, the star of so many of those wonderful old musicals, could have been a great medium in this life. "She has enormous ESP ability," Patricia said, "and she sees ghosts. She had a past life as a gypsy in Europe."

Stacy Keach Still Craves Excitement

A sample of Stacy Keach's handwriting informed Patricia that he had been the Earl of Kensington, a man used to wealth, a fanatical card-player, and an indefatigable womanizer. "The life of excitement that oyed in that time has carried over to his present incarnation—not always to his best advantage," Patricia said. "Stacy also had a Greek life. He served as a top-level soldier under Alexander the Great."

Peter Lawford and Marilyn Monroe: Swiss Sweethearts Who Found Each Other Again

Peter Lawford's heart line had a break in it that foretold romantic sorrow, the reincarnationist recalled. "Peter had what we term a 'simian' palm, in which the heart line and the head line move across together. This is the palm of either a very old soul or a newly evolved one."

The members of the Rat Pack—Frank Sinatra, Joey Bishop, Dean Martin, Sammy Davis, Jr., and Lawford—had been outlaws together in the Old West, Patricia said. "That was why they liked to make movies like *Ocean's Eleven* [1960], where they could play being desperadoes together again."

According to Patricia's past-life scan, Peter Lawford and Marilyn Monroe had been childhood sweethearts in a past life that they had shared in Switzerland. "They had always been attracted to one another in this lifetime," Patricia said. "Marilyn always turned to Peter for solace, and during the course of their many 'consoling' sessions, they fell in love. Peter was going to divorce his wife Pat Kennedy Lawford and marry Marilyn Monroe, but the Kennedy family warned him not to make waves until after the election."

Past Lives of the Kennedy Clan

Directing her past-life attunement to the Kennedy family, Patricia Rochelle Diegel saw that Joseph Kennedy, Sr., had been Julius Caesar and that Jacqueline Kennedy Onassis had been Calpurnia, his last wife.

"Jackie always went to Joe for advice while she was married to Jack," Patricia said. "Joe actually arranged the marriage between Jack and Jackie in order to get her back into his family. Peter Lawford had been a general in Julius Caesar's army. He was the one who brought Cleopatra to Caesar in that incarnation. Marilyn Monroe was an

GLI irresistibili

IL cavaliere dell'APOCALISSE

Una sera, dopo la proiezione di una pa[r]... girato, mentre riceveva le congratula... Ingram, di June Mathis e di molti altr... Rudy notò fra la gente che l'attorniav... credibilmente bella, con i capelli rosso... sava in modo insolito, muta, senza unirsi al... tazioni. Rudy provò per la prima volta in vi... inesplicabile. Forse era la stessa sensazione ip... ne provavano quando lui le guardava. Si se[n]... lizzato da quello sguardo, da quei grandi, fer... chi verdi. Il cuore cominciò a pulsargli affa[r]... ...lipsa creatur[a]... Continuò a... tutt'altro, e... la porta e... tto e più t... ne era stra...

(Contin...)

In 1923, Rudolph Valentino was the most popular motion-picture star in the United States. Few people knew that the Great Lover never made a move without consulting his spirit guide, Meselope. (FROM THE PERSONAL COLLECTION OF CHAW MANK)

John Barrymore, once the "Great Profile," sought to restore his waning personal powers by means of a mystical quest to India. Here, he appears in the 1921 film *Dr. Jekyll and Mr. Hyde* (*above*). (PARAMOUNT ARTCRAFT) (*above right*) Although she stresses that she does not want to become anyone's New Age guru, Oscar-winner Shirley MacLaine has brought metaphysical awareness to millions through her books, her seminars, and the 1987 television miniseries "Out on a Limb." (CAPITOL CITIES/ ABC) (*right*) Many find it difficult to accept Shirley MacLaine as anyone other than the actress who played all those kooky hookers and was the mascot of Frank Sinatra's old Rat Pack. She admits that it took a long time before she dared to reveal herself as a true spiritual seeker, but now she sincerely addresses herself to acquainting others with the "unseen reality." Here, for his *Cannonball Run II*, Burt Reynolds unites the Rat Pack, minus Joey Bishop and Peter Lawford. *Left to right*: Reynolds, Dean Martin, MacLaine, Sammy Davis, Jr., and Frank Sinatra. (ARAFIN B.V./CLARIDGE PICTURES, INC.)

Could Nancy Davis have fore-seen that she would one day be the First Lady when she played a custodian of a rich man's gray matter in *Donovan's Brain* (1953)? (UNITED ARTISTS CORP.)

It seems poetic justice that Charlton Heston, who played such heroes as Ben Hur and great spiritual leaders as Moses should have the only blood that can save a post-nuclear war world in *The Omega Man* (1971). (LOEWE'S INC.)

1724

Jack Nicholson has made a steady progression from portraying the demonically insane (*The Shining*) to Satan himself in *The Witches of Eastwick* (1987). (WARNER BROTHERS, INC.)

Jack Palance, the host of television's "Believe It or Not," was also the narrator of the 1978 film *Unknown Powers*. (JOHN COMO)

Alan Vaughan is one of the most tested and researched psychic-sensitives of our time. Psychic Alan Vaughan successfully predicted that actress Terry Moore, shown here in *Come Back, Little Sheba* with Richard Jaeckel, would establish her position as the wife of millionaire eccentric Howard Hughes and would once again become active in motion pictures. (PARAMOUNT PICTURES, INC.)

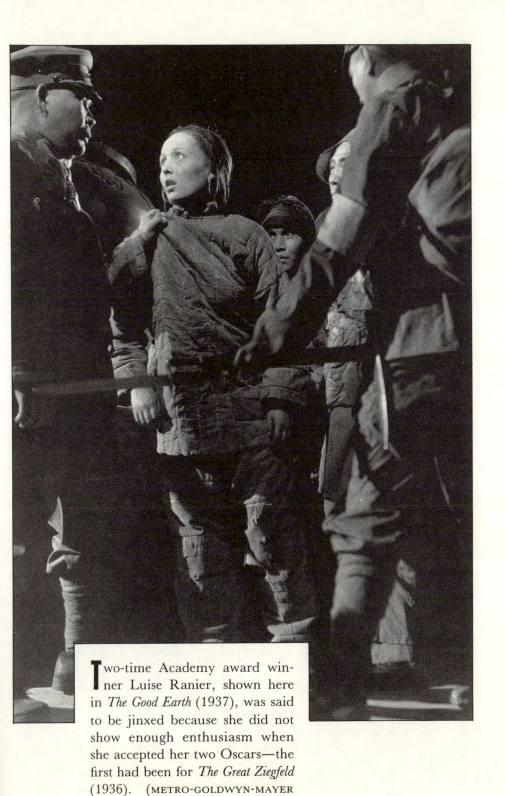

Two-time Academy award winner Luise Ranier, shown here in *The Good Earth* (1937), was said to be jinxed because she did not show enough enthusiasm when she accepted her two Oscars—the first had been for *The Great Ziegfeld* (1936). (METRO-GOLDWYN-MAYER FILM CORP.)

Since 1976, more than 85,000 people have attended past-life awareness seminars conducted by Malibu reincarnationist Dick Sutphen, pictured here with his wife, Tara.

Sylvester Stallone can recall a number of past lives, including one in which he was beheaded by guillotine. (LORIMAR)

A controlled experiment in regression sought to scan the possible past-life experiences of the entity who entered her present life as Frances Gumm and left as Judy Garland. (LARRY EDMONDS, INC., CINEMA BOOKSHOP) A tangible legacy of Judy Garland exists in her multitalented daughter Liza. Here, the two are rehearsing for Judy's 1963 television show. (UPI)

According to Ry Redd's computerized past-life reports, Clark Gable's most prominent past life was as a teacher on Atlantis.

A past-life reading of Bette Davis (here in the 1964 film *The Empty Canvas*) described her as one who was "unusual, highly intuitive, and psychic" but also "highly emotional, almost obsessive at times" on the Earth plane. (EMBASSY PICTURES CORP.)

Dr. Maxine Asher, head of the Ancient Mediterranean Research Association, feels intuitively that Marlon Brando is among the stars who come to their present lives with past memories of the lost continent of Atlantis. Here, Brando appears in *The Wild One* (1954).

The lives of Basil "Sherlock Holmes" Rathbone's entire family were saved because of his mother's vision. (UNIVERSAL STUDIOS)

Rolling Thunder, the great Shoshone medicine man, served as a consultant on the 1971 film *Billy Jack*. Tom Laughlin said that he would not have undertaken the ceremony with the seven-foot rattlesnakes if Rolling Thunder had not been present. Of Laughlin, Rolling Thunder commented: "In his heart, he is Indian. Being Indian is not a matter of blood; it is a way of life."

Yvonne Frost, high priestess of the Church of
Wicca, performs a ritual
blessing ceremony to bring
about good health and to
keep back the dark side of
the force. (THE CHURCH AND
SCHOOL OF WICCA)

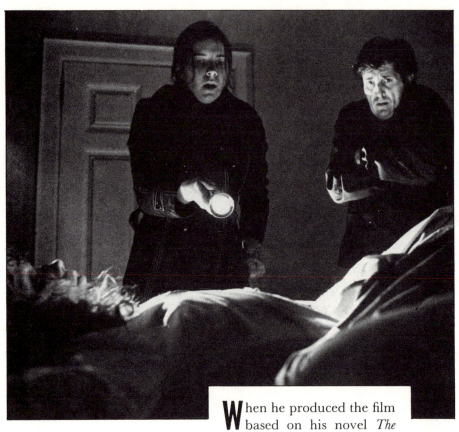

When he produced the film based on his novel *The Exorcist*, William Peter Blatty sought to convey the types of supernatural experiences that he had so often encountered in his own life. *Left to right*: Linda Blair (forefront), Kitty Wynn, and Jason Miller. (WARNER BROTHERS, INC.)

Mild-mannered and pleasant actor Robert Englund is transformed by make-up into child molester and Elm Street teen destroyer Freddy Kreuger, one of the leading screen horror villains. (NEW LINE CINEMA CORP.)

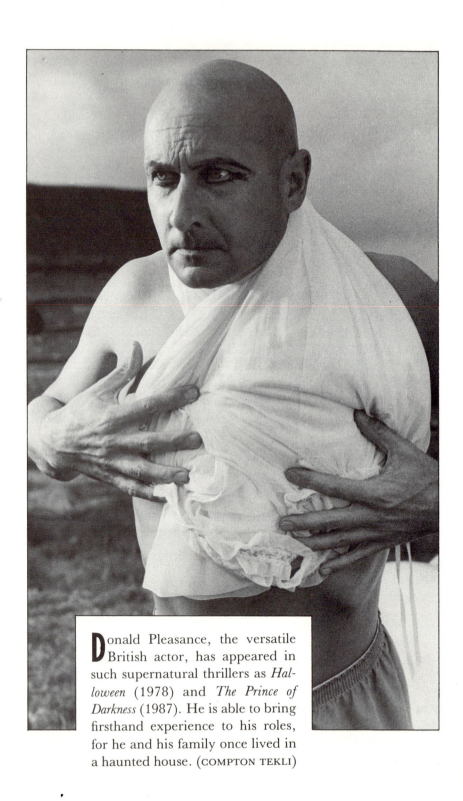

Donald Pleasance, the versatile British actor, has appeared in such supernatural thrillers as *Halloween* (1978) and *The Prince of Darkness* (1987). He is able to bring firsthand experience to his roles, for he and his family once lived in a haunted house. (COMPTON TEKLI)

A film that shows an authentic depiction of a haunted-house investigation is *The Haunting* (1963), starring (*left to right*): Claire Bloom, Russ Tamblyn, and Julie Harris as psychic-sensitives who have been gathered by researcher Richard Johnson. (METRO-GOLDWYN-MAYER FILM CORP.) Barbara Hershey portrays a woman brutalized by an incubus in *The Entity* (1981). Real-life ghost chasers Barry Taff and Kerry Gaynor served as consultants to the film. (PELLPORT INVESTORS, INC.)

oltergeist parents Craig T. Nelson and Jobeth Williams look on baffled as the young Heather O'Rourke announces, "They're here!" Children are often very sensitive to invisible guests in the home and are frequently the first to be aware of their presence. (METRO-GOLDWYN-MAYER FILM CORP.)

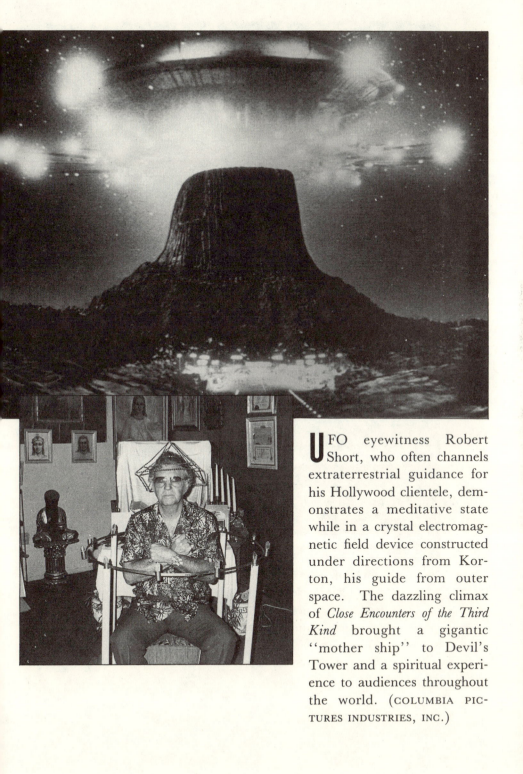

UFO eyewitness Robert Short, who often channels extraterrestrial guidance for his Hollywood clientele, demonstrates a meditative state while in a crystal electromagnetic field device constructed under directions from Korton, his guide from outer space. The dazzling climax of *Close Encounters of the Third Kind* brought a gigantic "mother ship" to Devil's Tower and a spiritual experience to audiences throughout the world. (COLUMBIA PICTURES INDUSTRIES, INC.)

A close friend and con-
fidante has revealed
that Elvis Presley claimed
to be a star person from
another planet. (FROM
THE PERSONAL COLLEC-
TION OF CHAW MANK)

It has been said that it was the spirit of actress Carole Lombard that guided Lucille Ball into taking a chance on the small screen and the television series "I Love Lucy." (METRO-GOLDWYN-MAYER FILM CORP.)

Kenny Kingston, one of Hollywood's most famous psychics and trance mediums, names Mae West as among the most psychic of movie stars, one who trusted completely in the "sweet spirits." (PARAMOUNT PICTURES)

Of Joan Crawford, his former client, Kenny King-
ston observed that her spirit
has not been very nice.

Marilyn Monroe told psychic Clarisa Bernhardt that she wanted all her fans to know that she did not commit suicide. (ESTATE OF MARILYN MONROE) Bizarre occurrences and the ghostly image of Marilyn Monroe have haunted Monroe look-alikes and impersonators in a mirror that was used frequently by the late love goddess. Some have said it is as if her ethereal image is telling would-be Monroes to "stay away" from her mirror. John Lennon was shot down on December 8, 1980, by crazed gunman Mark David Chapman outside the Dakota apartments in New York. Was it only coincidence that this was the same building in which Roman Polanski filmed *Rosemary's Baby* in 1967?

Richard Gere keeps tension from his body by maintaining a solid mind-body link.

Egyptian dancer, no one of fame or note, but she had known both Ted Kennedy, who was Tiberius, and Bobby Kennedy, who was Octavius and later named Augustus.''

President John F. Kennedy came through strongly to Patricia as having once been Marcus Aurelius. ''I had stated that for years,'' the reincarnationist said. ''Then one day I at last received confirmation of my impression. One of Jackie's maids told me that Jack kept only two books at his bedside—the Bible and Marcus Aurelius's *Meditations.*''

SCANNING JUDY GARLAND'S POSSIBLE PAST LIVES

On the eve of a solid week of controlled experiments of hypnotic regression into past lives—June 22, 1969—the beloved singer-actress Judy Garland died. Almost everyone alive at the time had his or her own private memories of Judy, from *The Wizard of Oz* (1939), musicals with Mickey Rooney, and jukebox Saturday nights with sodas and malts. We commiserated with one another over the passing of an era.

Someone in a research group suggested placing a subject in trance and asking her to attempt to travel backward in time to trace the evolution of Judy Garland through her various past lives. If certain metaphysicians are correct in their pronouncements about the Akashic Records, those esoteric impressions of each individual's lives, then it would be possible for an entranced subject to read these spiritual file cards in the manner of the ''sleeping prophet'' Edgar Cayce.

No amount of objective proof could be made available that would confirm any of the data revealed by our entranced subject. For those to whom such an experiment is utter nonsense, no amount of empirical evidence could possibly convince them of the experiment's validity. For those who are predisposed toward such concepts as reincarnation, karma, and the Akashic Records, the transcript may provide certain significant insights into the brilliant but tormented entertainer's life.

Our subject was directed to go back in time until she first contacted the soul entity who was known in this existence as Frances Gumm/ Judy Garland. Once contact had been established, the subject was told to observe the entity and report whatever activity the entity might be pursuing:

She is in a temple in Egypt. She is a temple priestess, so she has given up her name. She sings and brings the messages from the goddess. She has learned how a soul can raise another soul to spiritual elevation.

She was taught this in her sleep by a spiritual master. The master taught her how to sing so that her voice might prove a blessing to her fellow man.

Move ahead to a time in this life when the entity will be an older woman. At the count of three, tell us what she is doing. . . .

She teaches. She looks at the children to see which ones were born to be priests and priestesses, which ones were born to be healers, which ones were born with other gifts. She uses her spiritual gifts very well.

In the entity's next incarnation, Frances Gumm/Judy Garland was a raucous merchant named Ali Hasa who was not above cheating his customers or dealing in drugs. He dies when he is stabbed by other traders who had grown tired of his dishonest trade practices. His spirit-self wanders for a time in confusion and darkness. In the entity's third incarnation, she was an opera singer with a name "something like Rudmilla."

She is singing for the Austrian court, but she travels about from court to court. She is a court musician . . . and a courtesan. She is now twenty-nine years old.

At the count of three, you will move ahead ten years. . . .

She is singing. She dances; she laughs.

Move ahead another ten years at the count of three. . . .

She is still a court musician. She is popular because of her ever-youthful voice, and she is still a very good lover. She does not feel she is immoral. She feels that to make love is a necessary part of her work.

Another ten years . . .

She is still active in court life, but now she teaches more than performs.

Another ten years . . .

She is nearly seventy. She doesn't go out much anymore. She cannot sing anymore, but the young still admire her for what she once was.

At the count of three, you will go to her last moments as Rudmilla. . . .

She has been hurt. It was an accident. She is dying of injuries. She is leaving the body. She realizes that she has been happy but that she has been very vain. She has not thought much about a heaven or an afterlife.

The fourth life in the past-lives scan found the entity in 1836 as a young blond Swiss girl tending goats in a mountain pasture. She is bored with rural life and craves the excitement that she believes exists in the city. In time, she deserts her husband and takes her son to try her luck in a larger village. She bears an illegitimate child and attempts to survive in her wandering from town to town. When the entity is fifty years old . . .

She now thinks of her husband and wishes that she had not abused him so. Her son has gone away. The other child died. She ekes out a sparse living selling bread. She thinks now of the mountains that she forsook . . . the husband whom she deserted . . . the son who scorned her. She never did get to the city. She misses her son. She wishes she knew where her husband was.

Move ahead to the entity's last moments as Gisella. Tell us her last thoughts. . . .

How sad it is when one must stay all the time in one place yet yearn always for another. How sad it is to spend one's entire life being dissatisfied and to come to one's last moments and realize that one has not lived at all, that she has never really been able to do anything about her life.

She dies in her sleep. Heart attack. Paralysis comes in the night and she passes on. She is happy. She knows now that dreams are good but that one must have substance in order to live happily on the earth plane.

Move ahead in time. Maybe fifty years . . . seventy years. Drift with the entity until it once against assumes a physical form on the earth plane. One . . . two . . . three . . .

I see a baby.

What is its name?

Frances . . . Frances Gumm.

GLENN FORD'S THREE HUNDRED YEARS OF EXPERIENCE

"I smell horse!" cried the two-year-old toddler excitedly.

"I smell horse!" exclaimed the fifty-two-year old man suddenly.

The two cries came from movie actor Glenn Ford. The first one he uttered at the age of two at a time when he had not, to his mother's knowledge, ever seen a horse, let alone smelled one. The second cry came forth from deep hypnosis during which Ford also spoke French and recalled a past-life experience.

Glenn Ford, a hard-hitting, hard-riding man in the saddle through sixty-three movie Westerns, not only believes in reincarnation but he also claims to have recalled, under hypnosis, two previous lives. Ford's interest in psychic phenomena began many years ago when he was approached with a prospective script based on the life of Dutch seer Peter Hurkos. Glenn was so fascinated with the script, and with subsequent demonstrations with Hurkos, that he began his own research into the subject matter. Originally, he thought he had better investigate the field of psychical research to be sure there was really something to it before he invested any money for a film. Today, he is the serious owner of a good-sized library on parapsychology.

Glenn's research led him to interviews with members of the British Society for Psychical Research and similar organizations in the United States and he interviewed top psychics and researchers in the field, including Sybil Leek, Olof Jonsson, Jeane Dixon, and Dr. J. B. Rhine of Duke University.

Moving Back to Previous Life Experiences

His studies eventually led him to Dr. Maurice Benjamin, a Los Angeles physician. Beginning on December 1, 1967, a series of experiments was undertaken, culminating in Ford's own personal recall of two previous lifetimes. He was initially a difficult subject to hypnotize. Gradually, however, through several sessions, Dr. Benjamin succeeded in breaking down Glenn's subconscious resistance. While under hypnotic trance, Glenn was regressed to age sixteen, six, two, and one, then Dr. Benjamin urged him further back . . . beyond his entry into the world as Glenn Ford.

"Who are you now?" asked the doctor.

"Charles Stewart," came the reply spoken in a thick Scottish brogue. Further probing revealed that Charles Stewart lived in Elgin, Scotland, in the late 1700s and early 1800s. He had a sister, Elisa, who moved to Edinburgh, but Charles remained in his hometown where he earned his living as a music teacher. It was a profession he despised for most of his students were flibbertigibbety girls. He would much rather have been in his stables with his beloved horses.

When the hypnosis session was completed and Glenn listened to the recorded tape of his regression, he expressed a great deal of skepticism, wincing when he heard the brogue, knowing full well that as an actor he could simulate almost any accent.

The Eternal Horseman

There were, however, two things that really puzzled him. One was Charles Stewart's love of horses. The Scotsman had said that he loathed his giddy pupils so much that he would never marry but would devote his life to his horses.

Glenn Ford has never made such a vow of chastity, but a love of horses has certainly been with him throughout his current life. The first time he was ever in the saddle, at the age of ten years, he handled a wild black stallion that experienced horsemen had refused to ride. Glenn was praised as a natural in the saddle.

The second puzzling aspect was a bit more spine-tingling. Charles Stewart had been a music teacher. While in a hypnotic trance state, when Glenn Ford as Charles Stewart was led to a piano, he could play difficult compositions by Bach, Beethoven, and Mozart with ease. Outside of a trance, Ford could not even pick out a tune by ear!

These enigmas, of course, raised a question. If one could accept that these abilities were part of a past-life recall, then why would the easy facility with horses carry over and not the ability in music?

The actor answered that question himself. Psychologically, he reasoned, Stewart so hated teaching music that he developed a block against it. Horses, which were his one consolation in life, would more easily transfer to his next lifetime.

After this first and rather startling success, Dr. Benjamin proposed that he attempt to take Glenn back even further. The actor was most eager. However, at the suggestion to go beyond Stewart, Glenn began to show signs of intense distress. Dr. Benjamin immediately brought him out of the hypnotic trance and asked if Ford could remember anything.

Ford had a curious explanation: "Going back in time is like taking a journey by train. Each lifetime I could see a station, but it was all dark. I could not see anything at all."

Undaunted, Dr. Benjamin and Ford determined to have another go at it. This time, the doctor suggested that the actor go back until he saw light beyond a dark station.

A Cavalryman for Louis XIV

All at once, the actor exclaimed, "I smell horse!" When asked where he was, Ford promptly replied "Versailles," and the rest of his speech was in French! The waking Ford claimed to know about as much French as *parlez-vous francais* and *s'il vous plait*—and that with a bad American accent.

When Dr. Benjamin brought the tape of the hypnotic session to the language department of the University of California, it was confirmed that Ford was speaking fluent Parisian French of the 1670s.

The tape revealed some interesting information. Under questioning, Ford said that he was going into the front entrance of the Chateau, which is what the palace at Versailles was called in that time period. On the left, he could see the stables filled with horses. The doctor, being familiar with the structure of Versailles, disagreed with him, certain there were no stables on the left. When he tried to shake Glenn from what he believed to be an inaccuracy, the hypnotized Frenchman became so irritated that the subject had to be dropped!

Apparently during that particular lifetime, Glenn's name was Launvaux (spelled phonetically), a member of the elite horse cavalry and therefore an accomplished equestrian.

Launvaux's sense of smell was highly developed, and he described with extreme distaste the putrid smell of the sump that was being drained in preparation for the building of the Grand Trianon and later the Petite Trianon. Subsequent research on this detail pinpointed the year at 1684, definitely putting Launvaux under the reign of the Sun King, Louis XIV, who ruled from 1643 to 1715.

In this past lifetime, Launvaux/Ford expressed deep resentment and contempt for the aristocracy. For purposes of revenge, he courted and captivated a lady of the aristocracy. When her enraged husband found out, he arranged to have Launvaux executed.

The cuckolded aristocrat hired a more accomplished swordsman than Launvaux to deliberately insult the young officer. According to the structure of society in that day, Launvaux could not let such insults pass by, and he was honor bound to challenge the man to a duel. Thus, at the age of thirty-four, Launvaux perished according to the gentleman's code. As the rapier of his opponent pierced Launvaux inches below the breastbone, Ford writhed in pain in the hypnotist's chair.

Once out of hypnosis, Ford was eager to hear the tape and to do whatever research he could. He discovered an old map of Versailles that clearly showed the house of cavalry on the left, as one faced the Chateau entrance, during the time of Launvaux. It was also learned that the execution method of the irate husband was a common ploy in disposing of unwanted persons.

Glenn Ford's personal experiences with reincarnation have certainly expanded his beliefs and philosophies; in addition to his research into his own past lives, Ford has conscientiously undertaken a thorough study of the entire field of psychical research. He is convinced that he has lived other lives, and he is sure he will live more lives than this one.

In the 1970s, seeking further evidence of prior existences, Ford was regressed to a life as a cowboy, as a seventeenth-century British sailor, and as a Christian who was thrown to the lions in the Roman Colosseum. Death, the ogre of human existence, holds no threat for Ford. ''It is as though a great eraser rubbed out the fear of dying from my life,'' he said.

GARY COOPER: SPANISH ADVENTURER AND ANCIENT EGYPTIAN PRIEST

Past-life researcher Ry Redd has spent years recording and compiling past-life information from the readings of the great Edgar Cayce. In a forty-year period beginning at the start of this century, Cayce gave nearly fifteen thousand psychic and past-life readings and still managed to teach Sunday school on the side.

Redd distilled the essence of the Cayce readings, combined them with astrology, teachings about reincarnation from the ancient Hindu traditions, and other past-life information, and put it all on computers. Through the intercession of Redd's computer data, anyone can obtain his or her own past-life profile and come as close to an actual Edgar Cayce reading as anyone has managed to do up to this time.

The Edgar Cayce Past Life Reports, as delineated by Ry Redd, are based on the positions of planets at the time of the subject's birth as interpreted through the Cayce readings for individuals with the very same planetary positions at birth. Because famed star Gary Cooper's sun—Cooper was born May 7, 1901, at 5:45 A.M., in Helena, Montana—harmoniously aspected Saturn, the reading indicated that his soul for several past lives had been developing a powerful drive to succeed through trying fresh angles and making new beginnings. The son of a Montana Supreme Court justice, Cooper came to Hollywood hoping to become a cartoonist for a Los Angeles newspaper. In 1925, he began playing extras in cowboy movies. Destiny played a hand in 1926 when he was cast as the second lead in *The Winning of Barbara Worth* with Ronald Colman and Vilma Banky. The tall, soft-spoken actor was on his way to becoming one of Hollywood's top box-office attractions.

Entering the earth plane in this lifetime, Cooper came under the positive influence of Jupiter. "He was likely, then, to be attractive in appearance and to have a disposition that would lead him naturally to make friends while being slow to anger," the reading states. "Yet when anger did take hold, he became mad all the way through."

Laconic, with a hesitant delivery, Cooper came to be the very personification of the strong, silent American man of action: slow to wrath but always ready to fight should the need arise.

And arise it did in such film classics as *Sergeant York* (1941), *The Plainsman* (1937), *Beau Geste* (1939), *Northwest Mounted Police* (1940), *Unconquered* (1947), and *High Noon* (1952). He won the Oscar for Best Actor for *Sergeant York* and *High Noon.*

In his present life experience, Cooper came under adverse influences in the moon and Neptune. "This challenge brought him tendencies to be misled by others." Redd's Past Life Report noted that Cooper attracted to himself "strange, unusual, and mysterious people from previous lives. Also, because of his mercilessly high standards, he may have attracted souls in this lifetime who may have taken advantage of his vulnerability."

Ry Redd's "Cayce" report warned that Cooper should have taken special caution in his dealings with the opposite sex: "Such souls— again from past-life links—are the ones he was likely to be emotionally involved with and trust the most." A quick scan of the fan magazines of the day reveals that Cooper received extensive press coverage for his romantic flings with Clara Bow, Lupe Velez, Evelyn Brent, Marlene Dietrich, and many others.

According to the reading, Cooper's Venus in a harmonious trine pattern with Jupiter is "one of the most fortunate patterns to have at birth as it brings a deep religious faith and highly developed soul forces.'' Because of this harmonious trine, Cooper's past lives probably had in common their incarnations at times when far-reaching changes were coming about in the economic world, as well as in the intellectual, cultural, and religious thought of the planet's inhabitants. Ry Redd's report said that Cooper had at least one prominent life in the Holy Land, and souls that he contacted then would have been attracted to him again for his counsel and spiritual upliftment.

Cooper's sun in Taurus inclined him to be somewhat headstrong. Hence, the reading stated, he was not always understood, though he made long-lasting impressions on those with whom he interacted. Cooper the outdoorsman was also clearly seen in the Cayce reading: ''This love of nature was from one or more past lives spent on a farm or in natural settings. He lived in close contact with nature in the ancient Mideast and as a native of pre-Columbian America. A lifetime in Asia was also a part of his past-life experiences.''

With his moon in Sagittarius, Cooper quite likely felt the endless expanse of the oceans calling to him. ''Traveling long ago as a Spanish explorer, he crossed the oceans in search of a better world. He was then part of a strong, seafaring culture.''

Several of Cooper's past lives had a pattern of a strong inner commitment to faith, optimism, and group causes. ''He had past lives in humanitarian or spiritual service in Egypt and in the Holy Land,'' the reading said.

CLARK GABLE: ATLANTEAN TEACHER AND ROYAL MAGICIAN

As interpreted by Ry Redd through the Edgar Cayce readings, Clark Gable's most prominent past life was an Atlantean one, where he was quite influential in unifying teachings for the moral, intellectual, and material upliftment of others.

Because his moon was in an inharmonious aspect with Venus, Gable—born February 1, 1901, at 9 P.M., in Cadiz, Ohio—who in 1938 was named by film audiences as the King of Hollywood, might sometimes have experienced the painful emotions of feeling unloved and unappreciated. Redd's Cayce past-life reading said that the moon reflected emotions back to Gable from his previous incarnations on earth.

In one of his past lives, Gable had been unloving and uncooperative, thus blocking him from experiencing more love and cooperation from others in his present life experience. When he died of a heart attack on November 16, 1960, at the age of fifty-nine, he did not live to see the birth of his first and only child, John Clark, born to Kay, his fifth wife.

Gable's Mercury harmoniously patterned with Uranus blessed him with a high mental capacity, especially in writing or in speaking with others. Warlike, wrathful forces, which he experienced in the Mars realm between lives, prompted him to be incarnated in ancient Rome. Because this was a constructive lifetime, Gable was able to come to his present life with latent tendencies toward anger fairly well under control. Other lifetimes after his Atlantean incarnation included having been an astrologer or magician in the court of a king. The reading also saw Gable as a dedicated pioneer at the frontier of a new land and as a seaman who set sail for distant ports only to be carried away in search of lost legends.

In his films, Gable always cut a dashing figure: the white hunter in *Red Dust* (1932), the trapper Jack Thornton in *Call of the Wild* (1935), the mutinous Fletcher Christian in *Mutiny on the Bounty* (1935), and the adventurous Rhett Butler in *Gone With the Wind* (1939). In other life experiences, including his present one, he was labeled as a dreamer by more material-minded souls around him. With his sun in Capricorn, Gable was inclined to be one who was both a materialist and a person interested in spiritual matters. It was from a past life as a Native American that Gable developed a strong sense of independence and personal identity. Although he never played an American Indian on the screen, he did portray a mountain man married to an Amerindian woman in *Across the Wide Missouri* (1951).

Clark Gable's reading also placed him in Europe during the Middle Ages at a time when there was continual feuding and strife among the many fiefdoms, families, tribes, castles, and kingdoms that comprised European culture before its consolidation into a number of nation-states.

Although he was over forty, Gable joined the U.S. Air Force in 1942 after the tragic death of his third wife, Carole Lombard. He rose in rank from lieutenant to major and received the Distinguished Flying

Cross and Air Medal for having flown several successful bombing missions over Germany.

In one of his past lives, Gable was a member of the upper class of France, participating in jousting tournaments and making long journeys to join the Crusades against the Muslims in Palestine.

JAMES STEWART: PRE-COLOMBIAN NATIVE AMERICAN

According to Ry Redd's Edgar Cayce past-life reading, the revered actor James Stewart brought a great deal of positive energy from past-life accomplishments that is directly supportive of his spiritual development in his present lifetime. With his moon harmoniously aspecting the sun—Stewart was born May 20, 1908, at 12:10 A.M., in Indiana, Pennsylvania—he entered the earth plane with the positive afterglow of relationships from his cosmic past.

Stewart's successful personality integration is indicated in how he had gone forward in his soul development in this lifetime by the sheer force of his will. Hardly the conventional leading man with his gangling, skinny awkwardness and his halting delivery, he became the all-American Everyman in such films as *Mr. Smith Goes to Washington* (1939), *Destry Rides Again* (1939), and *The Philadelphia Story* (1940), for which he won the Oscar for Best Actor.

With his Venus conjoined with Neptune, he is a gentle, sweet, sympathetic person, likely to have a special fondness for animals and to have a strong, compassionate feeling for all those who suffer. In *It's a Wonderful Life* (1947), Stewart starred in a motion picture that is replacing Dickens's *A Christmas Carol* (1951) as America's most beloved Christmas story.

Stewart's Venus is in an inharmonious pattern aspect with Uranus: "He is an Atlantean as well as a Uranian," stated the Ry Redd reading. "This means that he is far more sensitive than the average individual because of latent urges from his experience between lives in the psychic realm of Uranus and from his past life in Atlantis."

His Jupiter harmoniously aspects Saturn, thus making him patient, persevering, honest, and sincere. "At the same time, he has marked executive abilities with a masculine mind and the ability to project goals and physically to carry them out."

During World War II, Stewart enlisted in the U.S. Air Force as a private and rose to a full colonel, subsequently flying twenty missions over Germany as a bomber pilot. When he retired from the Air Force in 1968, he was a brigadier general in the Reserve, the highest-ranking actor in the military service of the United States.

Capricorn's influence on his moon inclines Stewart to be one who is both a materialist and one who is interested in spiritual matters. "Before the white man set foot upon this land, James Stewart was a member of a Native American tribe that had an extraordinarily rich and meaningful culture. Many things associated with the American Indians are likely to be special to him. From one or more Native American lifetimes, Stewart developed a knack for being able to handle powerful changes in his life situation. He also brought with him into this life an appreciation of the balance and the organized interplay of Mother Nature and her creatures, as well as a natural ability to move with the flow of life around him."

Stewart's film persona matured in the 1950s when he began to portray Western heroes, private detectives, and criminal lawyers in such films as *Broken Arrow* (1950), *The Man From Laramie* (1955), *Vertigo* (1958), and *Anatomy of a Murder* (1959). Although Stewart's past-life patterns brought him a strong sense of independence and personal identity, he has also understood the necessity for people to live and work together as social beings. Because his soul recognized this need so strongly, he devoted himself to motion pictures, an area of structured communication.

A sense of order, responsibility, and structure—along with a capacity to grow with heavy changes in life—came with Stewart from a lifetime as a military officer during the Greek wars between ancient Sparta and Athens. Ry Redd's reading also pinpointed lives for Stewart in the days of the early Jewish-Christian church and later as an artist-musician in colonial America.

JAMES CAGNEY: BALANCED "OLD SOUL" AND MONGOL WARRIOR

With his moon harmoniously aspecting Venus, James Cagney—born July 17, 1899, at 9 A.M., in New York City—was blessed with a favorable pattern that was excellent for marriage and family life. "Souls should be attracted to you from your cosmic past who will take positive roles in the present—both as your helpmate and as your children," stated the Ry Redd Edgar Cayce past-life report for the actor.

When Cagney passed on in 1986, he and his wife Frances had been married for more than sixty years. The son of an Irish bartender and a Norwegian mother, the man Cagney was very different from his cocky, two-fisted screen persona, preferring a quiet, family existence on his farm. Because Cagney's Mercury harmoniously aspected Neptune, Redd's Past Life Report saw that his past lives had prompted him to be both the musician and the mystic. He was so gifted in these directions as to have true potential for creative, inspirational genius. Cagney was unique in that he could play musicians and dancers, such as his Academy Award–winning, immortal characterization of George M. Cohan in *Yankee Doodle Dandy* (1942), or, with equal aplomb, he could play criminal psychopaths, as in *White Heat* (1949). With his electrical energy sizzle from the screen, he could star in grade-B musicals, such as *West Point Story* (1950), then move on to portray an alcoholic in *Come Fill the Cup* (1951) and an eccentric naval officer in *Mister Roberts* (1955).

The Ry Redd report stated that the actor came into his present lifetime balanced in mind and body with a purity of purpose. Not only was he honest, but he was clean in his thoughts and actions. Over several lifetimes, Cagney had grown to reach a mature level intellectually, so that in the earth life just completed, he was in a position to produce creative additions to old principles. Competent and efficient, he had great self-control and reserve.

His Jupiter harmoniously aspecting Neptune revealed Cagney to be an "old," highly evolved soul, thus enabling him to benefit materially and spiritually in this lifetime. Ry Redd's reading placed one of Cagney's prior life experiences among the once-mighty Mongolian people of the ancient Gobi Desert. From such lifetimes as these, Cagney brought with him the ability to perform what was expected of him without being held back by his feelings.

According to the reading, he was "once a young Chinese woman who gave birth to many children, ran a large household, and pleased the master of the house. He may have done all this while quietly enduring the agony of brutally bound feet, which was once a cultural requirement of the true ladies of ancient China.'' Most film buffs know that James Cagney rose to fame portraying ruthless gangsters in such motion pictures as *The Public Enemy* (1931) and *Angels with Dirty Faces* (1938), but few fans were aware that Cagney began his show business career as a female impersonator. In another Asian past life, Cagney was a Mongolian warrior who fought to the death for his tribal leader, without hesitation or concern for his own injury or pain. Above all in these Asian past-life settings, the actor had dignity and he learned to cope with harsh conditions and challenges without wasting his energy on his personal needs.

Cagney often portrayed military men, warriors, on the screen. In such films as *Devil Dogs of the Air* (1935), *The Fighting 69th* (1940), and *What Price Glory?* (1952), he served in nearly every branch of the armed forces.

With his moon in Libra, Cagney's past-life analysis turned up a life when he lived among the great artists, sculptors, poets, and craftsmen of ancient India. He also lived in the Italian city of Florence and continued to express a love of culture, beauty, and an appreciation of art. Cagney brought such attributes into his present life, for he loved to sketch, paint, and write poetry.

Venus's influence through Libra made it extremely difficult for Cagney to accept anything that was crass or primitive. ''One of the challenges of Libra lies in being too liberal or too indulgent with oneself,'' the reading said.

The actor retired in 1961 after having starred in the successful comedy *One Two Three*. After a twenty-year hiatus, he appeared in a brief role in *Ragtime* (1981), his last cinematic portrayal.

BETTE DAVIS: A POWERFUL LEADER IN ANCIENT PALESTINE

With her sun in an inharmonious aspect with Neptune, Bette Davis—born April 5, 1908, at 9 p.m., in Lowell, Massachusetts—returned to the earth plane as a person the Ry Redd Edgar Cayce past-life reading characterized as ''unusual, highly intuitive, and psychic'' but also as ''highly emotional, almost obsessive at times, yet very calm at others.''

Fans and detractors alike would probably agree that the above is a rather accurate thumbnail sketch of the volatile leading lady of such films as *Of Human Bondage* (1934), *Jezebel* (1938; for which she won an Oscar), *The Little Foxes* (1941), and *All About Eve* (1950). When Bette Davis died on October 6, 1989, she left a dazzling legacy of motion picture classics.

The Ry Redd reading stated that she would go through most of her life "appearing to be peculiar to other people and rarely understood." At the same time, she would have "exceptional spiritual insight concerning soul development on the earth plane. Others would greatly benefit through their contact with her."

With her sun forming a square pattern with Uranus, Bette Davis had a tendency to be too abrupt or seeming to be rude. "Friendships will be strained or broken altogether," Redd's reading stated, providing a counterpoint to Davis's own observation: "You've got to have the guts to be hated."

Because of her moon being in an inharmonious aspect with Mercury, Redd's reading remarked that in spite of her high mental abilities, her temperament tended to be high-strung, restless, or nervous. Davis herself declared that she had been born during a thunder and lightning storm and that she intended to keep the fireworks happening.

"Her subconscious mind and emotions have a tendency at times to override common sense and rationality. She will frequently find herself enduring unnecessary personal hardships as a result of having said things that were not as well thought out as she might have wished them to have been." With her moon harmoniously aspecting the sun, she was born with a pattern for the high potential for a successful integration of the conscious and the unconscious mind: the outer and the inner self.

Bette Davis won her first Oscar for *Dangerous* (1935), her second for *Jezebel* (1938). Although the Best Actress award eluded her for *All About Eve* (1950), her role as Margo Channing was certainly one of her greatest performances. Bette's career waned in the late fifties, but she reclaimed the screen with a renewed vigor in such horror masterpieces as *Whatever Happened to Baby Jane?* (1962) and *Hush, Hush, Sweet Charlotte* (1965).

Ry Redd found that she had been morally and spiritually courageous in many of her past lives. "She was a religious teacher-warrior in ancient Israel and a Christian martyr in Roman times."

Her Venus conjoined with Mars, thereby creating her powerful sensuality, animal magnetism, and sex appeal. "While she had a great love for the beautiful," Redd's reading stated, "the desires for a home life were not pronounced. She was easily aroused to passion and anger. Moodiness, jealousy, and possessiveness were likely to have paralleled her expressions of love and affection."

Bette Davis often said that she found her greatest solace and fulfillment in her work. Four times married, after her 1960 divorce from number four, Gary Merrill, Bette stated that she was ". . . obviously a complete failure as a wife." Not long before her death, her daughter, B. D., published *My Mother's Keeper,* a book that declared that she had not been much of a success as a mother either.

The actress's sun was in Aries, bequeathing unto her inclinations considered by others as being headstrong. "This tendency toward self-determination is rooted in at least one lifetime in ancient Palestine. At that time, she was a powerful yet somewhat dogmatic leader." The Ry Redd Cayce reading also placed Bette Davis in ancient Rome, where she was an officer of high position in the military. She lived a later life in the hills around Galilee and in the desert near the Dead Sea, where the Essenes and others gathered to meditate and study. In the early period of the Christian church, she lived a celibate existence as a nun in a leading religious order.

"Regardless of specifics," Ry Redd's reading said, in her past lives, Bette Davis ". . . was always likely to be dominated by a sense of expectancy and mystery."

ATLANTIS AND THE PAST LIVES OF HOLLYWOOD STARS

Atlantis is traditionally believed to have been a continent in the Atlantic Ocean that was shaken by a series of violent cataclysms, causing it to sink below the surface of the waters. Apparently, humankind has desperately missed it ever since. Thousands of books have been written trying to prove the actual existence of what others dismiss as legend. Some years ago, a public opinion poll found that people in the United States would rank the discovery of Atlantis as a news story equal to the Second Coming of Christ.

In spite of the general public's enthusiasm for tales of the Lost Continent, the great majority of orthodox scientists evaluate the accounts of Atlantis as having been but philosophical parables recounted by Plato in order to provide a dramatic object lesson in civics for his students.

The famous "sleeping prophet," Edgar Cayce, envisioned Atlantis enduring two great cataclysms before a final catastrophe destroyed the island kingdom and transformed it from mighty nation to mythic realm. According to the seer of Virginia Beach, the first destruction ripped Atlantis, then a continent, with violent seismographic disturbances about 50,000 B.C. The second destruction broke up the landmass of Atlantis into five major islands in approximately 28,000 B.C. The final destruction, which placed the great sea kings beneath the ocean, took place about 10,000 B.C.

Dr. Maxine Asher, head of the Ancient Mediterranean Research Association, who has both the academic credentials and the enthusiasm to pursue Atlantis from Spain to Ireland, has become one of the foremost authorities on the Lost Continent in the world. With offices in both Los Angeles and Palm Springs, she has a heavy schedule of travel and publishing deadlines. Still, she was able to theorize about Hollywood and Atlantis.

A Lot of the Stars Act Out Their Atlantean Lives on the Screen

"Atlantis has always been an important part of the unknown," Maxine Asher said. "Creative people have always been fascinated by the possibilities of Atlantis, and actors, being creative, right-brained individuals, are very much intrigued by stories of the Lost Continent. I think that a lot of the movie stars are acting out their past lives in Atlantis on the screen."

Maxine has worked with the internationally known dancer-actress Ann Miller of *On the Town* (1949) and *Kiss Me Kate* (1953), who traveled with her to Egypt in 1976 to explore past-life memories. "Ann knows that she was also in Atlantis, and she wants to see its existence proven."

Sean Ferrer, the son of Mel Ferrer and Audrey Hepburn, has been intent on proving the reality of Atlantis since he was very young. "He's now the producer of our film on Atlantis. He's devoted to research on Atlantis and the Crystal Skull.''

One night, Maxine Asher was having dinner in a Los Angeles restaurant with Debbie Pryor, the former wife of comedian Richard Pryor. ''I had just completed telling her that she reminded me of a Nubian princess. I believe that records of Atlantis are buried somewhere in Nubia. We were discussing these things when a small earthquake rattled the building.''

''Maybe that's a sign of confirmation,'' Debbie said, smiling.

There Is Also Lemurian Energy in Los Angeles

Maxine Asher feels that there is a great deal of Atlantean energy in Los Angeles. ''But even more so, Lemurian. As you know, Lemuria was the parent civilization of Atlantis.'' One who possesses Atlantean energy is one who is in touch with the life force. Atlantean energy is mind-related energy.

''Those of Atlantean energy are tall, broad-shouldered, and relatively hairless, for a great portion of the energy of their secondary-sex characteristics goes to their brains. Most of them have the RH-negative blood factor. They are honest, forthright leaders.''

She speculated that many Hollywood actors are acting out aspects of their past lives in Atlantis in their movie roles. ''They may be living out in their art certain elements of their racial memory. Perhaps the memory of the destruction of Atlantis is encoded in their DNA.'' In her travels around the globe seeking physical proof of Atlantis, she has noted that Latin people are generally more receptive to such research. ''The Latins are definitely more 'into' Atlantis than, say, the northern Europeans. Perhaps more survivors of the sinking continent made it to what is now Spain, Italy, South America, and their descendants have a racial memory of the awful destruction of their world.''

Maxine Asher happened to mention that when she was a coed, she had served as the governess to Vanna Heflin, the daughter of actor Van Heflin, the star of *Green Dolphin Street* (1947), *Shane* (1953), and *Battle Cry* (1955), and his wife Frances. ''Van Heflin was definitely an Atlantean,'' she remarked. We asked her to name some other stars that she feels possess Atlantean energy. Among those she suggested were Ricardo Montalban, Sean Connery, Mary Martin, Robert De Niro, Robin Williams, Marlon Brando, Richard Pryor, Harrison Ford, Harry Belafonte, Carol Channing, Barbra Streisand, and Robert Goulet.

4 • ANGELS, REVELATIONS, AND VISIONS

Loni Anderson, the wife of Burt Reynolds, says she and her father always had a close spiritual link between them. Once when Loni was about twenty-three, she was involved in an automobile accident while she was on her way to spend New Year's Eve with college friends in Iowa. Back home in Minneapolis, her father awakened from a nap because he had "seen" Loni's head strike the dashboard.

The actress said that she was unable to call home for several hours because she had suffered internal bleeding and kept passing out. When she was finally able to make contact with her family, she learned that her father had been waiting by the phone. He had seen the accident exactly as it had happened.

Laboratory tests in ESP have long indicated that distance seems to have no effect on telepathy or clairvoyance. Equally remarkable results have been achieved when the percipient (receiver) was a yard away from the agent (sender) or when the experimenters were separated by several thousand miles.

Dr. S. G. Soal, the British researcher who conducted extensive tests with dozens of mind readers, once observed: "In telepathic communication, it is personality—or the linkage of personalities—that counts and not spatial separation of bodies. Minds are not spatial entities at all. There is no sense in talking about the distance between two minds. We must consider brains as focal points in space at which mind produces physical manifestations in its interaction with matter."

Creative, friendly people who believe in themselves and have a generally positive attitude toward others consistently score higher in ESP tests. Spontaneous psychic phenomena, however, most often occur when the percipient is in some kind of altered state of consciousness, such as daydreaming, sleep, fever, trance, hypnosis, fatigue, illness, or even while performing a movie scene.

British-born actress Ida Lupino was the descendant of a theatrical family that dated back to the seventeenth century. Although she despairingly referred to herself as a "poor man's Bette Davis," she solidly established herself as a commanding screen presence in such films as *The Light That Failed* (1940), *They Drive by Night* (1940), and *High Sierra* (1941).

In 1942, while the Nazis were carrying out their aerial blitz of her beloved London, the actress was working on a soundstage in Hollywood. Suddenly, in the middle of a scene, Ida interrupted herself in midspeech to shout: "My father has just been killed in London!"

Many of those on the set knew that she was the daughter of famed British revue and film comedian Stanley Lupino, and they did their best to reassure her that all was well at home in Great Britain. Two weeks later, Ida Lupino received a letter confirming her father's death. His passing had occurred at what, by London time, exactly corresponded to the actress's cognizance of the fact in Hollywood.

It is interesting to note that, on the average, a man is somewhat more effective as a sender and a woman as the receiver of psychic impressions. This seems to apply to spontaneous instances of telepathy and other functions of psi as well as to roles assumed under laboratory conditions. Controlled tests also demonstrate that percipients often achieve better results if the agent, the sender, is of the opposite sex. Perhaps this is one more indication that psychic ability is a fundamental and natural force that must be included in any total concept of what it is to be human.

What of the ability to foresee the future?

Basil Rathbone, the clever and aloof Sherlock Holmes in fourteen films in the 1940s, told of a prophetic dream that saved the lives of his entire family.

In 1896, the Rathbones were leaving South Africa, where Basil had been born in 1892, for their native England. Before their departure date, his mother, Barbara, had a dream in which she saw the ship sinking in the Bay of Biscayne off France. Her vision seemed so profound that Basil's father altered their plans and changed their departure for a later date.

It was as his mother had foreseen. The ship sank as prophesied, with considerable loss of life.

Rathbone also revealed the nightmare that he himself had experienced in the trenches while serving in World War I. He had suffered through the anguish of foreseeing the death of his brother John. A few weeks later, he once again was overcome by an ominous feeling, and it was on that date that his brother was killed in action.

There are certain kinds of precognitive experiences that can easily be identified as part of the normal process of the subconscious. A woman dreams of coming down with the measles and laughs it off. She did not succumb to the disease as a child, why should she weaken as an adult? In two days, she is in bed with the itching rash covering her body. Rather than judge this to be a prophetic dream, we might better regard the experience as an example of the subconscious mind being much more aware of the condition of the inner body than the superficial mind.

In other cases, a keen intellect and a great awareness of one's environment will enable one to make predictions. Much of the affluence of our economy, from stock market juggling to hemline raising, is based upon the ability of certain knowledgeable experts to make predictions concerning the preferences of a mass society. In contrast to these explainable predictions, however, are the many examples of men and women who seem beyond any doubt to have experienced true glimpses of the future. This power of prophecy resides within the transcendent self, which seems somehow to be aware of events that belong in the realm of the future for the superficial self. The transcendent self does not differentiate between past, present, and future but is aware of all spheres of Time as part of the Eternal Now.

The veteran character actor John Hoyt, so often cast as a German officer or a stylish criminal, as in *Rommel, Desert Fox* (1951) and *Duel at Diablo* (1966), enjoyed a career boost when he was featured as the grandfather on television's "Gimme a Break." As he told Dr. Franklin R. Ruehl, he would not have been around to participate in any projects after *The Conqueror* in 1956 if he had not listened to his inner voice.

The Conqueror was the ill-fated motion picture whose cast and crew received strong radiation effects from nuclear testing while they were on location near Saint George, Utah. It is believed that the fatal cancers that eventually claimed the lives of John Wayne, Susan Hayward, Dick Powell (in his directorial debut), Agnes Moorehead, Pedro Armendariz, and Thomas Gomez were activated by the fallout experienced during the filming of the epic about Genghis Khan.

Interestingly, Hoyt played the shaman, a wiseman, in the film. All of his scenes, with the exception of the exterior long shots, had already been filmed in the Hollywood studio when the cast was to travel on location. "My inner voice simply told me not to go," Hoyt said. "I felt that something very unpleasant would happen to me if I did."

The actor's outdoor scenes, faraway views of him riding a camel, were shot using a double, and he was spared the nuclear fallout that may have shortened the lives of so many of his colleagues.

ANGELIC WARNINGS AND COUNSEL

Billy Graham Asked Debbie Reynolds to Warn Marilyn Monroe

In early August 1962, Debbie Reynolds received a telephone call from a man she knew from the Bel-Air Presbyterian Church who worked at Twentieth Century-Fox Studios. According to her autobiography, *Debbie: My Life,* the man told her that evangelist Dr. Billy Graham had called him and said that he had been given a vision of Marilyn Monroe's death.

Graham had said that it was not yet Marilyn's time to pass, and he wanted Debbie to warn her fellow actress of impending death. Debbie explained that she did not really know Marilyn, but her acquaintance said that the evangelist was insistent that someone must tell Marilyn Monroe about his vision. Finally, Debbie wrote, she thought of Sidney Guilaroff, who had done Marilyn's hair. The hairdresser agreed to see Marilyn and give her the message of Billy Graham's vision. As fate would have it, however, he was thwarted on two separate attempts to speak with the actress alone. The following Sunday morning, Debbie learned that Marilyn Monroe had committed suicide.

Spirit Guides and Guardian Angels

Actress Stephanie Beacham created one controversy when she left her role as the sexy, scheming Sable on "Dynasty" and assumed the role of a nun on "Sister Kate." She inadvertently stirred up another when she announced that she had a guardian angel who looked after her—and that the angel had been a real-life nun.

The British actress told writer Joe West that her guide is Sister Cyrill, a nun who taught at the convent school that she had attended as a child in England. "Sister Cyrill became my spirit guide about six years ago while I was recovering from routine surgery," Stephanie said. "I decided to consult some psychic healers to assist the conventional medicine. All three psychics told me that I had a nun watching over me and that her name was Sister Cyrill."

According to the actress, Sister Cyrill is much more comfortable with her portraying Sister Kate than the sex-hungry vixen on "Dynasty."

Mickey Rooney's Busboy Came from Heaven

Mickey Rooney is convinced that a golden-haired busboy who told him that Jesus loved him was actually an angel sent from heaven to tell him to straighten up his life and become a good Christian again. The popular actor states that no one else saw the golden-haired entity that visited a busy, crowded restaurant in the Pocono Mountains of Pennsylvania.

"At first I thought he was the busboy," Rooney remarked, "but the waitress, the manager, and other customers around me didn't know what I was talking about." According to journalist Patricia Nolan, Rooney went on to say: "I desperately needed some meaning in my life, and the angel with the golden hair provided it. Now my life is much better. I know God loves me, as He loves us all."

The Belief in Angels and Spirit Guides Is Universal

Guardian angels, spirit guides, etheric masters—whatever the percipients choose to call them—the concept of multidimensional beings that materialize to help humans in times of crises appears to be universal. Generally, these teaching, preaching entities function in precisely the manner that the name angel implies, as messengers of God, intermediaries who deliver personal or group messages. In other instances, they may serve as rather militant entities who protect the spiritually vulnerable from the forces of disharmony.

Although certain of the orthodox religionists are somehow able to dissociate their saints and guardian angels from the mystical concept of spirit guides, masters, and teachers, it seems a matter of semantics and religious-cultural background that determines the title that one assigns to those ultradimensional entities who, for some reason, concern themselves with the activities of mortal beings.

TWO ANGELS FOR DYAN CANNON

Moviegoers who may think of Dyan Cannon only as that sexy blonde with the earthy laughter will be surprised to learn of her spiritual depth and of the angelic visitations that she has received.

Born on January 4, 1939, in Tacoma, Washington, the daughter of a Baptist insurance broker and a Jewish housewife, Dyan began her career as a performer by singing at a Seattle Reform synagogue. In the 1960s, she appeared in such low-budget fare as *The Rise and Fall of Legs Diamond* (1960), several television programs, and a number of Broadway plays that died on the boards.

Then, in 1965, Dyan achieved a sudden, secondhand fame by marrying screen legend Cary Grant. At the same time, she retired from show business. She bore Grant his only child, a daughter, and in 1968 obtained a divorce. In 1969, she returned to acting with the showcase role of Alice in *Bob & Carol & Ted & Alice* and firmly established her career with an Academy Award nomination and the New York Film Critics' accolade as Best Supporting Actress.

Dyan states that she nearly destroyed her life after a messy divorce from Grant. She admits that she sought any number of negative emotional outlets—smoking three packs of cigarettes a day, permitting her weight to balloon to one hundred and fifty pounds. She pursued Gestalt therapy, rolfing, and yoga to relieve her psychic pain. She now maintains herself with a fine mixture of work and metaphysics; in such a balance, she has found happiness.

In earlier interviews, Dyan had revealed that she had twice been visited by an angel. The initial visitation occurred at a low point in her life when she was beset by problems. She was sitting alone in a hotel room in Chicago when an apparition in white with long, flowing blond hair suddenly appeared before her. The being did not speak but communicated with her through gestures with its hands. The angel, Dyan stated, did not give her words but feelings. The visitation lasted for a few minutes, then, as she felt her problems dissolving, so did the angel.

Three months later, the phenomenon repeated itself. The actress says that the experience was identical to the first visitation except that the being was different.

"I really don't know how long the visitations lasted," she said. "It seemed like a minute or two. My problems melted away. I relaxed, then the angel was gone. Why do I say that it was an angel? I don't know. I just knew that's what she was."

LORETTA LYNN'S VISIT TO HEAVEN

Loretta Lynn, the Queen of Country Music, the coal miner's daughter, and vocal stylist of such legendary hits as "Stand By Your Man" and "D-I-V-O-R-C-E," says that she lost her fear of dying after a near-death experience in 1989.

On February 5, Loretta collapsed from an accidental overdose of painkillers. While the doctors were working to save her life, she felt herself leaving her physical body. Like so many others who have undergone a near-death experience, she found herself moving down a long, round tunnel with a bright light at its end. As she approached the light, she could see beautifully colored autumn leaves.

Loretta Lynn said that as she left the tunnel, she was struck with the realization that she had just experienced physical death. "Surprisingly, I didn't mind very much," she remarked. Then ahead she saw her mother looking youthful and lovely but wearing the dress in which she had been buried. Behind her, Loretta could behold a "big city of jewels . . . of every color in the rainbow." The singer knew that she was glimpsing heaven, for "nothing else could be so lovely."

Loretta wanted to embrace her mother, but she could see a whole host of people behind her. "Somehow I knew in my heart that these were all the people I'd loved in my life who had died," she was quoted by journalist John Blosser. "I could see my daddy and my son Jack. They were waiting there to greet me."

Loretta felt peaceful and contented. She knew that if she could just reach her mother and give her a hug, everything would be perfect. "But my mama pushed her hands out at me, as if to shoo me away. She said, 'Go back, honey. It's not time for you yet.' "

The country music singer said that she did not want to return to life on the earth plane, but she did so reluctantly. According to Loretta Lynn, the near-death experience gave her a "whole new lease on life." Now she knows for certain that there is an afterlife and that her mother, father, and her son are waiting there for her.

"I know I'm going to be with them when I die. I am the happiest woman in the world."

THE PSYCHIC VISION THAT SAVED ELKE SOMMER'S LIFE

Frau Rosa Bratter, a German psychic-sensitive, was sipping her coffee and paging through the daily newspaper when a shudder of revulsion made her fingers tremble. The infamous "Midday Killer" of Nuremberg, a demented slayer who always committed his murders at high noon, had struck again. His sixth victim had been an innocent man who may have accidentally jostled the killer on the street.

Wishing to escape thoughts of such horrible crimes, Frau Bratter turned the page of the newspaper. Ah, she smiled, much more pleasant news. There was a photograph of German-born actress Elke Sommer with a brief story telling of her plans to make one of her periodic visits to her mother, who lived in a little town about twenty miles from Nuremberg.

The year was 1972. Elke Sommer—born Elke Schletz, the daughter of a Lutheran minister—had become an international star with such films as *The Prize* (1963), *A Shot in the Dark* (1964), *The Art of Love* (1965), and *The Wicked Dreams of Paula Schultz* (1968). Suddenly, Frau Bratter gave an involuntary jerk and became aware of the fact that her psychic abilities were tuning in to something very urgent. Her whole being became suffused with what to her was a familiar vibration.

She was impelled to turn back to the page that carried the reports of the "Midday Killer" and his latest crime. As she was again focusing upon the story of the murder, the photo of Elke from the other page superimposed itself over the article. Surrounding the image was an aura of evil intent and horror. With the inner knowing of a sensitive, Frau Bratter was convinced that unless Elke Sommer altered her plans to visit her mother, she would be in great danger from the serial murderer.

Unable to contain the awful sense of danger that she felt for Elke, Rosa Bratter wrote a brief note to the star in Hollywood. She identified herself as a psychic and warned her of the mortal danger that she was certain awaited her if the actress did not alter her plans to visit the Nuremberg area.

The psychic's prayers were answered when, on the basis of her letter, the actress decided to delay her travel schedule.

Elke Sommer would have the rest of her life to be thankful that she did. On the day on which she had originally intended to arrive in the area, the "Midday Killer" struck again. This time, he killed a man who attempted to stop him after he snatched a woman's purse in a Nuremberg department store. On this occasion however, he was surrounded and brought into police custody.

Investigating officers who entered the murderer's apartment found a diary that recorded the man's criminal intentions. On the last page of the leather-bound volume, they discovered large block letters that read: ELKE SOMMER—KIDNAP HER!

The killer confessed that he had intended to capture the unsuspecting actress on her visit to her mother then ransom her for a large sum. The police found evidence of a much grimmer design. Among the possessions in the killer's apartment was a full arsenal of rifles, knives, hand grenades, revolvers, and pistols. One pistol was clearly marked for a specific victim. Deeply etched into the metal were two words: FOR ELKE.

The grateful actress, realizing that her sure demise had been averted by the German seeress, wrote Rosa Bratter to express her heartfelt thanks.

"I've always believed that beyond our everyday world, there lies the paranormal realm," Elke said, "and my experience with Rosa Bratter has only strengthened those convictions."

BOBBY DARIN'S SPIRITUAL ILLUMINATION
AT ROBERT KENNEDY'S GRAVE

Bobby Darin, the singer, songwriter, and actor, had long been an admirer of Senator Robert F. Kennedy, standing firmly behind the senator's efforts on behalf of peace, civil rights, and the war on poverty. Perhaps Darin's zeal for the senator's reforms was fueled by his own memories of having lost his father before his birth and of having to struggle for survival with his mother and the aid of welfare.

Just nine days before Senator Kennedy would be struck down by an assassin's bullet in Los Angeles on June 5, 1968, Darin had the honor of meeting his idol. There was only time for brief pleasantries, but Darin was deeply affected by the strength of Senator Kennedy's personality, his ideals, and his optimism. A dissatisfaction began growing within Darin, signaling an increasing awareness of the need for a change in his own personal approach to life.

When he learned of the young senator's assassination, Darin suffered great emotional turmoil while at the same time feeling that something important was awaiting him—some great change or resolution. With such ambivalent feelings churning inside him, he joined the mourners at the senator's funeral. At the conclusion of the services, something compelled him to remain at the graveside, a flickering candle clutched in his hand. At 12:45 P.M., it happened. A great ball of light swept throughout his being, illuminating his inner self. As the glowing ball of energy passed through him, it seemed to collect all of his frustrations, hostilities, and anxieties. In one great whoosh, Bobby recalled later, negative thoughts and feelings flew through the top of his head and away into space.

In its wake, the ball left an all-encompassing peace and calm. A deeper awareness suffused his entire being, and Bobby Darin understood that he had undergone a powerful illumination experience. Accompanying the illumination came a great sense of responsibility. He knew that he must translate the experience into physical expression or he would lose the insight that he had gained, and with this awareness came the realization that he needed to transform his entire life.

Darin's previous approach to life had been less than exemplary, arrogantly declaring to the world that he would be a legend by the time he was thirty years old.

In the late 1950s, he had launched a successful nightclub and recording career. In 1960—when he was twenty-four—Darin won two Grammy Awards for his version of "Mack the Knife." He found himself in the enviable position of being very young and very rich—a volatile combination in even the most balanced of psyches. Unfortunately, Darin's personality was not equipped to handle the fame for which he had hungered as a child. As his bank account swelled, so did the popular young singer's head.

The word was soon out in Hollywood that Darin was a talented performer who behaved like a spoiled brat, but still he landed roles opposite such major stars as Rock Hudson, Gina Lollobrigida, Gregory Peck, Steve McQueen, Stefanie Powers, and the pert and pretty Sandra Dee, whom he courted and married. After their almost inevitable divorce due to his immaturity, he assumed a madcap but unsatisfying life among the jet-setters of San Francisco. Although he may have proven too irresponsible to handle the role of real-life husband, he continued to turn in credible performances in both light and dramatic film characterizations. In 1964, he was nominated for an Academy Award for his portrayal of a shell-shocked soldier in *Captain Newman, M.D.*

But that day when Bobby Darin stood at the graveside of Robert Kennedy and experienced the marvelous sense of inner peace, he received the strength of knowing that he would be able to change his attitude toward other people, his image as a performer, his values, and his ambitions. Friends and coworkers noticed the changes almost immediately. Because Darin was at peace within himself, he could now be more open and sympathetic toward others. He also made a great effort to ameliorate his relationship with his former wife, Sandra Dee.

In January 1969, the new Bobby Darin walked purposefully onto the stage of the Copacabana nightclub. Instead of the flashy clothes of the past, he appeared in unpretentious jeans. Instead of the expensive toupee to hide his increasing baldness, he appeared for the first time in public as he naturally was. Backstage, the scene was even more changed. Gone were the sycophants, the flatterers, the hangers-on. Bobby had vowed on that day of transformation at Robert Kennedy's graveside that all the hypocrites and negativists would be banished from his life.

Next to go was the nightclub circuit. Darin began to concentrate on the college campuses and the coffeehouses, seeking to turn on young people to life and to show them where to take their energies. Bobby Darin had long been troubled with heart problems, and in 1973, at the age of thirty-seven, he died following an operation. Nevertheless, he had succeeded in building a new life based on age-old principles. He rejoiced in his rebirth and expressed his gratitude for being given a second chance with his life.

MICHAEL LANDON'S PROOF OF LIFE AFTER DEATH

Michael Landon has always been associated with family fare on television. He began in 1959 as Little Joe, the youngest brother of the "Bonanza" clan, joining the other Cartwrights—Dan Blocker, Pernell Roberts, and Lorne Greene. After the popular Western series ended, Landon served as director-writer-star of the long-running "Little House on the Prairie." As the patriarch of the Ingalls family on "Little House," he became a solidly sympathetic authority figure for youngsters throughout the world.

Although Landon's personal life has occasionally become rather stormy, both his admirers and his detractors have come to accept him as a sincere creator of programming that the entire family might watch without any awkward or embarrassing moments. Most of the episodes on "Little House" provided a solid "moral to the story" from which the viewers could learn if they could move beyond the suspicion that such idealized family life on the prairie was itself a bit supernatural . . . if not impossible! Squelching such doubts, the trials of the Ingalls family always contained enough universal human elements to touch our hearts and challenge us to make our own world better.

As soon as the Hollywood cynics heard about Landon's new television series, "Highway to Heaven," they got right on his case. Michael Landon playing an angel? Who did he think he was? Did he have a messiah complex? The skeptics and the materialists had to step to the back of the cosmic class, for the series was deluged with positive mail response. Landon's sincere approach to the subject matter of an angel performing good deeds on earth had enabled thousands of viewers to stretch, even change, their outlook on life.

Touched by the positive approach of the series, men and women wrote Landon to state how the program showed them the beauty of life. Letters testified to viewers having been given the courage to deal with grief, depression, and discouragement after watching an episode of "Highway to Heaven."

Landon told journalist Barbara Sternig that the show was all about "little miracles that love can bring about."

In earlier interviews, Landon had forthrightly stated that he had always believed in life after death. His heartfelt belief was given absolute proof when he heard his own father's voice speaking to him at the older man's funeral. In 1959, when Landon was a hit on television as Little Joe, the liveliest member of the Cartwright family, real-life grief shattered his reality when his beloved father, Sam, died. As Landon knelt before the coffin, weeping, he felt a soft touch on his shoulder.

"It's okay, kid," he heard his father's voice say. "Don't worry. I'm fine. Everything is going to be all right."

Michael knew then that a spiritual part of his father lived on and would always remain close to him. He was comforted by the awareness that he would be able to communicate with his father from beyond.

At that moment of mystical insight, Michael Landon made a resolution to one day create a film that would express his relationship with his father.

In 1984, *Sam's Son* was released, starring Eli Wallach as Sam and with Anne Jackson and Timothy Patrick Murphy. The autobiographical film, which told of an underdog kid who was a champion javelin thrower and his relationship with his frustrated father, a man who had never been able to pursue his dreams, was written and directed by Michael Landon, who told journalist Sternig that Sam's spirit actually helped him to write the script: "I felt my father's presence with me, enlightening my memories, helping me to commit to paper the feelings that I had about him. I really heard my father speaking to me from another dimension, filling my mind with just the right words. The story came so fast and was so right. In three days, the script was complete.

"To add to the miracle," Landon said, "financing—usually a lengthy process in the film business—was obtained in just two days after the completion of the script."

BILLY JACK'S GHOST DANCES AND RATTLESNAKE RITUALS

In the film *Billy Jack* (1971), actor-writer-director Tom Laughlin offered moviegoers the powerful film of a half-breed Vietnam veteran who drops out of the white culture in order to study ancient American Indian lore.

The modestly budgeted 1971 film became a counterculture classic, playing some cities in nine-week cycles and then returning to the same cities for full-house engagements. The story of the mystic-warrior who leaves his seclusion only to protect the students at an interracial Freedom School won the Grand Prize at the Festival of Nations in Taormina, Sicily, as well as Best Screenplay [Frank and Teresa Christina were the pseudonyms for Tom and his wife, actress Delores Taylor] and a NAACP Image Award.

Laughlin said that he was not only an aware exponent of Amerindian medicine power but was also an individual who had learned the validity of its magic through firsthand experience:

> I believe very strongly in dreams, and I do think the dream is telling me something about myself I don't already know. I also know that it takes me sometimes as much as a year or two after a dream before I fully understand it. I wouldn't intellectualize Billy Jack's use of clairvoyance throughout the film, but I think we indicate that Billy has a way of knowing that goes beyond what we are used to at this time. I think the Indian is in tune with what we might call the unobstructed universe. Billy Jack is clearly in touch with some source of communication that most of us don't know about.

The inspiration for the dramatic rattlesnake ceremony in the film came from the Shoshone medicine man Rolling Thunder, who is a very big force in both the Native American political and religious movements. Rolling Thunder came to us and said that he had been told that we were supposed to have that ceremony in the picture. He told me about it. He had previously taken some apprentices

through it, but, to my knowledge, no white men had ever seen that
ceremony before.

People I trust have told me that Rolling Thunder can walk down
a road in the Nevada desert, walk a quarter of a mile inland, and
there, under a rock, will be a rattlesnake. Rolling Thunder will talk
to the snake then come back on the road and go on his way. So
Rolling Thunder not only told us to put the ceremony in the movie,
but he remained with us throughout the entire filming.

The morning we shot the scene, we went through a special ceremony. Rolling Thunder was there with a seven-foot rattlesnake. I
wouldn't have submitted to the ceremony without Rolling Thunder
being there.

Rolling Thunder, impressed with Laughlin's sympathetic understanding of the mystical ways of the Indian, commented: "In his heart,
he is Indian. Being Indian is not a matter of blood: It is a way of life."

The sacred Ghost Dance is clouded in mystery to the white man,
but Laughlin was able to depict aspects of the actual ceremony in *Billy
Jack*. The Ghost Dance was the vision of Wovoka, a Paiute holy man,
who received a messianic charge while in a fever-induced trance and
who awakened with a long-sought prophecy of redemption for the Indian, a promise of the termination of white domination, a hope for the
regeneration of the Earth Mother, and the return of the buffalo. Wovoka advocated a code of conduct established upon the principles of
peace, brotherhood, forbearance, and nonviolence.

Tragically, it would be the hypnotic manifestation of the Ghost
Dance, which permitted every participant to mingle with the spirits of
his loved ones, that would evolve into the Sioux nation's version of the
"dance-in-a-circle" and would spin the participants away from their
aspirations of a bloodless victory and lead them in confusion to the
bloody massacre at Wounded Knee in 1892.

As Laughlin's personal medicine would provide, they were able to get
Andy Vidovitch, Wovoka's spiritual heir, on location. Laughlin recalled:

Andy was a very spiritual person. His wife, who had passed away
two years before, had been Wovoka's daughter. Just before we
started filming, Andy was preparing to die. A water heater had
blown up and burned eighty percent of his body. He was just lying

there, wanting to pass over, when the spirit of his wife appeared and told him that he could not die and allow Wovoka's message to die with him. He had to stay alive until he had helped get the Ghost Dance part in the movie. [Vidovitch died in April 1972.]

But Andy wouldn't help me write the speech for the Ghost Dance scene. He just kept telling me not to worry about it. The last day came, and I had to shoot something. Andy said, "You just go in there and the Holy Spirit will tell you what to say."

It was the most embarrassing time of my life. Honest to God, until I got back and saw the rushes, I had no idea what had come out of my mouth. I was amazed. I spoke about how the spiritual life in America had failed the kids and how they had gone to drugs and now they were looking for something more substantial. I was stunned to hear all that.

Andy smiled and said, "You didn't speak. Wovoka spoke."

[Laughlin explained that if Andy Vidovitch, Wovoka's son-in-law, had not been on location when the Ghost Dance was performed, there would have been trouble.] The Taos Indians were shocked to see that we knew the dance correctly. There are a couple fundamental things that make the Ghost Dance quite a different dance from the spiritual point of view. I went in trance during that scene. I have a rule when I'm acting that no one else can say cut. There are ten minutes of film in a camera's magazine. We started doing that dance, and when I finally said cut, I was shocked to find that twenty minutes had gone by. The camera had run out. Everyone was just standing there. No one dared to say cut.

I thought it had only been a minute or two. The colors just got so incredibly beautiful that I got fascinated with them. After a while, I thought, well, we've got enough film shot now. I was stunned to find that it was twenty minutes later.

So if that dance was performed properly all night long, I know what would happen!

IRON EYES CODY: INDIAN MEDICINE IS A STRONG POWER

Iron Eyes Cody has become internationally famous as the American Indian who, on those ecology television and print advertisements, sadly beholds the befouled environment and sheds a tear over the obscene violation of the Earth Mother.

Iron Eyes told us that he did not need to use the standard actor's aid of glycerin drops to provoke those tears of silent rage. They were real. Everything about Iron Eyes Cody is real, and that includes his visions:

> To receive visions is a great thing, but it is not always easy to have visions. Once I was in the sweat lodge. My son was heating the rocks. A man passed out. Another man was coughing so that he couldn't sing with the rest of us, then he saw his grandmother's spirit form in a dark place in the sweat lodge.
>
> You have to believe this because a vision is a matter of power of the mind. Visions come. You can see them, but you have to be strong-minded. Once we had a *Yuwipi* [spiritual society] meeting here in the darkroom of my photography studio. My wife was sitting next to the woman to be healed, then a bundle of feathers that had been on the other side of the room hit my wife in the lap. Nobody could have got there to grab those feathers. Magic is a strong power.
>
> If the medicine songs are sung properly, they can work great magic. I had been a technical advisor in films for years, but Cecil B. DeMille made an actor out of me when he filmed *Unconquered* [1947; with Gary Cooper, Paulette Goddard, and Boris Karloff]. "You speak Seneca," he said to me. "You know the Seneca songs. I want you to play Red Corn as well as be technical advisor." But the singing of such songs must be done correctly. In *A Man Called Horse* [1970], I was told to jump up and down and to throw powder in Richard Harris's face before the Sun Dance ceremony. I refused. I am a member of the medicine society of the *Yuwipi*. It is not done that way. An old medicine man, Richard Fools Crow, who was way up in his nineties, said, "I'm glad you said that, Iron Eyes. You stick to it."

Iron Eyes said that he told Elliot Silverstein, the director, that he would rather just quit the movie than to be unfaithful to his *Yuwipi* society.

"All right," Silverstein said. "Let's see you do it your way."

Iron Eyes conducted the ceremony in a very calm manner. "I put the eagle claws and the skewers through the white man's chest muscles, singing a song to defile the white man's magic, but the white man's power showed that he could do the Sun Dance, too. So at the end of the dance, I show that I admire the white man. I come in singing a blessing song.''

Iron Eyes stressed the point that he would never have sung proper ceremonial songs in some of the motion pictures in which he has appeared. In *The Great Sioux Massacre* (1965), Iron Eyes played Crazy Horse, the powerful spiritual warrior. ''Crazy Horse was a great man who saw visions and who sang strange songs. Things came to Crazy Horse that no one could explain. Nobody knew about the man, but they knew his ways and they followed them. He was a great man, and we use him now in songs. In this picture, they wanted me to be Crazy Horse singing the old songs. I would not do it.''

A Man Called Horse was the film that, according to Iron Eyes's inner knowing, most accurately expressed so many of the medicine ways and the beliefs of the mystic warriors. ''I did sing the sun vow song in *A Man Called Horse*. At first, I would not, but when the director allowed me to play the part in a spiritual way—the way I wanted to play it— that song came out of me as soon as I walked into the lodge.

''I did this great song—the *Wakan Tanka*—with feeling. I didn't see the cameras. I heard nothing that was going on around me. The *Wakan Tanka* is not a song that we sing everyday. It is sung only at the Sun Dance, and this was the picture in which it was to come out for all to hear.''

CLINT WALKER HAS LEARNED TO LISTEN TO HIS "STILL, SMALL VOICE"

In ''Cheyenne,'' his popular television series, and in such motion pictures as *The Dirty Dozen* (1967) and *The White Buffalo* (1977), tall, muscular Clint Walker was made to face cinematic death on many occasions; but when a ski pole pierced his heart in a bizarre, real-life accident, he learned that there was no scriptwriter or director to rescue him from what seemed to be a fatal wound. Clint discovered anew that one must obey the ''still, small voice within.''

Walker said, "There *is* a voice!" He had heard it many times before, usually in times of danger. The little voice had saved his life more than once. When the voice said, "Jump!" Walker simply asked, "How high?"

The episode with the ski pole was the one time that he did not listen. Clint, an amateur skier, was taking advantage of a break in his film schedule to learn how to negotiate a series of small hills on a larger hillside. As he was making his way along the slopes, a ski instructor, with whom he had spoken earlier, stopped and asked if he would mind if she were to give him some advice.

Clint eagerly responded, and she told him that his ski poles were too long and that he was not handling them properly in order to lean in on them for smoother, easier turns. Although she realized that her poles were too short for a man as tall as Walker, she urged him to at least try them so that he might get an idea of what she meant.

Clint agreed but found that they were far too short for him to use comfortably. He was about to hand them back to her when the woman shot away from him, shouting over her shoulder that they could exchange poles again at the bottom of the hill.

So there he stood with her ski poles, which, in addition to being much too short for him, did not have straps to secure them to his wrists. Walker figured because she was a pro, she did not need them, but he was a beginner and was used to having poles with safety straps—but his poles were now out of sight along with the well-intentioned instructor.

Then Clint heard his little voice: *"Don't use those poles!"*

His mental debate in response to his inner voice's admonition went something like this: "Oh, boy. What am I going to do? I can't just leave her poles here! What reason would I give her when I got to the bottom of the hill? Oh, well. It isn't *that* far to the bottom. I should surely be able to make it all right."

So Clint went ahead, proceeding down the slope with her poles, justifying his actions to himself as he went.

"To this day, I still couldn't tell you *exactly* what happened," he said, "but the next thing I knew, I was doing a flip in the air . . . a forward flip."

Strange Rings Emanating from the Hole in His Heart

Clint lost the poles in the fall. One pole landed in the snow, its sharp point aiming upward. As "luck" would have it, the actor fell directly on top of the sharp end of the pole with such force that the tip of the ski pole pierced his breastbone and moved through his heart.

"If it had not been for the basket being so firmly attached to the pole, the ski pole would have gone clear through my body, and I would surely have died," Walker said. "As it was, I hit the pole so hard that I bent it at a right angle. I managed to roll off the pole and stand up— of course, feeling extreme pain."

Walker noticed the hole through his sweater and saw blood coming out. He knew he was in trouble, but his sensations of pain and fear were diverted by a most astonishing sight. "I became fascinated by what I saw coming out of my chest! I saw 'rings' emanating from my wound. There was one ring after another. They looked just like smoke rings." While still mesmerized by the intriguing rings coming from his chest, grim reality hit. Clint knew that somehow he had to make it to the bottom of the hill, but his knees folded and he collapsed in the snow.

"The gist of the myriad of thoughts in my head was that much of what seems to be reality is really a fantasy, and a lot of times what we think is a fantasy is reality!"

"We Must Learn to Reason from the Seen to the Unseen"

"If we want reality, if we want the truth about life, then we must learn to reason from the seen to the unseen. Everything that we have in life—be it our house, our job, or even ourselves, for that matter—was *first* a thought or was preceded by a thought or a number of thoughts. Thoughts are invisible, yet they are the most powerful things in the world."

Many such realizations went through Clint's mind. A lot of the things in life that he had deemed important now seemed very insignificant. Other things that he had neglected because of his extremely busy, fast-paced schedule, he now perceived were the more important.

"I realized that it truly is *essential* to appreciate a hummingbird, a sunset, a butterfly . . . many little things that we so often overlook."

The great yogi Paramahansa Yogananda spoke directly about the truth that Clint Walker had discovered on that snow-covered hillside: "Everything that is visible is the result of the invisible. Because you do not *see* God, you do not believe He is here. Yet every tree and every blade of grass is controlled by the power of God within it. We should bathe our spirits in the deep pure feeling that stirs within us when we gaze on the glories of His creation. This is the way to know God as beauty."

Floating Away from Earth

"I closed my eyes," Clint said, "and I was not just floating above my body—I was up above the world. I could see the planet getting smaller and smaller, and it came to me that our world was just a dirty, little old bus stop in the universe. I saw, too, that time was an illusion. I could see the true nature of things so much more clearly. I realized that I had always seen through a glass darkly, and for that time it was as if I could perceive the answers to everything.

"I understood that I was smaller than the smallest grain of sand on the beach—yet I was also ten thousand feet tall, and both at the same time!"

Clint didn't know where he was going, but he felt at peace—and he felt good about his final destination. He suddenly became aware that it was possible to lead many lifetimes. He had always believed in God, but now he saw it was possible for the Creator to permit the soul to inhabit new bodies in different life experiences.

"The body is just a vehicle, a garment that we put on for a while," he said, "but the soul goes on forever. It cannot be destroyed." At the same time, Walker was struck by all the things that he wanted yet to do on earth. "I said, 'Lord, please, I want another crack at life,' and then I was back in my body. Now this leads me to speculate that we, ourselves, might possibly determine the time when we die."

Clint Walker has vague memories of the trip down the hillside in a toboggan and of lying in a hospital three hours later.

Already Pronounced Dead

"Two doctors had already pronounced me dead," he recalled. "A third doctor just happened to be passing through the room where I lay, taking a shortcut to somewhere else, and in a glance he believed I was still alive. He didn't even take time to wash his hands before he was opening me up. My eyes flickered, and I asked him, 'Do you really have to do that, Doctor?' And he said, 'Yes, I do, if I'm going to save your life.' "

Next Clint saw himself moving down a long tunnel. There were faces around him that he could not clearly identify. There were voices that he could not distinguish; but Clint asked God to allow him to live. Afterward, the doctor declared Walker to be a medical miracle. "You should have died," he told the actor, "or at the very least been left a vegetable."

Master Your Thoughts and Move Closer to Love

Clint Walker's statement that thoughts are things is a power-packed truth. We are responsible for our thoughts, and one of the most important lessons that we can learn is how to slow down the tape loop in our heads and begin to sort out and to understand our beliefs, our feelings, our values—and discover where they came from. With discipline, we can learn to master our thoughts; in so doing, we can move closer to the image of love.

An element cannot be changed without first changing its nucleus, and sometimes in life, that is exactly what happens: Our nucleus changes—perhaps to help us see a different center, a more appropriate balance.

Clint Walker told us that he has always felt a strong spiritual connection—although he went through a period, which many of us do, wondering if he was a square or just naive. However, it did not take him long to realize that he had his own inner convictions and guidance, and if that was square, it did not matter; he knew that he had to be himself.

If It's Not Real, It's Wrong

Clint shared a statement about his philosophy of acting that has a wonderful application to life: "I find if I have to work at something, it's phony; there's something wrong. I find in acting that if I can really get immersed in the part and really get concerned and involved with the problems of the individual that I'm playing, the rest of it, more or less, just happens."

Thomas Traherne said in *Centuries of Meditations:* "For God hath made you able to create worlds in your own mind which are more precious to Him than those which He created." Each one of us is unique and special and more loved and capable of love than we can imagine.

A Mysterious Attack by Four Very Strange Dogs

Five years later, Clint was told that he must have surgery to remove excessive scar tissue that had grown up around the old ski pole wound. Once again, he said, he traveled down the long tunnel with the misty faces and the mumble of voices. Once again, he asked God to allow him to live.

Walker never stays in a hospital any longer than he has to, so he was home convalescing within a few days. By his second day at home, he was out walking in his yard. By the third day, he was walking down the road toward his mailbox, weak but glad to be alive.

The rugged actor lived at that time in a remote canyon off Mulholland Drive, and he was walking on a dirt road when he saw a dog some fifteen feet away. Feeling full of good cheer, he said hello to the dog. "The dog stared at me in this very eerie manner, and then, suddenly, there were three other dogs with him. I knew that they were about to come for me. I scooped up a rock in each hand, being careful not to rip open my stitches from surgery, and I was barely standing upright again when they were on me."

Walker kicked one of the dogs under its chin and sent it sprawling, then pelted another with a rock. With angry growls and yelps, they beat a retreat.

He was about three-quarters of a mile from his home, facing a walk up a long, curving driveway. ''That's when my voice said loud and clear: *'Get a club. They're waiting for you!'* '' Clint found a thick branch and began to walk in anticipation of attack.

''Sure enough, when I went around a curve, they were waiting for me in the road. They were strange-looking dogs, like dogs I had never seen before.''

The brandishing of the club and a few well-aimed rocks sent the mysterious dogs back to whatever dark den had produced them. Once he was safe again in his house, Walker felt the unpleasant memory rush of a nightmare that he had experienced the night before.

''It was a nightmare that wasn't a nightmare,'' he said. ''It was a dream, I know, but it was also very real. A devilish face was grinning at me, and I knew the only way to whip it was with willpower, so I said, 'I reject you in the name of Jesus Christ.' I repeated that rejection and kept my will strong against it. There are evil forces, you know,'' Clint Walker said. ''I have learned that this is so, and we must stay strong against them and not give them power over us.''

Strangely, as the actor had been telling us about the eerie dog attack that he had endured, our own dog, an old guy that barks only to be let out to obey a call of nature, got to his feet and walked cautiously down the darkened hallway, growling at something only he could see.

As we shall see in Chapter Five, the dark side of the force seems to have secured a very special niche in Hollywood.

5 • UNHOLY NIGHTS—THE DARK SIDE OF THE FORCE

In George Lucas's mystical Star Wars Trilogy—*Star Wars* (1977), *The Empire Strikes Back* (1980), and *Return of the Jedi* (1983)— the initiate Luke Skywalker is told by his masters, Obi-Wan Kenobi and Yoda, that the force that permeates all living things has a dark side. The positive expression of the force that a Jedi knight who is pure of heart and purpose can channel as a great energy for good could be misused as a power for evil by one who has yielded to the lures and blandishments of the dark side.

Witchcraft . . . curses . . . demonology . . . satanism . . . secret occult rituals . . . human sacrifices. Frightening and diabolical scenarios have been derived from the dark side of the force and transformed into cinematic classics since the Hollywood of the 1920s. Tragically, the evil and demonic happenings that have occurred to certain Hollywood stars are every bit as grim as some of the most grisly scenes that have been concocted by any scriptwriter.

In the world of the supernatural, past and present may often blur into an eternal now. In 1926, Rex Ingram, the director of major films, such as *The Prisoner of Zenda* (1922), became intrigued by W. Somerset Maugham's early novel, *The Magician,* which had been inspired by Aleister Crowley, the notorious practitioner of the black arts. Ingram was convinced that an adaptation of the novel, together with a depiction of Crowley's love cult in Sicily, would make a box-office success. The director starred his wife, Alice Terry (Valentino's costar in 1921's *The Four Horsemen of the Apocalypse),* in the film and invested a great deal of their personal fortune. *The Magician* (1926) may have been popular among the Hollywood set, but nationwide it was blasted for its tastelessness, nightmarish sequences, and orgiastic rites.

During the 1950s, serious students of the occult insisted that Aleister Crowley had lived in Pasadena long enough in the 1920s to have founded a black magic coven, whose membership had remained active and had steadily recruited new followers. Anton La Vey, self-proclaimed High Priest of Satanism, is reported to be a former member of the coven. Sirhan Sirhan, the assassin of Robert F. Kennedy, and Charles Manson were also said to have been initiates of the cult.

Robert deGrimston, founder of the occult group The Process, traveled in the same social circles as Charles Manson and a number of his victims. Among Sharon Tate's friends were Jack Nicholson, Robert Evans, John and Michelle Phillips, Jay Sebring, Warren Beatty, Jane Fonda, Peter Sellers, Wojeciech Frykowski, and Abigail Folger. The circle in which Manson was said to associate also included other well-known entertainment personalities. According to some, there was a third circle that revolved around "Mama" Cass Elliot and a shadowy figure known as Manson II, an openly avowed Satanist.

Ironically, Roman Polanski, the director-husband of actress Sharon Tate, was a bemused skeptic who doubted the reality of the supernatural. In 1968, he had completed *Rosemary's Baby,* a film about a woman who is deceived into giving birth to the Antichrist. Based on the novel by Ira Levin, the motion picture boasted a superb cast, including Mia Farrow, John Cassavetes, Ruth Gordon, Maurice Evans, Ralph Bellamy, and Sidney Blackmer.

On the January 31, 1969, telecast of "The Tonight Show," an astonished Polanski informed host Johnny Carson about the censorship problems that he had encountered with the film in Great Britain. In genuinely baffled tones, the director explained that the authorities had been upset with certain scenes in *Rosemary's Baby* because ". . . there was quite a lot of this particular kind of witchcraft going on in Great Britain."

Polanski appeared incredulous and seemed to respond as though he had never considered the possibility that contemporary satanism could exist outside the pages of a screenplay or a book. In fact, he told Carson that his sole research for the film had been to examine one volume on the subject in order to obtain the symbols to be painted on Mia Farrow's nude body for the scene in which Satan impregnates her.

Seven months later, on August 8, 1969, Polanski's pregnant wife, Sharon Tate, was viciously murdered by assailants who were obeying the instructions of Charles Manson, a man who declared himself to be the Antichrist.

In Hollywood, the tendrils of the supernatural weave webs that stretch far and wide and ensnare many. According to the satanic teachings of Manson, the Helter-Skelter slaying of Sharon Tate and her three friends—Jay Sebring, Abigail Folger, and Wojeciech Frykowski—were supposed to set in motion a bloodbath that would take the lives of thousands and purge the planet.

SHARON TATE'S GHOSTLY PREVIEW OF HER MURDER

Terrible events are said to cast their shadows before them.

In 1966, before she married Roman Polanski, Sharon Tate dated Jay Sebring, a handsome and wealthy hairstylist who had purchased an expensive home in exclusive Benedict Canyon. In the early 1930s, the home had been owned by Paul Bern, the agent who had married Jean Harlow and who had committed suicide in the house after what was said to have been a night of sexual violence, as described in the Introduction to this book.

At the time, Sharon accepted Sebring's invitation to stay in his new home while he traveled to New York on business. She was eager to see the place, still notorious for the Bern-Harlow scandal; but as she later told writer Dick Kleiner, it had been an incredible night of feeling fear in the house, and she had been unable to sleep because of a "funny feeling" and strange noises.

The Ghost of a Creepy Little Man

Sharon turned on a bedside lamp and was startled to see something stirring outside her bedroom door. "I saw this creepy little man. He looked like all the descriptions I had ever read of Paul Bern."

The creepy figure came into the bedroom but did not approach Sharon's bed; instead, he moved quickly about the room, clumsily bumping into things, behaving like neither a ghost nor a prowler.

Frightened, Sharon put on a robe and ran downstairs, but what she envisioned on the staircase was far more horrible than the smallish, ugly man running around in her bedroom. She saw someone that she somehow "knew" was either Jay Sebring or herself tied to the staircase with his or her throat cut open. Sharon managed to find a bar and pour herself a stiff drink, but the terrible vision of a mutilated person, blood gushing from the throat, still remained tied to the newel post in the downstairs hall. Upstairs, she could hear the ugly little man still prowling about.

With a great effort of will, she managed to step around the bleeding figure on the staircase, dodge the clumsy ghost upstairs, and make it safely to the bedroom. Once in bed, she amazingly fell immediately to sleep. The next morning, Sebring returned and Sharon told him about the nightmarish night; never having had any kind of psychic experience, she did not know whether to laugh or cry.

In 1968, Sharon Tate accepted Roman Polanski's proposal of marriage, and they rented a house at the end of Cielo Drive, only a mile or so from the Sebring home in Benedict Canyon. It was here, less than two years after her vision, that the actress, Sebring, and two of their friends were cruelly slaughtered by the Manson family.

A PSYCHIC-SENSITIVE TRIES TO WARN HOLLYWOOD STARS OF IMPENDING DISASTER

Dr. Ernesto Montgomery, pastor of the Universal Metaphysical Church in Los Angeles, attended schools in the West Indies before completing his studies at Chicago and Indiana colleges. After graduation, he served with the British Armed Forces in World War II and with police departments in Jamaica and Texas. He has used his psychic abilities with a secret British intelligence agency and with law enforcement departments throughout the world. As was detailed in Chapter Two, in 1957, Montgomery pinpointed the area in Dallas's Dealy Plaza where he predicted a U.S. President would one day be murdered.

On June 16, 1969, the seer sent identical warnings to half a dozen show business personalities. As is the case with most mail that is sent to the home addresses of celebrities, the letters were returned unopened. In this case, such instant dismissal proved to be tragic. The text of Montgomery's letter predicted the Sharon Tate murders in great detail.

In his vision (Dr. Montgomery pointed out that he had *thousands* of accurate predictions to his credit), the seer foresaw the murder of five

HOLLYWOOD
·AND THE·
SUPERNATURAL

MAP

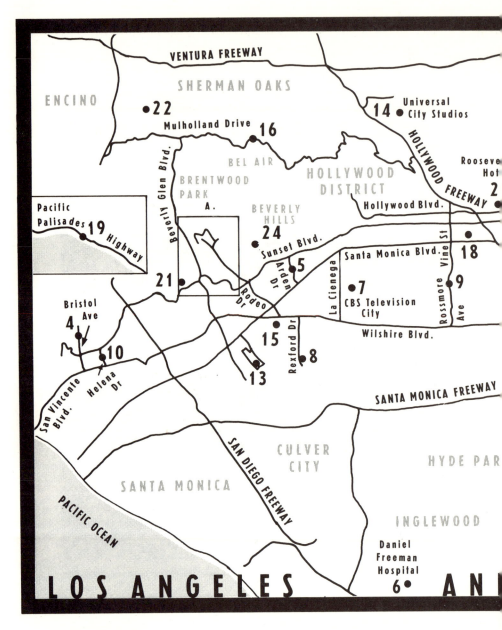

HOLLYWOOD SUPERNATURAL PHENOMENA

1. The spirit form of the Great Lover Rudolph Valentino has been seen in and around his former home, Falcon's Lair on Bella Drive.

2. Dr. Ernesto Montgomery foresaw the carnage that the Charles Manson "family" would wreak upon Sharon Tate and her friends on Cielo Drive.

3. Two years before her death, Sharon Tate stayed overnight in the Benedict Canyon home in which Paul Bern committed suicide after a night of sexual violence involving his wife, Jean Harlow. Tate not only saw the ghost of Bern, she received a psychic preview of her own grisly murder.

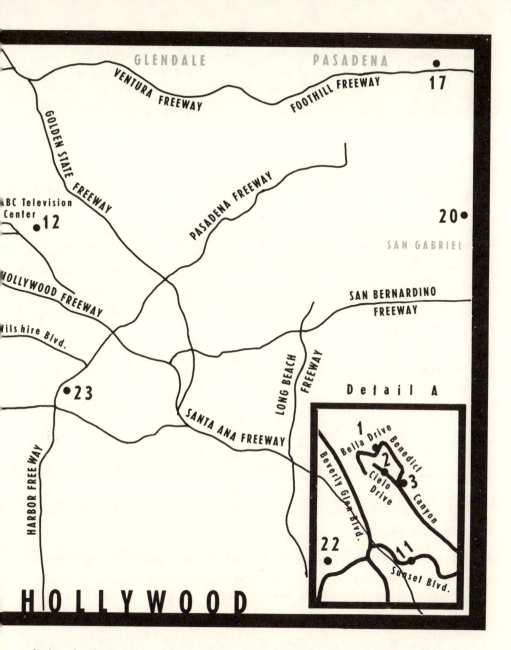

GLENDALE   PASADENA

VENTURA FREEWAY

FOOTHILL FREEWAY

17

GOLDEN STATE FREEWAY

PASADENA FREEWAY

BC Television
Center
12

20

SAN GABRIEL

HOLLYWOOD FREEWAY

SAN BERNARDINO
FREEWAY

Wilshire Blvd.

23

Detail A

LONG BEACH FREEWAY

HARBOR FREEWAY

SANTA ANA FREEWAY

Bella Drive

Benedict Canyon

1

2

3

Cielo Drive

Beverly Glen Blvd.

22

11

Sunset Blvd.

HOLLYWOOD

4. Joan Crawford's house on Bristol Avenue has an eerie history of mysterious fires that keep breaking out on the wall where the headboard of her bed once rested.

5. Mitzi Gaynor has a ghostly maid who helps dust the chandeliers in her home in Arden Drive.

6. While recovering in Daniel Freeman Hospital in Inglewood from a near-fatal motorcycle accident, Gary Busey saw a vision in

which the Grim Reaper informed him that it was not yet time to surrender his gifts.

7. A close friend of William Holden verified that a group of para-psychologists made contact with the actor's spirit during a controlled séance in a studio in KCBS-TV.

8. Psychic Kenny Kingston says that the spirit of Clifton Webb has made life very difficult for cigarette smokers and cat fanciers in his former home on Rexford Drive.

9. During a séance in her old home in the Ravenswood Apartments on Rossmore Avenue, the spirit of Mae West told medium Clarisa Bernhardt that she is now a member of the "Crossover Club," assisting the newly deceased to adjust to the "Other Side."

10. On the eleventh anniversary of her death, Marilyn Monroe materialized in front of her last earthly home on Helena Drive, in full view of former husband Bob Slatzer and friends.

11. When popular singer Englebert Humperdinck bought Jayne Mansfield's "Pink Palace" on Sunset Boulevard shortly after her death, he had no idea that he would encounter her ghost.

12. Medium Kevin Ryerson took the entire crew of Shirley MacLaine's television movie "out on a limb" when he brought along his spirit guides to speak their own lines for the production.

13. When the television series "Werewolf" put in a "werewolf hotline," they received more than 500,000 call. Over 5,000 callers said that they had witnessed real werewolves attacking victims—or that they, themselves, were true werewolves.

14. Kevin Ryerson, who served as a consultant to the film *Poltergeist II*, reports that many cast members experienced troublesome dreams and other eerie manifestations.

15. A Beverly Hills medical doctor states that many of his celebrity clientele have reported abductions by UFOnauts in which they were subjected to bizarre physical examinations aboard spaceships.

16. While recovering from surgery and walking in a remote section of Mulholland Drive, rugged actor Clint Walker was warned by his "inner voice" just in time to prepare for an attack by four mysterious savage dogs.

17. Persistent rumors stubbornly insist that Aleister Crowley, the "wickedest man in the world," lived in Pasadena long enough in the 1920s to establish the black magic coven that planted the seeds of evil that matured into the likes of Charles Manson.

18. Nick Nocerino, director of the Institute of Psychic and Hypnotic Sciences, a professional "ghost chaser," declares that there are more demonic, evil-type entities in the Hollywood area than anywhere else in California.

19. While driving on the Pacific Palisades, Kenny Kingston received a message from the spirit of former client Marilyn Monroe.

20. San Gabriel residents have reported an astonishing number of materializations of American Indian ghosts.

21. At a party in a home in the Bel Air hills, Elvis Presley confessed to a friend that he was a visitor from another planet.

22. In Jungleland in the suburb of Thousand Oaks, Jayne Mansfield watched in horror as a lion mauled her son in the attack that sent her to a satanic priest and may have caused her to make a deal with the devil.

23. A woman invaded a convention of fans of the gothic vampire television series "Dark Shadows" and bit more than 200 necks before it was discovered that she was the real thing.

24. The Spanish Colonial home that was once the love nest of Robert Taylor and Barbara Stanwyck is now the center of poltergeistic manifestations in which objects are tossed around the house.

25. Bizarre occurrences in the basement of the Roosevelt Hotel on Hollywood Boulevard centered around Marilyn Monroe look-alikes who used a mirror that once belonged to the late love goddess.

prominent people on Cielo Drive in Benedict Canyon—on or about August 9, 1969. He wasn't sure about the precise number of the address, but thought it was either 10060 or 1005.

Montgomery included the names of responsible journalists and business people who could vouch for his integrity and his accuracy, and he also enclosed a fact sheet that detailed his many clairvoyant accomplishments. The Tate murders occurred on Cielo Drive in Benedict Canyon, just as he predicted, and they took place on August 8. Would Sharon Tate and her friends be alive today if they had somehow received Montgomery's warning?

The prophet himself is uncertain whether or not the predictions of great cataclysms, such as earthquakes and hurricanes, can be changed—such major events may be truly destined to occur—but in the case of individuals who may exercise free will, Montgomery is convinced that each person has the power to change what may happen to him or her as a sovereign entity.

"An individual can use free will to decide whether or not he will remain in the vicinity that he has been warned to leave," he commented. "If the individual can be warned, as I tried to warn the victims in the Sharon Tate murders, then they can take the appropriate steps to prevent the occurrence."

On October 3, 1969, when the identities of the Tate killers were still unknown, Montgomery went into his psychic state and in a vision saw the name of the murderer.

"My vision indicated that a 'Charles Mansoon' was the leader of the murderers. My psychic insight had simply added a second 'o' to his name."

LUCIFER JOINS THE PARTY AT THE POLANSKI HOME

As veteran members of the Los Angeles homicide squad entered the grounds, they discovered the body of Abigail Folger, heiress to the Folger coffee fortune, lying near the swimming pool. A little bit beyond, sprawled upon the lawn, was the body of Wojeciech Frykowski, an actor and writer friend of Roman Polanski. In the car was the body of Stephan Parent, a guest of the Polanski's houseboy. Inside the house lay the bodies of Sharon Tate and Jay Sebring.

Folger, 26, had been stabbed in the chest and other parts of her body. Frykowski, 37, had been stabbed and shot. Parent, 18, died of multiple gunshot wounds in the chest and elsewhere. Sebring and Tate had been stabbed repeatedly and were linked by a white nylon rope that had been tied about their necks and extended over an exposed beam in the ceiling of the living room. A black hood covered Sebring's head.

Immediate pressure was leveled at the authorities to learn the identity of the killer or killers, and as the investigation got under way, a number of disturbing things were unearthed. When Jay Sebring's car was found to contain various drugs and torture implements, stories began to leak out about the kind of parties Sharon Tate's crowd liked to give.

The Real Party Began When the Straights Went Home

As one of the peripheral members of the group told it: ''The beginning of the party could be just like the normal-type party given anywhere in Hollywood, but then, around 1 A.M.—or whenever the 'straights' went home—Jay would bring out his goodies. That's when the real party would begin.''

According to certain individuals who claimed to have been participants in some of the parties, Jay's ''goodies'' generally included both hallucinogenic and hard drugs, as well as artifacts associated with satanic rites. Once, according to informants, Jay had even thrown a Lucifer party in which all the guests came dressed in black and were told to utter specific incantations as they entered the house.

The very instances under which the bodies of Jay and Sharon were found appeared to indicate the influence of black magic on the murderers. A popular starlet of the day claimed to belong to a white witches coven and offered to explain the significance of the manner in which Jay and Sharon were discovered.

Requesting anonymity, the actress used the *Witches Book of Moses* as her guide:

> The white cord tied around each of their necks, linking them together, indicated that the murderers believed that Sharon and Jay were adulterers. Everyone knew that they were lovers before her

marriage to Polanski, so the members of the Manson family probably assumed that they were still doing it.

The hood over Sebring's head was placed there to imprison his soul. The spirit of a dead man can rise from his eyes, nose, and mouth. The Manson family, being well-versed in Magick, placed the hood over these parts so the spirit could not rise and haunt them.

A lot of witches also believe that a dangerous spell can be cast upon the murderer who gazes into his victim's eyes, so that was probably another reason for the hood.

The cross that was slashed on Sharon's breast is supposed to serve the same purpose as the hood. It means that for her death is final, and she cannot return in spirit form to haunt her murderers.

A PSYCHIC BLOODHOUND TRACKS THE MANSON FAMILY

Before the identity of the assassins was discovered, concerned parties contacted one of Chicago's most famous psychic-sensitives, Joseph DeLouise, and brought him out to Hollywood to record his impressions.

"The fatal attack on Sharon Tate was a thrill murder," DeLouise reported to the Long Beach *Independent Press-Telegram*. "Their joy was killing, so it didn't matter if they killed ten or fifteen. The more they killed, the more joy they received. Also, they have no conscience. They don't feel sorry about it at all. On the contrary, they are excited about it."

The psychic's further impressions detailed a man weighing one hundred and sixty pounds with darkish-blond hair. The other he saw as shorter with dark hair. "One of the suspects could be in an institution in Texas, either a mental or drug institution, or in jail," he said. "There will be a break in the case on September 14 or 15."

Authorities later admitted that it was on precisely those dates that they first encountered the now-infamous Manson family. Charles Watson, six-foot-two, one hundred and fifty-six pounds, and with light brown hair, was arrested in Texas. Charles Manson, five-foot-seven with dark brown hair, was taken into custody as the leader.

DeLouise said that a girl by the name of Linda would be important to the case. He also felt that black magic and drugs had been involved in some way with the murders. The psychic's "Linda" turned out to be Linda Kasabian, the family member who turned state's evidence after her arrest and whose testimony helped to convict Manson. The bizarre family did practice strange rites based on a perversion of occult practices, and they were heavily into the unrestrained drug trip.

At the time of his investigation, Joseph DeLouise told his closest friends: "If the truth behind these murders ever really comes out, there will be a terrible black eye for Hollywood. Several big names will come out of the case if it is allowed to progress. A lot of Hollywood has been playing with black magic without knowing the problems that they have been bringing on themselves."

Today, in 1990, the rumors still persist. Authorities on satanism and various aspects of the counterculture state that the seeds planted by Charles Manson have not yet been uprooted and that there are many flowers of evil waiting to bloom.

RONA BARRETT SPEAKS TO SHARON TATE AT A SEANCE

Although in 1969 channeling was not at all as popular in Hollywood as it is today, there were attempts to contact the spirit of Sharon Tate and gain a more complete picture of just exactly what had transpired that terrible night in August. In the November 1969 issue of *Hollywood,* Rona Barrett reported a séance that she herself had attended with the express intent of communicating with the spirit of Sharon Tate.

Barrett reported that she, accompanied by two friends, met at the home of medium Zorina Andretz. Rona had brought with her photographs of Sharon Tate, Jay Sebring, Roman Polanski, and the others in the hope that the pictures might facilitate spirit contact. For several minutes nothing happened as the four sat around Zorina's large circular table. They were about to give up in defeat when Rona began to feel herself drawn into a swirling, dizzying vortex. Gradually, she became aware of a voice moaning over and over again: *"Why? Oh God, why?"* Then the voice explained brokenly that they had all been having such a good time that evening. "Sharon" said that they had been doing hard stuff that Jay had brought with him. The spirit entity answered in the affirmative when Rona asked if it had been Jay Sebring who had caused her to become hooked on drugs. (Roman had tried to get her to stop using them.) "Sharon" went on to explain that Jay had been jealous of Roman, jealous of the baby that she was carrying. Jay had tried to persuade her to divorce Polanski. The spirit that identified itself as Sharon Tate spoke next of the parties that they had given, particularly when Roman was away in London. At these parties, a secret society containing "some of the biggest stars in Hollywood" would show her the strange and intoxicating world of drugs. The secret society, "Sharon" said, was dedicated to pleasure and the unknown. Polanski had never been a member; he always drew the line at the supernatural and refused to participate in their black masses.

"Sharon" spoke of her love for Polanski but confessed that Jay held a terrible fascination over her. She had even helped him fill in names for a book of people who could be counted on to perform normal sexual acts in "a special way." On the fateful night of their last party, they had all been flying high on drugs and alcohol. They were preparing for the black mass, which was why, according to the spirit entity, Jay had the hood on his head. There were no lights on in the house. In the middle of her narrative, "Sharon" cried out in despair: "Oh, God! If I had only listened. The spirit of Marilyn Monroe tried so desperately to come back and to warn me about pills and drugs and the sex thing. She tried to come back and warn me, but I didn't listen."

Because she had been so heavily under the influence of drugs and alcohol, "Sharon" said that her last moments on earth were confused. "I bit and clawed and struggled, but I couldn't get away, and then the knife plunged into my chest. The pain! I never felt such pain. The expression on his face . . . he looked like Satan. Had we contacted Satan after all? Was this our punishment instead of the pleasure we expected? He kept carving on me. . . ."

As "Sharon's" voice became weaker, Rona Barrett was swirled through the vortex again and brought back to the reality of the present.

THE DEVIL LAUGHS WITH DELIGHT OVER THE HOLLYWOOD HILLS

While certain Fundamentalist preachers have always insisted that Satan invented motion pictures and founded Hollywood to serve his greater plan of worldwide spiritual enslavement, there is no question that the jaded and inquiring minds of far too many stars have become ensnared in an enormous variety of satanic webs.

Around 1973, Anton La Vey of the Church of Satan granted a lengthy interview, with a number of questions having to do with the rising influence of satanism on the films being produced by Hollywood during that time:

> Aleister Crowley said, "Every man and woman is a star," but he neglected to mention that there are stars of varying magnitude. The nebbish who has been a nothing all of his life who takes up satanism to get an ego boost will certainly be confronted with the cold, hard truth that he is like the inner tube with the leak in it that has been blown up out of proportion and put in the bucket of water so that all those leaks can show up. Satanism does separate the men from the boys. Rational self-interest is what satanism is all about, not an excuse or a license to do whatever people feel like doing.

> *What is your opinion of the occult dramatizations that one sees almost every week on television? Satanic themes are becoming very popular.*

> Oh, I am consulted on most of these things. Some of the presentations are not exactly what I would like, but they at least spur interest and get people to probe a little deeper into what satanism is really all about—or at least get them wondering.

> Recently, [a television network] did *The Terror at 37,000 Feet.* It was good because there was a doubt at the end and the forces of so-called darkness were not defeated.

> The prognosis of films of this nature is that they will lead us to more and more dramas where the forces of darkness win out—and not as evil forces! It has already been done, in a sense, in *Rosemary's Baby* [1968], but it wasn't as explicit as the public perhaps could have been fed. They are not quite ready to see the devil turn out to be the hero and ride off into the sunset with the white hat. That is the inevitable end result, but what we are seeing now are impasses where evil is not really defeated.

> Joseph Cotton is a swell guy. He loves to do these movies. In the past, he always played a fair-haired, very staid, very conservative Southern gentleman type, so it is a lot of fun for him to do these things.

His *The Devil's Daughters* [1972; on television] was great for us. He, the saintly attorney, turned out to be the devil in the end. It was excellent! It showed that all those people who appeared to be such nice folks were really the satanists. And this, of course, is the way it really is!

That nice couple next door or that executive whom you think is Mr. Nice Guy himself is the satanist. The kindly doctor you know or the guy that might be running the boys' club or the local little league or something like that happens to be a satanic priest. This is the way it really is.

The satanic age began about the year 1966, and now we are beginning to see in *Jesus Christ, Superstar* [1973] and *Godspell* [1973] Jesus as fallible, no different from any other man, which is originally what Satan was supposed to represent—man with all his shortcomings and all his potential. So Jesus has really attained the sort of status that Satan originally had.

Take *Jesus Christ, Superstar*. A superstar is a nova, and a nova is always a star or constellation that flares up at its brightest just before dying. If there is a hidden message in that title, *Jesus Christ, Superstar*, it is indicative of a flare-up just before the death of Christianity.

THE DEMONIC MALEDICTION THAT TOOK JAYNE MANSFIELD'S LIFE

In spite of what appeared to be an all-consuming passion to become a major movie star, Jayne Mansfield seemed trapped in a role rut, condemned to play the same bosomy, dizzy blonde in role after role.

A bride at sixteen, a mother at seventeen, Vera Jane Palmer, who was far brighter than her public image suggested, attended drama school at the University of Texas and later at UCLA. Her first big break came when, in 1955 at the age of twenty-two, she appeared on the Broadway stage clad only in a towel as a breathless Marilyn Monroe clone in *Will Success Spoil Rock Hunter?* In 1957, she re-created the role in the movie version, expecting to become Hollywood's hottest new star. Instead, she got stuck in a groove deeper than her own cleavage as she starred in such forgettable films as *The Sheriff of Fractured Jaw* (1959), *Playgirl After Dark* (1960), *It Happened in Athens* (1962), and *Las Vegas Hillbillys* (1966).

It may have been as a last desperate move to revitalize a career that had never really begun that Jayne Mansfield came to explore satanism. Some friends say that she was merely curious about its philosophy. Others state that she came to embrace its doctrines in order to curse her former husband, Matt Climber, and to ensure her receiving custody of her fifth child, Antonio.

According to a friend, it was in November 1966 that Jayne and her boyfriend, Sam Brody, drove with a press agent of the San Francisco Film Festival to the black magic cathedral home of Anton La Vey, the self-proclaimed High Priest of the Church of Satan. Her friends say Jayne merely went to talk with the black magician and to view his satanic home. Others claim that the actress went to La Vey to ask his help in strengthening her career.

The only agreement among friends and witnesses centers upon the intense dislike that Brody and La Vey expressed for one another. One account has it that the satanic High Priest displayed two human skulls and a chalice with the warning that anyone who touched them would die. Brody laughed at the malediction and touched the artifacts, defying La Vey, who supposedly told Brody that he was doomed and demanded that he, Jayne, and the publicist leave the satanic church at once.

Nevertheless, Jayne and Brody did return. Some say that they did so in an effort to placate the High Priest of Darkness. Others assert that the actress was hungry for publicity and knew that La Vey always got extensive press coverage for his antics. The occasion for their return visit, states one account, was to allow Jayne to pose with Anton La Vey for a photo layout as an act of propitiation for Brody's sacrilege.

La Vey brought out his two sacred skulls, a silver chalice, and a "demon weapon." He asked that Jayne pose in her trademark bikini, but she refused and wore a dress. She did, however, with the High Priest's permission, pose with the fateful objects in her hands.

Brody had been opposed to Jayne's posing with La Vey, but he promised to be on his best behavior. Then, according to one account, he began to fondle the holy statue of a naked woman that stood at the altar of the satanic church. When La Vey commanded him to cease, Brody sneered at his admonition and blew out several black votive candles that surrounded the statue.

Infuriated, La Vey proclaimed that Brody had angered Satan with his acts of disrespect and that he would die within a year. Then, as Jayne's friend May Mann remembers it, La Vey turned to the actress and warned her that if she continued her relationship with Brody, she, too, could face a tragic and sudden death.

Brody and Jayne made the decision to blow the curse off and to divert their attention from the malediction by enjoying a good dinner at La Scala. It was on that night that the first of their narrow escapes in a car occurred. Brody had just given Jayne a new sports car, and on the way home from the restaurant, they were hit by another car and the Mansfield vehicle was totally demolished. Brody and Jayne barely escaped with their lives. About a month later, Jayne's five-year-old son, Zoltan, accompanied her to Jungleland in the suburb of Thousand Oaks, where she had agreed to pose for publicity photos. While she looked on in horror, a so-called tame lion suddenly and without provocation jumped on Zoltan and began to maul the child.

As the boy underwent several emergency surgeries and his life hung on a perilously fragile thread, Jayne, according to Milo Speriglio of Nick Harris Detectives, flew to San Francisco to plead with La Vey for Satan's intervention to save her dying son. Speriglio says that La Vey, dressed in a satanic ceremonial gown, climbed to the top of Mount Tamalpais, just outside the city, and, in a driving rainstorm, performed a ritual that brought Satan's assistance for Jayne's son.

Zoltan survived, and it is said that the actress credited the miracle to Satan and asked La Vey's forgiveness for Brody's blasphemy. Should La Vey be powerless to avert the wrath of his satanic majesty, then Jayne begged that her children be free of the curse.

Speriglio, who says that he was working for Sam Brody in 1966–67, stated in the December 1988 issue of *Celebrity* magazine that Jayne Mansfield's problems had just begun: "A short time later, while on a visit to Japan, her treasured diamonds were stolen and never recovered. Soon after, while in Britain, she was publicly humiliated and had a performance canceled when she was falsely accused of not paying a hotel bill. She was hit with a charge of tax evasion from the Venezuelan government, robbed while in Las Vegas, and attacked at *Carnival* in Rio de Janeiro by a crazed mob who stripped her to the waist."

On Wednesday, June 15, 1967, Jayne's oldest daughter, Jayne Marie, left home and placed herself in the protective custody of the courts, claiming that she was a victim of child abuse at the hands of her mother and Brody. She refused even to speak to Jayne about her terrible accusations. The charges were dropped, and Jayne Marie was released into the care of relatives.

On Wednesday, June 22, Sam Brody was on his way to pick up Jayne for a charity luncheon when his luxury car was hit by another car. It was crushed, and Brody was hospitalized with a broken leg and ribs.

On the Wednesday following Brody's accident, Jayne, Sam, and three of her children left the Biloxi, Mississippi, nightclub where she had been appearing to travel by car to do a guest spot on a New Orleans television show. En route, the sedan in which the Mansfield party was riding slammed into a parked truck on U.S. Highway 90. The top of the car was sheared off, leaving Jayne Mansfield decapitated. Sam Brody, the driver of the car, was also killed instantly. Jayne's three children, who had been sleeping in the backseat, escaped with minor injuries.

May Mann says that when a photographer friend of Jayne's informed Anton La Vey of the tragic deaths, he intoned quite simply that the devil's prophecy had come true. "Perhaps the most eerie finding of my investigation," Milo Speriglio wrote, "was the fact that just before Mansfield's death, La Vey had 'accidentally' cut the head off a picture of the actress with a pair of scissors."

May Mann flatly refuses to believe in the reality of a curse or to ascribe any real power to the self-professed devil's High Priest. She does admit, however, that Jayne's many close scrapes with death, the many thefts that plagued her, the charges pressed by her daughter—all tumbling head over heels to crowd themselves into the last months of her life—certainly seem to suggest that some inexorable hand of fate was moving toward Jayne, reaching out to snatch her into the waiting jaws of death.

Bandleader-psychic Chaw Mank had exchanged Christmas cards with Jayne Mansfield for many years. Hers always seemed to have a more home-loving touch to them, he remembered. When the yuletide card for 1966 arrived, Chaw recalled that he had "seen" black crepe around it. He seemed to know, in some inexplicable way, that she was under psychic attack, that tragedy could soon strike the actress or some member of her family. Immediately, he sent off a note to her, warning her of fire and fast cars.

When the news was broadcast of Jayne's death on June 29, 1967, Chaw sadly went through the cards and letters that he had received from her, regretting that no more would ever come. Then he discovered a letter in which Jayne had shared with him her favorite prayer: "Gentle Jesus, meek and mild/Look upon thy little child./Pity my simplicity./Suffer me to call to Thee!"

One can only hope that in those last terrible seconds before she knew her death was imminent that Jayne Mansfield called out to the gentle Jesus and not to the avenging Satan.

DID SATAN TAKE HIS REVENGE ON THE PRODUCER OF *THE EXORCIST*?

When *The Exorcist* (1973) became a huge financial success, psychic sensitives feared a spiritual backlash. After all, William Peter Blatty's novel and the screenplay that he crafted from it showed the devil for what he really is—a liar, a deceiver, a molester of the innocent, and a possessor of the helpless and defenseless. The devil would seek his due, they warned.

Producer Noel Marshall had been a powerful, driving force behind the motion picture adaptation of the best-selling novel. He was well-rewarded for his efforts as the film collected millions of dollars and brought immediate success to Marshall, who was married to actress Tippi Hedren, Hitchcock's cool blonde in *The Birds* (1963) and *Marnie* (1964).

Marshall now wished to leave tales of possession and demons behind him and begin work on his dream movie, a project that could become a reality because of the commercial triumph of *The Exorcist*. The producer had always wanted to do a film about lions, the royalty of the animal kingdom. It was his goal to illustrate what he believed to be remarkable similarities between humans and lions. Using his profits from *The Exorcist*, he began obtaining lions, tigers, panthers, and jaguars for their one hundred-acre ranch compound in a canyon north of Los Angeles. Amidst the big cats, Marshall built a home and sets for the motion picture.

He gave his film the title of *Roar* (1981), but all he received from prospective actors and actresses were loud whimpers. It was not that they were against participating in a film that featured animals. While it is true that no actor likes to be upstaged by four-legged costars, such films as *Lassie Come Home* (1943), *Benji* (1974), *The Black Stallion* (1979), and the Tarzan epics can make a lot of money for the two-legged thespians.

The main problem with *Roar* lay in the grim fact that Marshall wished the big cats to remain untrained in order to demonstrate his thesis that man and lion can live in peaceful coexistence, even in the wild state. Since there were no other takers, it was decided that the major roles would go to family members. After all, this was the family that boasted the glamorous Tippi Hedren and her daughter Melanie Griffith, who much later, in 1988, would win the Academy Award for Best Actress for her role in *Working Girl*.

There was still the problem of the film crew, however. Not every cameraman aspires to film *National Geographic* specials, and there probably does not exist a grip who sees himself as fast food for a lion. On one occasion, an entire crew walked out on Marshall in the midst of a productive day of shooting. They could not handle being knocked down and mauled by the tigers and jaguars. When he hired another crew, it lasted only long enough to witness the mauling and near death of two of its members. His third crew proved to have enough diehards in it to stick with the project until its completion. Although Marshall would probably protest that the interaction between the lions and cast members went fairly smoothly, he himself was bitten ten times—once so seriously that it appeared he might lose an arm.

Tippi Hedren required thirty-eight stitches in her head after being chomped on by a lion. Later, her leg was crushed by a four-ton elephant. Their son, John, who needed fifty-six stitches to close his head wound, said that he could actually feel "the lion's teeth scraping" his skull. Jerry, a second son, nearly lost his foot and had to spend a month in the hospital.

Melanie had her face opened by a lioness. Although the required twelve stitches were not of themselves that bad, she needed plastic surgery in order to retain her movie star glamour.

A spokesperson for the Antelope Valley Medical Center in nearby Lancaster jokingly commented that they should rename the hospital the "Noel Marshall Memorial" in honor of the many emergency room visits that the producer had brought to them.

Three years of filming and $3.8 million worth of property were destroyed overnight when a flash flood struck the canyon and demolished the multimillion-dollar set and the Marshall home. The unexpected flood also removed fences, thereby allowing the big cats to wander out onto the highway, thus necessitating the summoning of sheriff's deputies to help round up the lions, tigers, and jaguars.

The determined Marshall, already deeply in debt, surveyed the damages and decided to rebuild and reshoot. The budget had stood at nearly $4.5 million before the flood. After borrowing additional funds and selling more property and personal holdings, Marshall regrouped the project for close to $9 million.

Even then, the suspected curse had not been lifted.

The Marshall ranch proved to be in line for one of Southern California's worst forest fires in decades. A set on the eastern edge of the compound that was to be used in one of the final scenes of the film was consumed by flames.

Although *Roar* was finally completed after eleven years of planning, distribution problems have prevented it from being seen in the United States. Marshall's dream movie cost him virtually all the money that he had acquired from *The Exorcist*—$17 million, according to some sources—and *Roar* has the dubious distinction of being the most accident-plagued film project in the history of Hollywood.

Perhaps after completing *The Exorcist,* Noel Marshall should have read I Peter 5:8—"Be vigilant, because your adversary, the devil, walks about as a roaring lion, seeking whom he may devour."

WAS JOEL DELANEY SHIRLEY MACLAINE'S TURNING POINT?

The following is an excerpt from the May 1972 issue of *Show,* the magazine of film and the arts:

The Possession of Joel Delaney is a psychological thriller dealing with a form of witchcraft called Espiritismo—the spirit of a dead person taking possession of a living human being. Portraying the older sister of the "possessed" Joel Delaney [Perry King] is Shirley Mac-Laine.

Shirley MacLaine?

How surprising to find Miss MacLaine taking a crack at a *Diabolique*-type shocker, but then the lady has been doing a number of surprising things lately—surprising, that is, to everyone but herself.

Shirley MacLaine certainly kept right on surprising Hollywood!

To place the above excerpt in its proper context, we must remember that the Shirley MacLaine of 1971 was hardly the Shirley MacLaine of 1990. Although there were increasing numbers of folks who were happily announcing the dawning of the Age of Aquarius, the Hollywood scene back then would have had a difficult time reconciling everybody's favorite film comedienne, typecast as either a kook or a hooker—or perhaps a kooky hooker—with UFOs, possession, spirit guides, and metaphysics.

It was true that Shirley MacLaine had occasionally escaped her cute-kook roles and provided ample evidence of her serious dramatic abilities—as in *The Children's Hour* (1962), *Some Came Running* (1958), and *The Apartment* (1960)—and she had twice been nominated for an Oscar. But in the early seventies, there would have been few people in Hollywood—or in the rank and file of theater audiences—who would have been prepared to listen to Shirley MacLaine espouse New Age teachings.

From the vantage point of the present examining the past, so many of Shirley's statements in that old *Show* article seem wonderfully prophetic of the woman who would one day surprise the world with her spiritual vision:

You can search for the navel in the orange all your life, but sooner or later you've got to stop and ask yourself: ''Hold it! What do I believe?''

I'm much more revolutionary than Jane Fonda. I don't want to free just the Black Panthers; I want hard hats to be free, too. Sometimes I'm afraid that she provokes the violence and *then* reflects on it. I [have seen] dehumanization all over the world, and it filters through every level of society. After you realize that you really do care, that you're optimistic enough to believe mankind still has a chance, you have to make a decision. I asked myself: "What can a movie actress do?"

The most intelligent manner of "crusading" is to work at expanding the human consciousness. I'm my own best invention. I try to keep from going bananas myself. One has to start with oneself. There's no other way to hack it.

My home is inside my own head. That's what is true—my life and my feeling of amalgamation with being alive.

British astrologer Fredrick Davies once stated his belief that Shirley MacLaine experienced the turning point of her own spiritual awakening during the filming of *The Possession of Joel Delaney.* He said that Shirley was noncommittal when he asked her if she had had any psychic reactions to the dramatic and controversial shooting of the exorcism scene in the film, but Davies felt intuitively that things had stirred within the actress that prompted an acceleration of her own awareness of the spirit world.

Director Waris Hussein confided to Davies that during the vital scene in which an exorcist performs an actual ritual of deliverance from a possessing entity, the actor playing the part collapsed. Several other actors and crew members had "unusual and inexplicable metaphysical reactions" to the ritual.

"Some of the cast and crew asked that they, themselves, be exorcised," Hussein told Davies.

In 1977, Shirley MacLaine made a film entitled *The Turning Point* with Anne Bancroft and Mikhail Baryshnikov, and Davies remained convinced that *The Possession of Joel Delaney* and the strange occurrences that surrounded the making of the film served as the turning point of her own spiritual awakening. The accomplished astrologer expressed his opinion that Shirley—born April 24, 1934, at 3:57 P.M., in Richmond, Virginia—was predisposed by the Taurean influence to hard work and an open mind.

"Perhaps it was her Venus in the sign of Pisces that made her first want to be a dancer, as Pisces rules the feet. Taurean determination could also be seen when, in the course of a long career, she had been nominated for an Oscar five times before she won on her sixth nomination.

"After her spiritual regeneration, her mystic disciplines combined with Taurean strength and her Mercury in Aries, and she learned to project and to visualize what she wanted in life," Davies explained. "She visualized the winning of an Academy Award, the writing of a best-selling book, and the success of her revue on Broadway, and she achieved all three goals."

FILMING THE DARK SIDE OF THE FORCE

William Peter Blatty, the author of both the book and the Oscar-winning screenplay for *The Exorcist* (1973), has experienced paranormal phenomena around him since his earliest childhood. Blatty feels that he has demonstrated psychokinesis—mind over matter—on numerous occasions, and he is convinced that he has powers of precognition—the ability to glimpse the future.

Blatty has said that he believes that we retain an electromagnetic field when we die that can, in fact, move physical objects also within an electromagnetic field. This theory, he suggested, explains poltergeist phenomena. His powers of precognition assisted him greatly in writing *The Exorcist.* The entire work was a subconscious creation, he said, so the actual writing was merely "the discovery of preexisting territory."

The Exorcist Sought to Create Absolute Terror

When he worked on the film, Blatty's principal objectives were to convey the types of supernatural experiences that he had so often encountered in his own life and to create in an audience a feeling of absolute terror. He decided that it was important for the audience to know these experiences in aural as well as visual terms.

He experimented with sounds that the members of the audience might not consciously be able to identify "but that part of you recognizes." When the possessed girl, Regan, arches backward and an apparition of the devil appears, the special effects people created an unforgettable scream of a demon in pain, a demon being driven from its earthly habitation.

"It was the sound of bees trapped in a jar," Blatty said. "It was the sound of bees trying to get out of a jar, multiplied hundreds of times, combined with the screams of swine being led to slaughter. Your unconscious knows what that sound is. It works on an audience fantastically. I'm sorry about the effects that the book and the movie have had on some people. In certain eastern cities, little girls who unfortunately read the book when they shouldn't have been allowed to do so began to manifest the so-called possession syndrome—which looks a great deal like hysteria except in cases where paranormal phenomena are involved.

Blatty Believes in Possession

"The Exorcist is, of course, based on an actual case that is factual, documented. I haven't any doubt that the case was true. I believe in such things as possession. One can doubt everything, but we do make prudent judgments in life, don't we? I've made a prudent judgment based on the evidence, and I believe there are authentic cases of possession. By that I mean cases in which there are unquestioned paranormal phenomena that are exterior and can be witnessed and verified.''

Pressed for more of his opinions on the subject of demons, Blatty said that he saw them not so much as monsters with horns but as ''malign, disembodied intelligences,'' capable of seizing on the human body and possessing it. ''A demon wants the kick of being married to a human nervous system. Like Henry the Eighth wanting to eat a thirty-course meal again.''

We Were Seeded Here on Earth: Benevolent Angels Created Us

Blatty's fascination with the supernatural has led him to speculate that humankind was seeded on earth by creatures from another galaxy.

''I have no doubt of the existence of UFOs,'' he told celebrity bestselling author Charles Higham. ''Pursing this idea one step further, we come to the concept of devils and angels, to the idea that angels were the benevolent creators of the human race from another galaxy. That God created them, that they were the intermediaries, and that the demons were from that same or another galaxy and have interfered. This is one explanation of the existence of evil. I believe *creatures* created us.''

The Phenomenon of Love Is Paranormal

Blatty once said that we do not need the so-called paranormal or the occult to prove God or life after death: "The phenomenon of love is paranormal—really it is. In a mechanistic universe where the atoms that make up a man are rushing as blindly as the rivers to the seas to accomplish their selfish ends, how is it that there is love? How is it that a man will give his life for another?

"That's occult enough and sufficient proof enough for me of the existence of the soul. Love is a proof that there is a God. There was great love in *The Exorcist*. When Damien Karras [Jason Miller], the Jesuit psychiatrist, hurls himself out the window and gives his life for the possessed girl, Regan MacNeil [Linda Blair], it is a love that is totally unsolicited, unexpected. He never knew the little girl as the lovely thing that would win one's heart. He knew her only as a wretched creature, and he gave his life for that."

Mercedes McCambridge: Fear of Offending God Forever

One of the actors who was invisible on the screen but who contributed to the soundtrack of *The Exorcist,* one of the film's most horrifying features, could have used a great deal of the healing love of which Blatty spoke so eloquently.

In an article for the *New York Times,* later collected in his 1979 *Celebrity Circus,* Charles Higham recounted the anguish that the "voice of the devil," Mercedes McCambridge, experienced both during and after the filming of *The Exorcist.*

McCambridge told Higham that she thought perhaps God might be punishing her for playing the voice of the devil. She said that she had performed more than the devil's voice—she had also accomplished all of the demon's sounds. Her chronic bronchitis had helped with the wheezing. The wailing just before the demon was driven out was the keening sound she had once heard at a wake in Ireland. The moaning cries she had used when playing Lady Macbeth for Orson Welles. For the groaning sounds, she had pulled a scarf tight around her neck and almost strangled herself.

"In Order to Play Evil Incarnate, I Had to Think Evil"

Mercedes testified that she was a devout Catholic, the product of convent schools. "Speaking those vile, blaspheming words was an agony for me. For sixteen years, I sat in front of a pulpit hearing about the horror of evil incarnate, and now I had to play evil incarnate. I had to think evil."

She had to imagine Lucifer. She had to envision the eternal agony of a lost soul. Mercedes even drew upon her experiences as an alcoholic and the times that she had seen people in state hospitals. In the classic scene in which the possessed girl spews out a stream of green vomit, McCambridge swallowed eighteen raw eggs and a pulpy apple to make "the ugly sounds of violent expectoration." To convey the feeling of the demon being trapped, she had the crew bind her hand and foot. Sometimes she left the studio so exhausted that she had to spend the night in a nearby motel, unable to drive home. Her voice was ruined. For weeks, she could not speak above a whisper.

"If there was any horror in the exorcism," she said, "it was me!"

Wes Craven Is Busy Creating Nightmares

One might expect Wes Craven, the director of such assaults on the psyche as *A Nightmare on Elm Street* (1984), to have sprung full-blown from a body-snatching pod that drifted to earth from an alien world. In actuality, the father of nightmarish Freddy Krueger, that burn-scarred, steel-taloned, unkillable child molester, is another purveyor of the supernatural who, like Blatty, was reared in a religious family.

Born to strict Baptist Fundamentalists who separated when he was four, Craven had to endure the trauma of his father's fatal heart attack a year later. It was his nightmares during this period that planted the frightening seeds of *A Nightmare on Elm Street.* Wes realized the childhood terror of going to sleep each night. "Sleep is the one place where your parents can't come with you."

The only movies Craven saw as a kid, he told writer Jeffrey Book, were Disney classics and newsreels. "The first years of my life occurred during World War II, so I would go from seeing *Bambi* [1942] to dead Yanks on Normandy beaches. That was very strange at the time."

Craven's admitted goal is to create films that are strange and bizarre yet "completely related to something very powerful and intimate in people's subconscious." Because everyone has dreams and nightmares, Craven wants his ideas to relate to memories of the first years of life "because that's where many people have their most powerful emotions buried."

As Craven sees it: "It's those parental figures, the mysterious house, the bully on the block that stay with us into adulthood and affect how we cope with similar situations on more complex adult levels."

Brian De Palma Depicts Physical Horror

Brian De Palma, the director of *Carrie* (1976) and *The Fury* (1978), is another who specializes in depicting the physical horror of human existence. He has also declared that his films are the products of his nightmares.

Quite obviously inspired by Hitchcock, De Palma places his victims in vulnerable positions in showers and in bedrooms and disguises his villains so that they might all the easier commit their evil and bloody deeds. Both *Carrie* and *Dressed to Kill* (1980) end with grisly scenes that turn out to be a last nightmare of the protagonist that the audience gets to take home with them and transform into their own disturbed dreams.

Can these cinematic nightmares become externalized beyond the motion picture screen and bring havoc upon those very magicians who play fast and loose with the collective unconscious?

Director James Whale, who collaborated with Boris Karloff to animate the dread Frankenstein monster, was found dead in his swimming pool under mysterious circumstances.

Willis O'Brien, the Hollywood special effects master and creator of King Kong, watched in horror as his two sons were shot just before the release of *Son of Kong* (1933).

Piercing the Dark Side with Rays of Spiritual Light

Gale Anne Hurd, producer, and James Cameron, writer-director, have collaborated on three action-adventure films with definite spiritual overtones—*The Terminator* (1984), *Aliens* (1986), and *The Abyss* (1989).

They believe that it is possible to film the ''Dark Side of the Force'' with a balanced perspective.

While some viewers will recall *The Terminator* only for the scenes of violence involving the indestructible android, played by Arnold Schwarzenegger, it must be remembered that the vicious robot has been sent from the future to murder a young woman who is destined to become impregnated by a Christ-like man. If she gives birth to this messianic entity, he will one day eliminate the murderous androids. Film critic Richard Corliss pronounced the film, ''A hip retelling of the Annunciation.''

Sigourney Weaver survived the devastation of director Ridley Scott's *Alien* (1979) to star in the Hurd and Cameron sequel, *Aliens* (1986). The climatic scene is pure good versus evil as surrogate mother Weaver squares off mano a mano with the great bitch monster that has been laying all those terrible alien eggs.

Without Cameron, Hurd produced *Alien Nation* (1988), which used the scalpel of science fiction to peel back layers of racial prejudice.

As life often imitates art, the story of *The Abyss* (1989) has its central characters, played by Ed Harris and Mary Elizabeth Mastrantonio, separated and in the process of obtaining a divorce. A remarkable underwater illumination experience resuscitates their drowning marriage. Hurd and Cameron, wed for more than three years before embarking on *The Abyss,* were unable to achieve vicarious salvation of their marital union through their fictional creations' rebirth of love. Nonetheless, their undersea saga retained its highly moral, even biblical, connotations.

Hurd commented that her father was Jewish and her mother Roman Catholic so she got guilt from both. Cameron attended Sunday school regularly and came from firm Protestant stock.

''Parts of *The Abyss* are like a religious experience,'' Cameron was quoted by Beverly Walker in the June 1989 issue of *American Film.* ''It has a message of hope . . . and a warning that we have to change. It's about contact with an ultimate force, which is in a position to judge us.''

''I want to make movies that make the world a little bit better without preaching,'' Hurd said. ''Popular entertainment with the right message. I like stories that show that ordinary people can be in power. The world has grown so fast, and people feel so insignificant. We need to realize that the little things we do contribute to the future.''

6 · HAUNTED HOLLYWOOD

The mystery of death and what lies beyond its veil undoubtedly holds an enormous fascination for people. Surely a large measure of the continued popularity of the ghost story over the centuries—and throughout the history of Hollywood—lies in the fact that regardless of how gentle or how grim the ghost, its very presence is a testimony of the survival of the human spirit after death.

There is an interesting situation that has been created by the flickering reality of the motion picture. In a very real sense, once an actor has committed his image to film, he has created his own ghost, his own shadow that will continue to talk and walk and act out a prearranged drama whenever that film is shown.

Years of research investigating the phenomena of ghosts and of hauntings have convinced us that a real ghost performs more like an animated memory than a creature of independent intelligence. It is as if something has impressed a memory pattern upon a certain environment; the pattern, like a brief strip of film being fed into a projector, keeps remembering the same bit of action night after night. (This continual replay was interestingly portrayed in the 1988 movie *High Spirits,* starring Peter O'Toole, Steve Guttenberg, and Daryl Hannah.) The ghost-actor is as indifferent to the observers who see its performance as an actor on film is to the audience in a theater or in front of a television set. It would seem as out of character for a real ghost to take notice of someone and engage that person in conversation as it would be for an image on a strip of film to suddenly step off the screen and begin shaking hands with moviegoers in the front rows—despite Woody Allen's charming portrayal of just such

154

an event in his 1985 *The Purple Rose of Cairo,* staring Mia Farrow and Jeff Daniels.

It must be emphasized that we are now referring to ghosts, not to spirit entities or souls. The excited cry, "Elvis still lives!" that we frequently hear arising from different parts of the country reflects the collective sorrow of devoted fans who do not wish to accept the reality of their idol's death.

Yet Elvis *is* alive, and so are Clark Gable and Spencer Tracy and James Cagney and Marilyn Monroe and all the other film personalities who have left their indelible imprint upon the magical mixture of light and celluloid. All of these actors achieved another dimension of life on film. They attained an immortality that will last as long as there are motion picture projectors to give animation to their films.

The advent of television and home video sets has made the film stars of Hollywood even more accessible to the mass consciousness than ever before. As Dr. Franklin R. Ruehl observes, "We now have millions of people living unreal lives. The movies create a fantasy world for our entertainment, but because of the immediacy and the proximity of this unreal world, more and more people are entering into the world of fantasy. There is an interesting paradox here: As our technology has increased, we have become more fantasy prone. Too many of us are living life vicariously through our television sets."

Another fascinating element of transference has occurred since the golden days of Hollywood. For the average person, the movie star used to belong in the theater—remote, glamorous, removed from the routine of a humdrum existence. With the advent of television, the movie stars are now in our homes. We eat, sleep, and get up with them in the morning. Small wonder, then, that we have diminished the barriers between the material and the nonmaterial and that we may not be surprised to see the ghost of a departed Hollywood star walking among familiar landmarks.

Of course, as we steadily learn in this book, the stars, themselves, encounter ghosts.

Susan Olsen, who played the youngest of the six children on television's "The Brady Bunch," had decided to elope to Greece with her husband-to-be. She changed her plans when she saw the spirit of her dead grandmother appear to advise her not to elope and hurt the family's feelings but to invite everyone to a simple ceremony at home.

Since he starred in *Halloween* (1978), the versatile and accomplished actor Donald Pleasence has appeared in numerous cinematic offerings about ghosts, phantoms, and demons. Pleasence is able to bring first-hand experience to his roles for he and his family once lived in a haunted house.

"I was scared to death when we first began to hear strange noises," he admitted, "but then it hit us. When we had remodeled the house and knocked down the walls, we'd allowed the ghosts of children to run through the place as they had done years before. The ghostly sounds were, after all, sounds of joy."

There definitely appears to be something in those Hollywood hills that stimulates hauntings; before we begin to explore a wide range of manifestations, a few definitions would seem to be in order:

- A **ghost** is a stranger to the one who perceives it. Remember our explanation of the animated memory pattern that somehow springs to a kind of transient life.
- An **apparition** is well-known by the witness and is instantly recognizable as the image of a parent, sibling, spouse, or friend. An apparition usually appears at a time of crisis—most often that of physical death—and usually appears only once.
- A **vision** is the appearance of a religious figure, such as the Virgin Mary, an angel, or one of the saints.
- A **poltergeist** is a projection of psychic energy that most often finds its center in the frustrated creativity of adolescence and emanates, therefore, from the living rather than from the dead. A poltergeist is a ghost only in common parlance. What links the two is the spooklike nature of the poltergeist that causes the invisible pseudoentity to prefer darkness for its violent exercises of tossing furniture, objects, and people about the room.

Now that we have defined the various types of haunting phenomena, we will probably all go right on using "ghost" to describe any eerie encounter that seems to involve the image of a human being that we strongly suspect is no longer physically with us on the earth plane.

THE HAUNTED HOLLYWOOD HILLS

Charlene Tilton, who achieved international fame as Lucy Ewing on "Dallas," may well have been the center of poltergeist activity as a child. She has described doors opening and closing of their own volition, pockets of cold air around her, and a sense of something invisible following her.

She recalls the instance when a neighbor asked her to turn down her blaring radio. In a teenage tantrum, Charlene refused. "Then things began to happen," she told writer Virginia Smith. "The plug jerked out of the wall without anyone being near it. When I pushed it back into the socket, it was jerked out again so violently that sparks flew. The neighbor stood there frozen with terror."

Now that Charlene is married to gospel singer Domenick Allen, she has come to view the mischief-making ghost that tormented her childhood as a guardian angel that was seeking to keep her on the "straight and narrow." In her present view, she has identified the entity as the spirit of her grandfather who sought to provide her with ghostly discipline.

During our visits to Los Angeles, author and parapsychologist Barry Taff has shared a number of his Hollywood ghost-chasing experiences with us. On one occasion, the three of us sat down for a quick meal and didn't move until three hours later as Barry regaled us with the details of a recent investigation.

In her book *Haunted Houses and Wandering Ghosts of California,* Antoinette May tells of Taff and his partner, Kerry Gaynor, investigating a home where they were told "books just flew around by themselves." The house, an attractive Spanish colonial, had a romantic past— Barbara Stanwyck and Robert Taylor had once lived there. The present owner said that a houseboy had just quit his employ because "cabbages had chased him about the house."

On May 14, 1976, Taff and Gaynor found that their investigation must have touched a psychic maelstrom. An ice tray flew from the kitchen into the dining room. A shower head from an upstairs bath floated downstairs into the living room. Coins fell on them from the empty air. A heavy pewter goblet struck a wall with enough force to scatter plaster. A member of a news team ducked a flying shoe that nearly struck his head. Another newscaster was chased down the stairs by a *World Book Atlas*. Other members of the group said that the book appeared almost birdlike as it pursued the hapless journalist.

Apparently it was not determined whether the haunting phenomenon had anything to do with either Robert Taylor or Barbara Stanwyck. It would be interesting to learn what may have occurred in the home after her death on January 20, 1990. According to certain of her friends, the 82-year-old actress spoke to the ghost of Taylor for nearly a year before her own passing. Barbara never made a secret of the fact that Taylor, who died in 1969, was the love of her life. It is said that the actress, the star of television's "The Big Valley" and more than eighty motion pictures, welcomed death so that she and Taylor could begin their love affair anew.

John Newland Took Hollywood One Step Beyond

In our opinion, the most authentic television presentation of the paranormal was John Newland's "Alcoa Presents: One Step Beyond," which ran from 1959 to 1961. Newland's polished voice and mannerisms assured audiences that they were not about to watch some wild story that had been concocted by a writer of weird tales because each story contained a "substantial kernel of provable fact."

When the tale concluded, whether it dealt with ghosts, prophecy, or reincarnation, Newland returned with a carefully worded signature: "What you have just seen . . . To whom it happened, we know. Where it happened, we know. How or why it happened—who knows?"

Even though the writers and its urbane host did their best to present an attitude of open-mindedness rather than proselytism, Newland told us that the offices were deluged with tons of angry letters accusing them of doing the work of the Antichrist.

"We answered each of the hostile letters by reminding the writers that we lived in a nation where free speech and free opinion were cherished. It is the fear of the unknown that makes it so difficult to deal seriously with the subject matter of hauntings and other paranormal phenomena in the media,'' Newland said. ''You can give them fiction and far-out stories, but you cannot say that an incident actually happened.''

On ''Alcoa Presents: One Step Beyond,'' students of psychical research recognized many classic cases presented in a balanced manner but with the actual names and places changed. Newland explained that this was done for all the obvious legal reasons and to make some of the incidents more entertaining. It was the writers' intention to capture the essence of the true experiences rather than to present strict documentaries.

''Alcoa Presents: One Step Beyond'' will always stand as a landmark series on the paranormal, but when an attempt was made to revive the program a few years ago, the episodes had little of the excitement or the feelings of verisimilitude that the former series had evoked.

''When we did 'Alcoa Presents: One Step Beyond,' '' Newland said, ''no one interfered with us. Alcoa gave us the money to prepare the episodes, and [the] television [network] put them on the air. In the case of 'The Next Step Beyond,' Procter and Gamble completely and tediously involved themselves in everything. There was no way that they would permit the slightest hint that any of the documented experiences had actually occurred. They strictly enforced the broadcast code that forbade the indeterminate sciences to be presented as fact. Our sponsors totally de-energized the series.''

Newland characterized himself as a believer in the paranormal, but he is apparently a nonreceptor as he has not yet seen a ghost, visited a haunted house, or spotted a UFO.

''I certainly am open to the experience,'' he said, ''but as of this time, nothing has seen fit to manifest through me.''

The Making of *Poltergeist*

Steven Spielberg, the producer of the supernatural thriller *Poltergeist* (1982), has referred to something manifesting through or around him, but he chose not to reveal the details. ''It is a very, very personal thing that I won't discuss. I've always wanted to see a UFO, and I never have. But ghosts—that's another story.''

As a kind of teaser, Spielberg suggested: ''Probably every fourth person you talk to has had an experience with a poltergeist or ghost—or knows someone who has.''

Tobe Hooper, the director of *Poltergeist,* saw no reason to be coy about his own experiences. Hooper, who first gained fame for his creation of the cult classic *The Texas Chainsaw Massacre* (1974), may actually have undergone a kind of textbook example of a poltergeist. He was nineteen when his father passed away. ''For three days after he died, glasses broke, knickknacks were shattered on the floor a good distance from the shelves where they should have been—and a lot farther than they would have naturally fallen. Even Dad's favorite rocking chair started rocking with no one anywhere near it. Then, the incidents just stopped.''

JoBeth Williams, who costarred in the film with Craig T. Nelson, remembered her one and only experience with haunting phenomena.

She was in residence with a summer stock company in New Hampshire. One night she was awakened from her sleep by the violent shaking of her bed. She thought nothing of it at first, assuming it was a dream—until she realized that she was not asleep and that the bed was in fact shaking, and the room had become very cold. The next day, she told the owner of the house about her experience. The owner was not at all surprised. She said that someone had died in the house.

Beatrice Straight, who plays the parapsychologist in *Poltergeist,* stated that she owns a farmhouse in Connecticut that dates back well into the 1800s. Her children used to wake up in the night complaining that they heard noises and that someone was tugging at their covers. ''My housekeeper and I used to hear someone calling, 'OOOO-who-OOO-who,' '' she recalled. ''We once had a well-known psychic come to the old farmhouse, and, believe it or not, we brought out a Ouija board that spelled out the words 'Younglove,' 'drown,' and 'lake.' ''

Since there was a lake near the farmhouse, they all went to visit it. ''According to the psychic, an Indian named Younglove had drowned in the lake and his spirit was thanking us for caring.''

The actress added that documents had been discovered that indicated that Indians had lived in the area and had been friendly with the family that had lived in the house many years ago.

Steven Spielberg did not hesitate to point out that *Poltergeist* walked the thin line between the scientific and the spiritual. ''The film has some incredibly spiritual things in it. It also has a good amount of humor and terror and fright; but we show the spectral light that comes to earth, piercing a hole in time and space into the home of a suburban family.''

He went on to state that he had taken the premise that poltergeists were disembodied spirits or souls from people long since dead ''who come back or who have never left.'' Although such a definition is somewhat at odds with the more standard parapsychological portrait of a poltergeist, Spielberg explained: ''In our film, they are spirits or ghosts who don't know they are dead and who need a guide to take them into the next plane of existence through a gateway of spectral light.''

Joan Rivers Moves into a Haunted Apartment

Joan Rivers recently moved from Los Angeles to a luxury apartment in Manhattan's East Side in a concerted effort to begin a new life after the death of Edgar Rosenberg, her husband of twenty-three years. Rivers went through a devastating period of mourning, suffering through the many painful emotions that accompany the tragedy of her husband having taken his own life. Her bravery, honesty, and willingness to deal with her feelings have given many people the courage to face similar situations in their own lives.

Now it would see that her remarkable strength is being put to another test. The swanky apartment building into which she has moved is reputed to be haunted. Many tenants there have attested to bizarre noises and strange occurrences. Many have even canceled leases rather than stay in their eerie apartments.

According to writer Jill Evans, Joan Rivers is not at all disturbed by the prospects of residing in a haunted building. She has even expressed a feeling of comfort that one of the spirits might be that of her late husband.

The Ghost of Humphrey Bogart Haunts Statues of the Maltese Falcon

It may be the power of suggestion or the dynamics of mythic association at work, but reports have been made of the appearance of the ghostly image of Humphrey Bogart in connection with replicas of the Maltese falcon, the legendary statue from the 1941 film classic. In the motion picture, Bogart plays Sam Spade, the private detective who must avoid a series of double-crosses and the Fat Man, whose lust for the statue leads him to murder.

The sculptor who had fashioned the replicas said he has no idea why Bogart's ghost has allegedly materialized in conjunction with the statues, but he stated that certain purchasers of the Maltese falcon have reported seeing the actor standing near the statue in his trademark trench coat and fedora.

A psychic sensitive commented that the replica of the Maltese falcon may act as a kind of magnet to draw Bogart's image from the Other Side. "Perhaps those who claim to have seen him have strong feelings about him. He may represent another more idealistic and direct era to them, and they are seeing him as they best remember him."

If there is any truth to these sightings of Bogart's ghost, we wonder if just before he vanishes he might not mumble under his breath, "Here's looking at you, kid."

PHOTOGRAPHING REAL GHOSTS WITH NICK NOCERINO

"I'm working on a case right now where the home is haunted by the ghost of a little boy," Frank R. ("Nick") Nocerino told us. "He's scaring the hell out of the kids in the family. There's black stuff oozing out of the walls. It's a nasty haunting."

When Nick calls it a nasty haunting, he has nearly fifty years of experience upon which he bases such an assessment. "But please, don't call me a 'ghostbuster,' " he said.

Nocerino, the director of the Institute of Psychic and Hypnotic Sciences in Pinole, California, has been pursuing "whatever ghosts are" as a parapsychologist, a psychic researcher, or a consultant on the paranormal since 1944. He is one of the most respected photographers of the supernatural in the United States, and we have known him since 1976.

Working most often with his associate, Charles Pelton, Nick explains that the team uses tripods and cameras and ASA 400 black-and-white film. They set up the cameras, preset the focus and exposure, and then shoot in a radius around a room that they have been told—or that they sense—is a center of ghostly manifestations. The only available light in the entire house comes from one candle that is used to draw out the psychic energy. When Nick or one of his associates begins to sense something in the room, he points the camera in that direction and clicks away.

Presenting us with photographic files that covered the years from 1950 to 1985, Nocerino emphasized that the hundreds of pictures now at our disposal were not taken for publication. "These are all on-the-spot case photos," he said. "Nearly every one of them was taken with just one candle that was lighted in a room where energy was felt. You can judge for yourself the energy that was produced by looking at the photographs. When we shoot outdoors, in cemeteries and so forth, we use only available light—which at night is very little. When making notes, there is usually one light on inside a room for about half an hour. We usually photograph between 9 P.M. and 5 A.M."

Nick informed us that while there were more conventional-type hauntings reported in Northern California, the southern part of the state, especially the Los Angeles/Hollywood area, reported more demonic, evil-type disturbances.

"The ghosts in the Los Angeles area are meaner," Nocerino stated, though he was reluctant to speculate as to why this might be so other than to reflect that it may have something to do with a peculiar magnetic field in the area. "We've just been called in on another nasty haunting in Los Angeles. One by one, all of the pets have been killed by the phenomenon—the dog, the birds, the cats. The owners of the home have so far asked the help of a minister, a priest, and a rabbi, seeking all the traditional religious types of exorcisms. The minister had his Bible burst into flames; the rabbi was bodily ejected from the home by the unseen entity; the priest had his cross glow red-hot and burn his flesh. I don't intend disrespect toward anyone's faith, but sometimes an orthodox exorcism only makes the entities angrier."

Could such occurrences result from a magnetic field that appears to produce more than its share of demonic entities in the Hollywood area?

"I have only unconfirmed data at this time," he said. "There may be some kind of dimensional opening in the area." Nocerino stated that they had investigated a number of houses where people had disappeared, simply vanished. A policeman had gone to investigate and he too, vanished. As the occupants before him, he simply never left the house.

"That kind of thing smacks of some sort of dimensional opening rather than a haunting—mean or otherwise," Nick told us.

Why does Nick Nocerino feel that real ghosts and restless spirits manifest at all? And why, sometimes, in such violent ways?

First, he explained, there is the ghost of someone who has been murdered and whose death has been improperly recognized. "Maybe it was officially recorded that the death was a suicide or an accident, but the spirit of the deceased wants to set the record straight and have it known that he was murdered. A close variation of that kind of haunting," Nocerino added, "is the type that is set in motion because a body has been improperly buried."

Second, there is the confused spirit of one who had been forcibly kept away from society. "We encounter the ghosts of men and women who were kept chained in cellars or in attics," he said. "You know, maybe they were insane or mentally retarded—or maybe their families decided they were when they weren't. Well, a lot of those spirits have not yet found peace. They are still disturbed."

A third common haunting is precipitated by someone bringing home an antique or a Native American relic. "In one particularly dramatic case involving an ancient Chinese vase, the owner became so desperate that we all went along to throw it in the ocean. We all saw it sink into the waters, so imagine our consternation when we returned to the house and found it waiting for us."

Fourth, there is the spirit that travels with people from a haunted area. "There was a bar that had a ghost that would follow customers into their cars then manifest while they were driving, grabbing at the steering wheel, pushing at the brakes. A lot of accidents were caused by this entity."

Which brings up an uneasy point. Can ghosts harm people?

"Not directly," Nocerino answered. "Not physically, but sometimes it would appear that they can. In this one cemetery where lights manifested and ghosts materialized, even members of our research team ran screaming from the place. One of our investigators said that he was thrown over a tombstone by an entity. I don't believe ghosts can really injure people, but I believe that they can put all kinds of things into people's minds and cause them to believe that all sorts of terrible things are occurring that really might not be happening in physical reality. Or they can cause people to injure themselves.''

Which brings up yet another queasy point. Is Nocerino now referring to spirit possession?

The fifth category of ghostly phenomena does most certainly have to do with invading spirits that people can pick up from a negative environment when they are depressed, angry, emotionally imbalanced, or under the influence of drugs and alcohol. ''That is why a psychical researcher must be especially well-balanced and must steadily work at keeping himself or herself in harmony and at peace,'' Nocerino said.

INDIAN GHOSTS IN HOLLYWOOD STREETS

When Wanda Sue Parrott was a reporter on the staff of the *Los Angeles Herald Examiner,* she stated that the bulk of ghost reports received by the newspaper consisted of incidents involving the spectral manifestations of American Indians.

A Mrs. P. told Wanda that she and her husband had many encounters with an Indian spirit before their marriage. After her marriage, she had her first visitation with the entity in 1961, just before a serious illness. ''He came to warn us of danger ahead,'' Mrs. P. said, ''and he protected me.''

A Mrs. W. was told by the ghost of an Indian man that he would leave her apartment only if she disposed of the Amerindian artifact that she had recently acquired. She obeyed the spectral Indian, and even though he was true to his word and left with the artifact, Mrs. W. found herself so unnerved by the eerie incident that she consulted a psychiatrist, who consoled her with the astonishing statement that there was nothing wrong with her: many of his patients had had similar experiences with the ghosts of American Indians!

Wanda Sue found that a number of San Gabriel Valley residents had shared in the Indian ghost experience. ''Men, women, and children alike have reported seeing a male Indian appear in their yards, bedrooms, and living rooms at all hours of the day and night. Most of the witnesses agree that he seems friendly enough. He stays for a moment or two then fades away.''

The Indian Ghost That Gave People a Hotfoot

Clarisa Bernhardt, who has gained international fame as a psychic-sensitive, is half-Cherokee, the granddaughter of Chief John Muskrat of Tahlequah, Oklahoma. However, being the relative of a chief provided her with little influence when she encountered the ghost of a Shumash chief who greeted people with a hotfoot.

As one of the spirit's victims put it, ''You'll believe it after he comes into the room while you are in bed and burns your foot. Then nobody will believe *you!*''

Clarisa's friend Flo owned a haunted house, but had not experienced any unusual spirit phenomena until after the place had been restored; then no one could spend the night there without waking up with red marks on fingers or toes and without experiencing burning sensations.

''The house had been built next to and over a Shumash graveyard,'' Clarisa recalled. ''Flo met the ghost of the chief, got the hotfoot, but eventually made peace with him and things settled down for her.

''You can feel a presence in that house as soon as you enter it. I have the privilege of seeing people on the other plane. I met the chief in the hallway. He was in feathers. There was a very high vibration there. The Shumash were apparently a very evolved people.

''At first the spirit was hostile to me, but after a couple of visits, he was all right. He just wants to be certain that nobody's going to do anything to violate his tribe.''

LIVING IN A HAUNTED HOUSE IS GOOD PREPARATION FOR ACTING IN ONE

Although millions of television viewers know Lar Park Lincoln as one of the glamorous ladies of ''Knots Landing,'' she has also achieved popularity as the telekinetic Tina, who successfully battles the monstrous Jason in *Friday the 13th, Part VII—The New Blood* (1988).

Lar thinks nothing of playing such contrasting characters. To switch from being Linda Fairgate, Michele Lee's overzealous, health-nut daughter-in-law on ''Knots Landing'' to a mental patient whose psychic abilities reactivate Jason from his watery grave is all part of paying her dues as an actress. Besides, she also played a teenaged prostitute in the award-winning *Children of the Night* (1985).

When we asked Lar (short for Laurie and pronounced Lar-eee) if she had been affected by starring in one of the gory *Friday the 13th* episodes, she said that the sheer mechanics of filmmaking really prevented her from getting terribly caught up in the horror of the story line. As a matter of fact, "I didn't get to see [Jason's] 'beautiful' face until the finished picture was edited. They did my reaction one time— and I had to react to what I guessed would be a pretty gruesome guy— and then they put in Jason's face later. As you know, films are shot in bits and pieces and edited together later. We shot very late at night, and we would come back to the hotel all dirty and bedraggled."

The actress laughed when she told us that they did have a time with the maids not wanting to clean her room or Jason's room. They filmed *The New Blood* in Alabama, and the reputation of the series had placed some of the local citizenry a bit on edge.

Lar said that she had been especially interested in the role of Tina, who is a mental patient with unusual paranormal abilities. "I have my own thoughts and concerns about who it is who determines mental illness or mental health," she said. "My husband, Michael Lincoln, works with autistic children, and sometimes it seems as if they are in the right and we are in the wrong."

Nevertheless, Lar said that it was fun having such incredible psychic powers in the film. "Even though I was aware of the crew moving on the catwalk above me, pulling the wires like puppeteers, it was great to be able to simply move my head and a television set would fly across the room."

Sometimes, just to have fun with her, the crew would move things that were not scripted to fly about the room. "That was freaky," she said, laughing, "and it really gave me a sense of what it would be like to have such powers."

During one scene, filmed at seven o'clock in the morning, Lar admitted that she did become "giddily hysterical" when the script called for her to touch a dead man's head in a cooking pot. "The special effects people take great pride in their work. The head looked and felt so real that I simply panicked. I would not touch it."

Although Lar may not be too keen on slasher-type horror films, she does like movies about the supernatural that emphasize mystery and suspense. Perhaps the fact that she lived for a time in a haunted house helped to prepare her for such roles as Tina.

She was reared in a military family, and while stationed in Texas, they lived in a house that was haunted. "The television channels would change right in front of us while we were watching. The lights would go on and off, and we could see the switches moving. The toilets would flush by themselves, and we could watch the handle actually pressing down."

The actress also described an odd odor that permeated the strange house. "One night, my older sister and I were awakened by the sounds of our parents making coffee in the kitchen," Lar remembered. "We could hear all the normal noises that would be involved in such an activity. Then we happened to look toward Mom and Dad's room— and we could see them both sleeping in bed!"

The sisters awakened their parents and told them that intruders were in the kitchen. Their story was convincing enough to cause their father to get his revolver and go downstairs to investigate.

"The kitchen was completely empty," Lar said, "but when Dad got down there, the light in the garage flicked on and off."

MITZI GAYNOR'S PET GHOST HELPS WITH THE HOUSECLEANING

We first met the multitalented dancer-actress Mitzi Gaynor many years ago when we appeared together on a television talk show in Chicago. Mitzi was promoting her personal appearance at a Windy City theater and we were on the show to discuss our book *The Psychic Feats of Olof Jonsson* (1971). It's about the remarkable Swedish-born mystic Olof Jonsson, who had participated with astronaut Ed Mitchell in the controversial moon-to-earth ESP experiments during the February 1971 flight of Apollo 14.

Both Mitzi and her husband, Jack Bean, seemed interested in the possibility of controlled psychic abilities and in the reality of the paranormal, so we were not surprised to learn in 1989 that Mitzi had encountered a ghost in their house. The star of such screen musicals as *Les Girls* (1957) and *South Pacific* (1958), Mitzi said that one terrified maid quit after she witnessed sheets and pillowcases rise off a table and fly around the room.

Mitzi has come to call the ghost "Mrs. Walker," after the previous owner, who had died in the house. Shortly after they moved in, the actress said, she had several chandeliers hung in various rooms. Evidently "Mrs. Walker" didn't approve of two of them. Both crashed to the floor, and the electricians who had been hired to install them could not determine how they could have fallen.

Mitzi has come to accept the eerie and expensive fact that "Mrs. Walker" will destroy those chandeliers that she does not like. "On the other hand," the actress told journalist Paul F. Levy, "she doesn't allow those she does like to get dusty. Now and then during the night, we enjoy the faint musical tinkling of the crystal prisms on our chandeliers, which tells us that 'Mrs. Walker' is going about her task of cleaning them. That's one chore the maids never have to do—dust the chandeliers."

VAMPIRES AND WEREWOLVES

Handsome and perpetually tanned George Hamilton, who is known to fancy the company of beauties, was not long ago seen in the company of beasties. For Halloween 1989, Hamilton hosted the syndicated special "Dracula, Live from Transylvania," a documentary that traced the myths and realities of vampires and professed to include encounters with actual "creatures of the night."

George, who played the eternal count in the 1979 film *Love at First Bite,* explained his beliefs about the phenomenon of vampirism: "In medieval times, there were people who seldom saw the sun or ate anything fresh. This caused their gums to recede, which made their teeth look like fangs. Their bad diet also created pernicious anemia, which made the sufferers crave blood."

Rumor had it that Hamilton had a unique breed of groupies following him in the hope of being interviewed for the special, claiming that they actually were vampires.

How would one conduct a casting call for real vampires? Carefully, very carefully—and maybe while wearing a fang-proof turtleneck.

A not-so-funny thing happened at a 1984 convention of fans of the popular television series "Dark Shadows"—a real vampire dropped in to bite a few necks. In fact, according to Dr. Stephen Kaplan, founder of the Vampire Research Center, she managed to bite nearly two hundred conventioneers before it was discovered that "Misty" from San Diego was the real thing. Jonathan Frid, who played the vampire "Barnabas Collins" on the series, found himself upstaged by the attractive young woman who spent most of her time in a borrowed hotel suite feasting on the blood of willing victims.

Kaplan and his wife Roxanne completed their third worldwide vampire census in 1989: not of the undead who turn into bats or wolves or puffs of smoke but living people who crave human blood and who may display some well-developed fangs.

Their census form asks such questions as "Do you sleep in a coffin?" "Are you now or have you ever been a member of a satanic cult?" "How often do you drink blood?"

The Vampire Research Center divides its creatures of the night into three basic categories: 1) Fetishists erotically attracted to blood; 2) vampire imitators who adopt the traditional trappings in search of powers of domination, immortality, sensuality, and charisma, and 3) true vampires—those men and women who have a physical addiction to blood, who drink it, who believe it will prolong their lives, and who experience sexual satisfaction through the blood-drinking ritual.

According to the 1989 census, the average female vampire appears to be twenty-three years old, has brown eyes and black hair, is five-foot-six, and weighs one hundred and twenty pounds. In the previous census conducted in 1983, the average female vampire appeared around twenty years old, had green eyes, blond hair, was five-foot-eight, and weighed one hundred and eighteen pounds. The average male vampire in the 1989 census appears to be twenty-six years old, has brown eyes and black hair, is five-foot-ten, and weighs one hundred and seventy pounds. In the 1983 census, he looked to be around twenty-one years old, had blue eyes and brown hair, was five-foot-ten, and weighed one hundred and fifty pounds.

The Kaplans estimate the vampire population to be about five hundred worldwide, with approximately three hundred of them in North America. Estimates show that California has twenty vampires; New

York and Texas have fifteen each; Oregon has ten; and Pennsylvania and Maryland each have nine. The rest are scattered from Illinois (seven) to Hawaii (two). Among the two hundred known foreign vampires, Australia has the most, followed by Spain, Germany, France, and the United Kingdom.

Accurate demographics are exceedingly difficult to determine, for the Kaplans have found that more than three hundred vampires frequently move from one state to another or from one country to another, crossing borders by car, plane, or boat, thus making it very difficult to identify them within a specific area.

In the November 1989 issue, *Psychology Today* addressed itself to what it envisions as pop culture's current preoccupation with vampires, a "craze in the computer age" that may forecast what to expect from the 1990s. Writer Katherine Ramsland quoted Stephan Martin, editor of the journal *Quadrant* for the C. G. Jung Foundation of New York, on the popularity of vampires: "Vampires are living parts of our humanity that people in a technological age have ignored. They have to do with the darkness and magic that is not given its due. If we ignore the unconscious, it becomes avaricious, voracious . . . the vampire is another side of our culture that needs a voice."

Kaplan told us that when he served as the consultant on "Werewolf," the cable television series, more than half a million telephone calls were received on their "werewolf hotline." "People were invited to call in if they thought they knew a real werewolf or if they felt they had ever seen one in real life," Kaplan said. "They were also invited to call if they *were* werewolves."

Most of the callers requested additional information, but five thousand insisted that they had seen actual werewolves apart from the motion picture or television screen. An astonishing number of callers stated that they, themselves, were real werewolves, with some describing very convincingly how they killed their victims. Others claimed to be "latent werewolves," the result of werewolves who had mated with humans. "It was really great," Kaplan said. "[Television] was helping me research *wolves!*"

He had his first encounters with real werewolves—both female—in the late 1970s, but he did not go public with this aspect of his research until 1985. As always, he is very cautious in conducting interviews with self-professed werewolves. "Many of them have spent time in mental institutions. Many have killed as teenagers and were committed, and the full moon does affect them."

Kaplan emphasized that he had never observed a metamorphosis from human to werewolf in the manner of Lon Chaney, Jr., or the hapless fellow in *An American Werewolf in London* (1981). "But many do have fangs, unusually long canine teeth. They are affected two days before the full moon, two days during, and two days after, so for six days they are werewolves."

Because of their obsession, Kaplan said, male werewolves may go for that period of time without shaving, thus adding to their hairy effect. A six-foot male may walk on his toes, wolf-style, thus adding to his height and appearing three or more inches taller. "The voice, the posture, the personality changes. In some cases, even eye color changes. They become full-blown 'schizoids.' Some of them will actually use artificial hair to give a stronger emphasis to their werewolf appearance."

The researcher said that he knew a New York psychiatrist who was treating two werewolves in Queens. Also, the werewolf hunter does receive angry threats.

"A couple of werewolves in Pittsburgh were disturbed because I had maligned their kind. They took exception to hearing me on a radio talk show state that werewolves ripped, mutilated, raped, and sometimes devoured a portion of their victims. How dare I say such terrible things? So they threatened to kill me as an object lesson."

Kaplan theorizes that werewolves may be the genetic result of the more aggressive Yeti—the so-called abominable snowman—who came down from the mountains and eventually crossbred with humans. Werewolfism may skip a generation, he noted, before leaving us with an unsettling thought: "One of the most common causes of accidents on the playground, in nursery schools, in primary schools, is kids biting each other. How many latent werewolves do we have out there among us?"

ANN MILLER MEETS A FIERCE INDIAN GHOST

Dancer Ann Miller, who, in such musicals as *On the Town* (1949) and *Kiss Me Kate* (1953), displayed one of Hollywood's brightest smiles and

two of its longest legs, is the great-granddaughter of a Cherokee medicine woman who was esteemed for her psychic abilities. But being
part Cherokee did not prevent Ann from being frightened by the
ghostly appearance of a scowling Indian brave.

She had just moved into a home that she had purchased as an investment in Sedona, Arizona. Her accountant, Joan Gibson, was in
the guest room and Ann was sleeping in the master bedroom. "I was
awakened sometime during the night by the image of a fierce Indian
brave standing glowering at me," she said. "I was frightened by his
appearance, and I thought at first that I might be having a terrible
dream. I shook my head and took a sip of water—but he was still
there. He was real, not a dream."

When the ghost at last disappeared, Ann found the courage to leave
her bedroom and walk into the front room to investigate. "There,
glaring at me through the front picture window, was a coyote—with
the same fierce look that the Indian brave had fixed on me! I felt that
I was not wanted in that house."

The next evening, she was having dinner with a Hopi medicine
teacher and his wife. The shaman explained that it was possible for
spirits to assume the form of coyotes or other animals. He told her that
the son of the pioneer Arizonan who had built her house had been
killed during its construction. The sorrowing father had asked a medicine priest and a tribal chief to bless the house and to help his son find
peace. A fetish had been placed in each corner of the house, and a
special blessing had been bestowed upon the kiva, a small house used
for religious ceremonies, that was situated behind the larger dwelling
place.

Somehow, it seemed that Ann Miller's presence in the home had
provoked the materialization of a guardian Indian spirit that had been
placed there long ago by the medicine priests and their blessing ceremonies.

Ann called a psychotherapist friend who also performed exorcisms.
"She did a complete and total cleansing of the house, and she worked
extra hard to clear the kiva. Now the house is at peace. No more ghosts
with fierce expressions wake me up in the middle of the night."

The author of a new book, *Tapping into the Force,* Ann collaborated
with another friend of ours, Dr. Maxine Asher. Although the dancer
had given evidence of psychic talents even as a little girl, she had never

been able to discuss her experiences with any of her famous costars. "It just wasn't time then. They would have thought that I was loony tunes."

As always, she has used her paranormal talents to help others, but never herself. "Great-grandmother predicted that one of her grandchildren would inherit her abilities. I guess that was me."

"MOMMIE DEAREST" MAY STILL BE A LEADING LADY— AMONG HOLLYWOOD'S GHOSTS

Few actresses have rivaled Joan Crawford for star glamour and staying power as one of Hollywood's top movie queens. Her stardom spanned an amazing five decades and included such films as *Our Dancing Daughters* (1928), *Rain* (1932), *Johnny Guitar* (1954), and her Academy Award–winning performance in *Mildred Pierce* (1945). Joan Crawford epitomized the essence of the Hollywood rags-to-riches story—a poor shopgirl who, in the 1920s, becomes the very embodiment of America's "flaming youth" and then transcends the role of "dancing daughter" to emerge the heroine of America's favorite melodramas.

In 1978, Christina Crawford, Joan's adopted daughter, wrote *Mommie Dearest* and shocked the United States with her heart-wrenching story of what it was *really* like growing up with one of Hollywood's most famous leading ladies. *Mommie Dearest* was on the *New York Times* best-seller list for forty-two weeks and was made into a 1981 film starring Faye Dunaway.

We had heard rumors of haunting manifestations in Joan Crawford's former home, and Christina seemed genuinely surprised that we knew about the stories. "Not many people know that the house I grew up in may be haunted . . . it is not in print anywhere."

When asked if there were manifestations or hauntings that she could remember as a child living there, Christina recounted the following:

> I have vivid memories of some things, but when you are severely abused, you tend to block out other things. I'm positive that there were manifestations occurring when I was little . . . I saw them! There were places in the house that were always so cold that nobody ever wanted to go in them.

As a child, I was always told that I had an active and vivid imagination; I was *always scared* by things, but people just told me that I just had an "active imagination." Years later, I thought, oh well, maybe that was good to have had an active imagination, and I became a writer because of that.

But as a child, I *saw things in the house!* There was, of course, no context or framework in which to put what I saw and felt. I had nobody to speak to about the occurrences . . .

Any time I would become extremely frightened and would get out of my bed to try and find somebody, I was always treated as though I were just being a "bad child" that didn't want to go to sleep. I always expressed my fear to my mother because it was she that I went to find to help me . . . because I would be very upset and I'd be crying.

I used to have terrible nightmares and that kind of thing, but a lot of it had to do with the fact that I *saw things* in the night; so the solution to that finally was just to leave the lights on everywhere. One of the things I saw seemed like an apparition of a child . . . or children, but as I said, I may have blotted out a lot.

Christina told us that she had not been back to the house since she was seventeen. "That was when I went to college [in 1956], at which point, Crawford still owned the house."

Christina recalled her last day there:

I remember the woman who had taken care of me and my two younger sisters since I was four years old just watching me, without saying a word. I was going from room to room in the house, without saying anything, just standing in the middle of each room, then going on to the next one. She finally asked me what I was doing. I told her that I would never see this house again, therefore, I was saying goodbye to it.

Many years after I had left, we met again. She was now an elderly woman and had retired. We always had been quite close. She told me she had always remembered the look on my face when I said my goodbyes to the house. It seemed a strange thing to do, to say, 'I'll never see this house again,' when at that time there was absolutely no inkling of the house being sold. In fact, it was not sold for another two and a half to three years, and, indeed, I never have been back.

Christina had learned recently that the current owners of the house had called in the Reverend Rosalyn Bruyere of the Healing Light Center to work with the house:

Rosalyn described what she had seen in the house when she went there. She picked up on some things that astounded me because they seemed to validate what I may have seen and experienced when I was little. It gave me goose bumps when Rosalyn told me that she discovered so many spirits in the house and there had been signs of ritual abuse in one of the rooms. Many of the spirits had "underworld" connections.

I was sent to boarding school when I was ten years old. I came home infrequently after that. I always believed that I was sent away partly because I was too much the eyes and ears of the world—a witness. I saw too much, I guess. Some of the things that I saw that were going on were very violent. Her [Joan Crawford's] relationship with men, a number of men, was extremely violent. I was getting too old, and I was beginning to understand what was going on. That house is so weird! Now, evidently, the walls are starting to catch fire! Other people have heard children's cries in the walls! Every single owner has had trouble. The *first one* was Crawford. She built the majority of the house. It was a small cottage when she bought it, but most of the house, she built. She sold it to Donald O'Connor, who sold it to the Anthony Newleys. They sold it, I think, to the current owner, who is a friend of the Reverend Rosalyn Bruyere, and they asked her to "work" on the house.

Every single family that has lived in that house has had horrible things happen . . . illnesses, alcoholism, addictions, relationship problems, and now, evidently with the current owner, *the walls are breaking out in flames!* I've heard that in particular it's the wall that was behind Crawford's bed.

Although the scene is in her book, *Mommie Dearest,* Christina reminded us that the last words that Joan Crawford uttered were to a woman who was kneeling at the foot of her bed, praying for her. "As she was dying," Christina said, "Crawford opened her eyes and said directly to the woman, 'Don't you *dare* ask God to help me!' . . . and then she died."

It was such arrogance, Christina said, that she believes is a major part of the difficulty with the seemingly accursed house.

> And that has nothing to do with me! So it would not surprise me in the least if the "haunting" spirit that is in the house is Crawford! She was capable of real evil. If you have never experienced that "look" from another human being, it is almost *impossible* to believe that such an experience could even exist! I think perhaps that's why so many people are unwilling to deal with the shadow side because they can't really get themselves to believe that such a dimension exists.
>
> My brother and I were absolutely terrified of her. In fact, there is a passage in *Mommie Dearest* that describes "the look" on her face when she tried to kill me when I was thirteen. We all saw "that look." My brother and I talked about it extensively . . . it was not of an ordinary human being!

Later, we were able to contact the Reverend Rosalyn Bruyere of the Healing Light Center, who kindly agreed to share her thoughts on the manifestations in Joan Crawford's former home. "It is true that the house was afflicted with spontaneous fires, primarily in the wall behind where Joan Crawford's bed used to be. However, I did not pick up that Joan Crawford's ghost was there."

The Reverend Bruyere expressed her opinion that the house had been poisoned in some way before Crawford had moved into the place but that the evil in the house had added to Joan's neuroses. The actress had apparently built onto a preexisting cottage in a very chaotic manner. "Nothing is where it should be," Rosalyn commented. "She added dining rooms and hallways that led to other dining rooms. It all combines to form an H-shaped house. Turn a corner and you're lost."

The noted healer, who in this case served as an exorcist to clear the home, said that she found the haunting existing in levels. "It was a place of conspicuous negativity. I called it an 'Astral Central,' a gathering of spirits that were attracted to the negative vibrations. People had been tied up and tortured in that house. I picked up on gangland figures, corrupt politicians. There is an area in the house where a child [not Christina] had been tortured and molested. Terrible things went on in that house.''

The Reverend felt that ghosts themselves were trying to burn the house down. ''Once the Beverly Hills Fire Department spent four days there attempting to solve the mystery of the spontaneous fires that would break out on the walls. I feel the spirits were trying to burn the house down to protect some horrible secret. There is something hidden there. I am certain that there are bodies buried in that basement.''

She said that there had only been one recurrence in the house after she had exorcised and cleared it. ''The house had become an astral dumping ground, but it seems clean now.''

DEALING NATURALLY WITH THE SUPERNATURAL

John William Galt has appeared in hundreds of industrial films and television commercials, a dozen or more dinner theater and stock productions, and thirty motion pictures. He especially likes roles in films that deal with the supernatural or the unknown, and the fifty-year-old actor has a magnificent background for such characterizations. Indeed, he has interacted with the paranormal all of his life.

''My grandmother was a great teller of ghost stories,'' John recalled. ''She used to tell us about 'pookas' and other entities. It has been exciting sharing supernatural experiences with other actors. I did seventy-six weeks on the road with Mickey Rooney in *Three Goats and a Blanket*. Mickey is a fabulous gentleman who has had a lot of paranormal experiences.''

Galt spotted his first UFO when he was a youngster. His mother worked on the James Conley Air Force Base; his father was in the army: ''My brother Neil was with me when I saw the UFO. I had a pair of World War II German binoculars that went up to 30-power, and the object showed up very clearly, like a little moon wearing a snow cap. After hovering for a few minutes, it just zipped away at an enormous rate of speed.''

John tells of the time when he was a bachelor father living with his sons in an apartment on Laurel Canyon Boulevard. He had just taken his son Joey to audition for a television commercial, and while he waited in the car, his younger son, Eddie, was sleeping in the backseat. "Suddenly, Eddie wakes up and says that he has had a 'really dream.' He's upset about a car crash—which he describes in detail—and says that I am a hero. I'm glad I am a hero in his dream, so I calm him and tell him that when Joey is finished, I'll treat everyone at Great American Hamburger in Santa Monica."

On the way there, John said, they witnessed a violent accident: "A car runs a red light, strikes another. A man, bleeding profusely from a head wound, is trapped in his car. I run over to the smashed car, pop open the door, and pull the man free. That's when I realize that the accident has fulfilled all the details of Eddie's 'really dream,' and the kid is yelling at me from our car, 'See, Dad! You're a hero, just like in my 'really dream.' "

Eddie had another 'really dream' some months later. "He woke up from a nap, yelling that Joey is in the middle of the street and got hit by a car. I told him to stop crying. Joey is sitting right here, watching television with me and his friend Ralph." The next day, Ralph pounded on their apartment door and brought John running out to the street. "This time it really happened, Mr. Galt!" Ralph was sobbing. "A car just hit Joey."

Eddie had once again dreamed "real."

"This story has another kicker," John said. "While Joey was lying there in the street, he said that his grandfather, Benjamin Franklin Pace, walked up to him and told him, 'Lie still, son. You must lie still.' Grandpa Pace had always thought that Joey was the cutest baby ever, and he loved him very much, but Grandpa Pace had died when Joey was just a few years old."

It was good that the spirit form had cautioned the boy to lie still. "He had a shattered femur," John said, "and he spent the next two and a half months in the hospital."

When the Galt family moved to Texas and John married his present wife, Dian, they took occupancy of a home in which Eddie talked to an old man in a chair. "We took that in stride," John recalled, "but then he began to speak of this woman who would come into his bedroom every night. He was becoming pretty agitated, so I thought I would investigate the next night at the time when Eddie said the ghost would enter the room. I opened the door just in time to witness the circuit breaker, which was in the room, burst into flames. If I had not been there at that moment, Eddie could have been terribly burned—or worse—along with the entire house. It is very possible that the ghost set the whole thing up so that I would be on hand to prevent a tragedy occurring in our family.''

John relates these accounts in a very straightforward manner. In addition to working diligently at the craft of acting, he also strives toward achieving his second-degree black belt in t'ai chi ch'uan kung fu. Dian and the four children also follow the discipline imposed by a serious study of martial arts. And Eddie with his ''really dreams''? He, too, works to balance mind and body. The night we visited with John William Galt about his family's mystical experiences, Eddie was leaving home to become one of the youngest professional martial arts instructors in the Southwest.

THE HAUNTED HOUSE WAS TOO MUCH FOR SUSANNAH YORK

She may have played *Superman*'s mother in the 1978 motion picture starring Christopher Reeve and Marlon Brando, but Susannah York has decided that she will leave the heroics to her cinematic characterizations. In real life, the supernatural can be a bit too much to handle.

Reared in a remote Scottish village as a child, the blond, blue-eyed leading lady of such outstanding films as *Freud* (1962), *Sands of the Kalahari* (1965), and *They Shoot Horses, Don't They?* (1969) had long had her heart set on a beautiful country manor. Why, it even had its own drawbridge over a moat. If she chose, she could live as her character Sophia Western did in *Tom Jones* (1963), the bawdy classic of life in eighteenth-century England.

What is more, she was told, the manor even had its own ghost, and a lady ghost, at that.

Susannah would be the first to admit that she has just a bit of an eccentric streak, the kind that the British seem to prize. She would actually not mind at all if she shared a lovely country estate with a friendly spirit or two. The trouble was, the ghost in the manor is not a particularly pleasant one. By all accounts, it is the spirit of a woman who had committed suicide by throwing herself from an upstairs window.

When the lady ghost manifests, she does so in a very sinister manner.

Susannah had come to spend a night in the manor with the full intention of making an offer on the place first thing in the morning. She had no sooner settled in for the evening when she was suddenly struck by the feeling that she could not move. It was as if she found herself walled in by some invisible barrier. The actress actually fainted from fright.

The next morning, she stated that her entire being seemed suffused by "a terrible feeling of gloom" and the sensation of "being trapped." Susannah felt cold and began to tremble.

As soon as she was able to free herself from the awful spell, she picked up her bags and fled. She was so terrified by the experience that she abandoned all plans to purchase the country manor. As far as Susannah York is concerned, the nasty lady ghost can keep it all to herself.

7 · CLOSE ENCOUNTERS OF THE HOLLYWOOD KIND

Some may question the inclusion of a chapter on UFOs in a book about supernatural experiences. Many of the reports of alleged alien encounters sound so very much like accounts of individual mystical experiences that we often find it difficult to determine where an authentic UFO report ends and a narrative of a supernatural encounter begins.

Quite frankly, we consider UFO research to be among the most important work being conducted today, for as we view the mystery, it touches all aspects of human endeavor on the planet and carries with it implications that strongly suggest that we are living in the most important time in history.

It was the late Dr. J. Allen Hynek, the astronomer who for more than twenty years served as a consultant to the U.S. Air Force on the Project Blue Book study of UFOs, who coined the term "close encounters of the third kind" to classify an interaction between a citizen of earth and a humanoid occupant of a UFO. His other categories include "encounters of the first kind," a sighting of a UFO from a close distance, and "encounters of the second kind," when some kind of physical evidence is left behind by the UFO.

Sherry Hansen-Steiger, the coauthor of this book, had the privilege of serving as Dr. Hynek's publicist and manager until the time of his death in 1986; she learned that the Center for UFO Studies had more than eighty thousand reports of such sightings and encounters on file from more than one hundred and forty countries. Dr. Hynek estimated that there are about one hundred UFO sightings worldwide every day. Indeed, some of these reports may turn out to be weather balloons, conventional aircraft, or many other known objects, but at least ten percent remain truly "unidentified."

He admitted that he had assumed the entire matter was foolishness when he first began his work with the Air Force on Project Blue Book. "Now after nearly forty years of research, I can say that the study of UFOs is certainly not nonsense," he told Sherry. Dr. Hynek was impressed that a large number of UFO reports are made by highly responsible people from all walks of life, including military and civilian pilots, engineers, technicians, scientists, doctors, teachers, astronomers, ministers, law enforcement officers, and even space program personnel. He also emphasized that for every UFO reported, at least a dozen remained unreported for fear of ridicule.

The astronomer-researcher once made the observation that one could view the UFO phenomenon as a kind of conditioning process for the human race, ". . . a forced nudging, a pushing us to a deeper awareness of the universe."

Producer-director Steven Spielberg and Dr. Hynek corresponded frequently, and the motion picture *Close Encounters of the Third Kind* (1977) contained events based on actual UFO reports that had been filed with his nonprofit Center for UFO Studies in Evanston, Illinois. The astronomer became a technical director on the film and made a brief cameo appearance in its climax, the dramatic encounter scene atop Devil's Tower.

Before his passing, Dr. Hynek made the following pertinent statement: "The existing evidence may indicate a possible connection between the UFO and extraterrestrial life, the probable existence of which is generally accepted. If such life does exist, if there is any possibility of establishing communication with it, our scientific knowledge of that life might even be critical to our own survival."

There are several theories as to the UFOnauts' actual place of origin and their true identity. Generally, such arguments are distilled to the central issue of whether the UFO intelligences are essentially nonphysical entities from another dimension or physical beings who have the ability to attain a state of invisibility and, on occasion, to materialize and dematerialize both their bodies and their craft.

Perhaps both theories are correct. We may be visited by extraterrestrial *and* multidimensional intelligences in our spiritual, intellectual, biological, and evolutionary progress on planet earth. On the other hand, we earthlings may have been discovered by an unknown intelligence that has a physical structure totally unlike ours and that has the ability to present itself in a variety of guises in order to accomplish a goal of communication with our species.

UFO contactees—men and women who feel that they have been contacted by outer space beings—abound in the Los Angeles and Hollywood area. Robert Short of Joshua Tree speaks often of an impending New Age wherein humankind will attain a new consciousness, a new awareness, and a higher state—or frequency—of vibration. Short channels an extraterrestrial guide named ''Korton,'' who, along with other communicating outer space entities, regards each physical body as being in a state of vibration and says that all things vibrate at their individual frequencies.

The UFO intelligences may come from the Pleiades or Alpha Centuri or any number of extraterrestrial sources, the contactees agree, and yet the Space Brothers also exist in higher dimensions all around us that function on different vibratory levels, just as there are various radio frequencies operating simultaneously in our environment. The contactees believe that we can attune ourselves to those higher dimensions in much the same manner as a radio receiver tunes into the frequencies of broadcasting stations. Different entities travel on various frequencies according to their vibratory rate.

Dr. Fred Bell of Laguna Beach says that he is in contact with a starwoman named ''Semjase,'' a UFOnaut that he and others describe as a beautiful, goddesslike blonde. Semjase, a Pleiadean, has told Bell that divine intervention occurred on earth in 1980 as a messianic energy began to stimulate more people to the presence of their brothers and sisters from the Pleiades. After the year 2001, lost souls from the astral plane will slowly begin to reincarnate on earth as super souls, entities with advanced physical powers.

Many contactees are convinced that our planet shall experience a global UFO encounter in 1999; they say that personalities in the media have been the knowing or unknowing recipients of an active extraterrestrial campaign of positive programming to ensure a hospitable reception for such a visitation. Although most of them request anonymity at the present time, we have spoken with many actors, producers, writers, and directors who confide that they believe themselves to have been guided in their work by UFO intelligences.

It is interesting to note that the bug-eyed monsters that came to brainwash us in *Invaders from Mars* (1953), to replace us in *Invasion of the Body Snatchers* (1956), or to destroy us in *War of the Worlds* (1953) gave way for a time to the cute and cuddly aliens of "E. T.," "Alf," and MAC of *MAC and Me* (1988).

In *The Day the Earth Stood Still* (1951) Michael Rennie's somber alien messenger became the prototype for the Space Brothers appearing to warn humankind to clean up its act and to end its wicked, wasteful ways. Contrary to many viewers' memory of the film, the dignified alien came only to warn us, not to save us. He is firm in stating that we may exercise free will and choose to destroy ourselves—it is just that the Outer Space Council does not wish to catch any of our fallout should we decide to blow our planet to radioactive atoms.

Stanley Kubrick's and Arthur C. Clarke's *2001: A Space Odyssey* (1968) told us of an ancient alien artifact that had stimulated the brain of prehuman ape creatures so that the evolution of our intelligence might be accelerated in order to propel humankind back to its place of origin. A seemingly traitorous computer named HAL warned us of relying too heavily upon our technology when our own brains are always there to serve us.

Gene Roddenberry's television series "Star Trek" emphasized a partnership between humankind and aliens—embodied by the friendship of Captain Kirk and Mr. Spock—that is sustained by mutual respect. Roddenberry's scripts indicated that it is such unions that will truly permit humankind to go boldly to new frontiers beyond the stars.

The mythic Star Wars Trilogy—*Star Wars* (1977), *The Empire Strikes Back* (1980), and *Return of the Jedi* (1983)—focuses upon conflicts between intergalactic cultures that occurred aeons before our world had come into being. At the same time that we are witnessing a transplantation of human emotions and dreams, Yoda, a pointy-eared reptilian humanoid, is teaching Luke Skywalker and us about the existence of a force that interpenetrates all of matter and that may be controlled by the psyche of a disciplined practitioner, a Jedi.

Close Encounters of the Third Kind (1977) was Steven Spielberg's brilliant cinematic way of making sense of what would appear to be random UFO sightings and contacts. Spielberg's greatest gift to theater audiences lay in his permitting us to have a spiritual experience when the dazzling mother ship touched down on Devil's Tower. The combination of the haunting theme, the appearance of the humanoids, and the beautiful light show bombarded our psyches with archetypal shocks of recognition.

In the summer of 1982, in *E. T.—The Extra-Terrestrial*, Spielberg introduced us to an entity that is at first frightening and fearful to the boy Elliot and to ourselves; then as we, together with Elliot, come to know "E. T.," he is transmogrified from the grotesque into a cute little member of our collective cosmic family. We are humbled when we learn that he literally lives on the love vibration and that he is a member of an extraterrestrial species that has been monitoring our flora, our fauna, our soils, and ourselves for what may have been aeons.

Starman (1984) picked up on the paranoid possibility that aliens could replace us and look just like our husbands and wives but made the whole situation less frightening when the DNA-borrowing alien, played by the talented Jeff Bridges, assumed the human form of Karen Allen's deceased husband and conducted itself in a gentle, nonthreatening manner. As in *E. T.*, the government scientists pursuing the alien were made to become the villains.

Superb acting and excellent production values transformed *Cocoon* (1985) into a marvelous crossover film. Although the senior citizens discovered a fountain of youth that really worked, the aliens were only indirectly responsible for their rejuvenation. It is made clear in the film that it is mature attitudes and actions that will win cooperation with alien life forms—and win an invitation to visit their paradisiacal planet. The aliens themselves are shown as brightly glowing light beings that must artificially assume human form.

Alien Nation (1988) takes us to the near-future when *it*—contact with an alien world—really happens. They look mostly like us, and they have good guys and bad guys, honest people and sleazy crooks, blue-collar workers and white-collar executives just like we do. They don't seem any wiser, but they are a bit stronger physically and have certain advances in their technology. Salt water affects them as if it were hydrochloric acid, and they get high on sour milk. All in all, they seem to be as varied and individual as we do. They certainly are not angels, but neither are they demons.

Currently, both on the cinema and television screens, behind the cameras and off the sets, Hollywood is coming nearly full circle to "war of the worlds" scenarios with frightening talk of alien abductions of our citizenry and fervent accusations of political conspiracies that have kept the truth about UFOs from the general public.

Whitley Strieber's *Communion,* first a best-selling book and then a late-1989 theatrical release starring Christopher Walken, together with the research of Budd Hopkins as expressed in his book *The Intruders,* has once again brought up the issue of aliens that may not always have our best interests at heart—aliens that, in fact, may hurt us, haunt us, and cut us apart for terrible experiments. The unpleasant possibility of nasty aliens out there with the benevolent ones and the cute ones becomes even more complex when accounts of kidnapped earthlings serving as unwilling participants in programs of interspecies cross-breeding are discussed at group meetings in the Los Angeles area.

A Beverly Hills medical doctor has stated that many of his celebrity clients claim to have been abducted by aliens from other worlds or dimensions. A team of investigators informed us that a number of actors, directors, and producers have said that they were teleported from their homes directly into alien spaceships. There is a psychological axiom that maintains that whatever the conscious mind represses, the unconscious embodies in allegorical form, either in dreams or in conscious creative imagery. Demons, for example, often serve as personifications of undesirable emotions, such as jealousy and hatred. The Pleiadean space beings, with their inspirational messages of universal oneness, could be the angelic externalization of religious feelings that have been progressively denied expression in an increasingly secular world. The UFO abductors that provoke fear and pain are most frequently described as grayish-skinned reptilian or insectlike entities with large eyes, not at all far afield from traditional descriptions of demons.

The fact that the space beings' contacts, as well as the Grays' abductions, seem to be accelerating both in the Los Angeles area and throughout the world at large could constitute a serious expression of contemporary humankind's need to fashion a new religious structure that will satisfy the basic spiritual requirements of the psyche while, at the same time, presenting a modern adaptation to space-age society.

Father Andrew Greeley, the Roman Catholic priest who is also a novelist and a respected sociologist, has observed that humans maintain a "hunger for the marvelous." According to Father Greeley, "If you give up angels and devils—which I think is an awful mistake—

some people are going to turn to aliens. Life seems to be full and unexciting, especially if you're just a yuppie, so you have to hunt for something marvelous enough to bring back the excitement.''

There is always plenty of excitement on the UFO scene as one deals with rumors of alien bodies recovered from crashed spacecraft, secret alien bases beneath our oceans, and government agencies that interact with aliens directly and keep our various presidents and prime ministers informed. With charges of a top-secret government agency known as ''Majestic-12'' being dismissed by some as paranoia and championed by others as fact, one wonders if our first Hollywood President, Ronald Reagan, knows even more about UFOs than he does about astrology.

In June 1982, Steven Spielberg screened his soon-to-be-released film *E. T.—The Extra-Terrestrial* to President Reagan at the White House. After the movie had ended and the lights had been restored, Reagan confided to Spielberg, ''You know, there aren't six people in this room who know just how true that really is.''

Before Reagan could elaborate, we are told, their conversation was interrupted by well-wishers at the screening. Three years later, in December 1985, while addressing Fallston, Maryland, high school students, Reagan mentioned the subject of space beings once again. Recalling his recent conversation with Soviet leader Mikhail Gorbachev, the President said: ''I couldn't help but say to [Gorbachev] how easy his task and mine might be . . . if suddenly there was a threat to this world from some other species from another planet outside in the universe. We'd forget all the little local differences . . . and find out once and for all that we really are all human beings here on this earth.''

Again in September 1987, in a speech before the entire United Nations General Assembly, Reagan remarked: ''In our obsession with antagonisms of the moment, we often forget how much unites all the members of humanity. Perhaps we need some outside, universal threat to make us recognize this common bond. I occasionally think how quickly our differences worldwide would vanish if we were facing an alien threat from outside this world. And yet I ask you, is not an alien threat already among us? What could be more alien to the universal aspirations of our peoples than war and the threat of war?''

Perhaps one day we shall learn that President Reagan's unusual references to alien threats were the result of confidential information received during briefing sessions with top-secret agencies responsible for the investigation of visitations to this planet by alien starships.

HOLLYWOOD STARS AND PERSONAL UFO SIGHTINGS

The distinguished actor James Earl Jones, who provided the deep, resonant voice for the ultimate villain Darth Vader in the Star Wars Trilogy, expressed his disagreement when that film series and *Close Encounters of the Third Kind* (both 1977) were given credit for evoking a new wave of interest in science fiction and UFOs.

"I also did a television project called *The UFO Incident* [1975] with Estelle Parsons that came before *Star Wars* and *Close Encounters,*" Jones told Douglas Bakshian of *Fantastic Films* in August 1981. "It was about a documented UFO incident in New Hampshire that involved a real-life couple, Betty and Barney Hill [whose UFO abduction experience occurred in 1961, long before either of the motion pictures in question]. I find that all very, very fascinating."

No one can deny that impressionable, creative people may be influenced by motion pictures that achieve mythic status in our popular culture. As serious UFOlogists, we know that in the late 1960s, the popularity of "Star Trek," the television series, influenced to some degree the susceptibility of certain UFO sighters who wished to see alien craft in our skies. *Close Encounters of the Third Kind* had a powerful impact on the psyches of UFO believers and nonbelievers alike, as, to a lesser degree, did *Star Wars,* released the same year. It must always be firmly noted, however, that the citizenry at large, as well as the Hollywood stars, were sighting UFOs long before such films were a part of the collective unconscious.

"All Things Are Possible with God"

Eddie Bracken has been in show business since he was three. He first gained fame as the "poor little rich boy" in the original, silent screen *Our Gang* comedies. Most recently, the star of such films as *The Miracle of Morgan's Creek* and *Hail the Conquering Hero* (both 1944) was seen as

Wally of Wally's World in the popular 1983 Chevy Chase comedy *National Lampoon's Vacation.*

Bracken stated that he had a UFO sighting in 1965 while he was playing golf on Long Island with a group of seven other people. "It was in the middle of the afternoon, and suddenly someone pointed to a huge object hovering high in the sky. I saw planes passing beneath it, so I realized the object had to be at a tremendous altitude. It certainly wasn't anything that we or anyone else had built—it was much too big. It was hovering absolutely still—and then all of a sudden it just shot off and was gone. UFO experts tell me that what I saw was probably a 'mother ship.' All things are possible with God. If the Creator was able to place life on earth, he could assuredly have placed it elsewhere in the universe."

"A Huge Object Shaped Like a Toy Top"

Singer-actress Lillian Roth was a child celebrity when she was five and the toast of Broadway and Hollywood before she was twenty. The star of such films as *The Vagabond King* and *Animal Crackers* (both 1930) fought back from the despair of alcoholism and a tragic personal life to write a triumphant autobiography that was transformed into the motion picture *I'll Cry Tomorrow* (1955), starring Susan Hayward.

Her first UFO sighting occurred in April 1951, when she and her husband Burt were spending the night at an out-of-the-way motel in the Arizona desert.

"I was out walking my dogs when I caught a glimpse of a huge object shaped like a toy top. It was perhaps one hundred and fifty feet in diameter. It hovered in one position at what would be the height of a fifteen-story building. It had a metallic body. All around the hull were small portholes, which were lit up with different colored lights."

After hovering for about fifteen minutes, the object shot upward at a fantastic speed. "But as quickly as it had risen," Lillian said, "it returned, remaining stationary for another two minutes. Then it began moving away at a gradual upward angle, toward the east. Soon it was out of sight."

Lillian Roth had another sighting in Florida in March 1952 when she and her husband were heading from Fort Lauderdale toward Palm Beach: "We were in an open stretch of road with an unobstructed view in all directions. Without warning, as if from nowhere, a huge, cigar-shaped craft appeared. We sat there at the side of the road watching it for two or three minutes when the gigantic ship suddenly faded away into nothingness.''

"A Long Cylinderlike Object Passed in Front of Our Car"

DeForest Kelley, who played Bones McCoy on ''Star Trek,'' reported a UFO sighting that occurred several years before he could have imagined that he would become an icon to Trekkies around the globe.

''In 1950, long before the series began, my wife and I and a friend—a very solid kind of man—were driving in Louisiana. It was around six in the evening, a summer night in July. We were going through the swamp country when a long cylinderlike object passed in front of our car. It was probably four or five hundred yards away from us and five or six hundred feet above the ground. It had a red light flashing, and there were what appeared to be blue and green flames floating off the side of it. When we got to Montgomery, Alabama, and stopped to get a bite to eat, the newspaper in front of the place said, 'Mysterious Object Sighted over Southland.'

''Today I read things about UFOs and say, 'That can't be.' Then I think back to what we saw. It still seems far out to me.''

Nothing on This Planet Could Maneuver in Such a Fashion

Academy Award–winner Cliff Robertson (for *Charly* 1968), lost his skepticism toward UFOs when he sighted a mysterious object in July 1963 while living in a house that overlooks the ocean in Pacifica Park, California.

''It was a clear day, not a cloud visible in the sky, around 3 P.M.,'' Robertson recalled. ''I was standing on an observation deck that overlooks the sea, watching the gulls fly by. Suddenly, my eyes were diverted toward an object high in the sky. It was traveling from south to north, sparkling like a diamond as it reflected the rays of the mid-afternoon sun.'' Completely baffled as to what he was viewing, Robertson picked up a pair of binoculars and focused on the object. ''By no means was I prepared for what I saw. I have been a pilot for years, and I have never encountered anything remotely like this. There, in front of me, was a weird, alien contraption, a cylindrical-shaped craft made of highly polished metal.''

The UFO hovered motionless for more than ten minutes before it finally shot straight up and disappeared from sight. ''It was definitely a UFO, like so many other people have seen around the world,'' Robertson said. ''I was awed by its sleek design, its trim appearance, and the fact that one minute it could hover on a dime and the next blast off into space at a fantastic speed. I don't know of anything on this planet that could maneuver in such a fashion.''

Gyrating Through the Heavens in an Erratic Course

Kaye Ballard, the talented actress-singer-comedienne who has appeared in *The Girl Most Likely* (1957) and *The Ritz* (1976), saw her UFO in Palm Springs, California.

It was in May 1970, around nine-thirty in the evening. She was sitting in a car with three other people at a drive-in movie. The sky was crystal clear when she just happened to glance up and catch sight of an object gyrating through the heavens.

''It followed an erratic course, zigzagging all over the place,'' she said. ''I knew it couldn't have been a falling star because it was going in all directions—stopping and reversing its course. Besides, it was several times more brilliant than the brightest star visible. Finally, without a sound, the UFO shot straight up and disappeared.''

The UFOs Outdistanced the Air Force Planes with Ease

Ed Asner, who achieved star status as the slow-burning Lou Grant on ''The Mary Tyler Moore Show,'' says that he became caught up in an extensive UFO scare that shook the top brass at Fort Monmouth, New Jersey, where he was stationed in 1952.

''Many of my buddies in the Signal Corps were seeing UFOs on a regular basis—almost every day,'' Asner said. ''In addition to visual observations, the unknowns were also being picked up on radar.'' He recalled one sunny day, just after noon, when a formation of flying saucers transformed the base into utter chaos. The men were kept busy for several days tracking the strange discs through binoculars and calculating their speeds, which Asner was informed were astronomical.

At the height of the UFO flap, Asner said that an emergency call was placed by a high-ranking officer at Fort Monmouth to a nearby Air Force base. A request was made that pursuit planes be sent to pursue the UFOs. "Our planes were never ever to get very close," Asner said. "The UFOs outdistanced them with ease."

It was at that point that the enlisted personnel at the base were told to keep quiet. According to Asner: "One day at class, we were all formally told that if we saw a UFO yesterday and if we told anyone that we saw such an object, we would now tell that person that we had not seen a UFO. The implication of such a statement was perfectly clear. I guess they didn't want us to know too much. After all, we were just a bunch of Army slobs—privates. It wasn't our business."

"It Was There—As Big As Life!"

It was around 1950, when he was about twenty-two years old and returning from a squirrel hunt, that rugged actor Clint Walker, star of television's "Cheyenne" and such movies as *The Dirty Dozen* (1967) and *Sam Whiskey* (1969), had an unexpected encounter that proved to be much more exciting than the pursuit of fuzzy-tailed treehoppers.

Clint was driving on the old river road that led north to a quiet, secluded area near Alton, Illinois. It had been a beautiful fall day and it was now about an hour and a half before sundown. There was absolutely no wind, no clouds in sight, just a serene, crisp day. The Mississippi River was on the right side of the road, and limestone bluffs, some of which towered two hundred feet, were on the left. Suddenly, the actor noticed something coming in over the river toward him. He became so entranced with the object that he almost drove over the side of the road, right into the river! Pulling over to the shoulder, Walker got out of the car and to his amazement saw the object come in and hover right in front of him.

The size of this object seemed to be twenty-five to thirty-five feet long and six to eight feet wide. As it came toward him, Clint estimated it to be traveling at about thirty-five to forty miles per hour. At that particular time in his life, he was employed as a steeplejack, currently painting a one-hundred-and-five-foot water tower, so he considered himself to be a good judge of height and distance. The object appeared as if it were two saucers, one on top of the other. It seemed to be made of a highly polished aluminum or stainless steel. Walker was intrigued by the fact that he could see no windows, no portholes, no exhaust—and it made absolutely no sound.

"Yet it was there—as big as life!" Clint said. His first thought was that it was going to crash into the limestone bluffs, but it stopped about seventy-five feet in the air, approximately one hundred and fifty feet or less in front of him.

Walker was extremely curious, for he had been interested in such things. The craft seemed to hover silently for ten to twelve seconds before it tilted at a four- to five-degree angle and seemed to slip backward about twenty-five to thirty feet, then it shot forward.

Clint was able to watch it for about fifty to sixty feet, and then . . . it was gone!

Like so many, he did not tell anyone at the time about what he had seen, figuring people would just think he was crazy. "I had not been drinking," Clint said. "I did not—and do not—use drugs. I saw what I saw. I don't know what it was or where it came from, but I know one thing for certain, it was definitely there!"

GENE RODDENBERRY, STAR TREKKING INTO THE UNIVERSE

The genius of Gene Roddenberry, the producer-creator of "Star Trek," has influenced millions of people all over the world and acquainted them with areas of the mind that permit them to go where they have never been before.

We are by now quite familiar with the thoughts and the philosophical positions of Captain James T. Kirk, Mr. Spock, Bones, Scotty, and the other familiar characters of the starship *Enterprise,* but what of the beliefs of their creator?

We asked Roddenberry his opinion of the space kids, the star people who appear to be manifesting all over the planet and demonstrating unusual psychic abilities, similar to those of famed Israeli sensitive Uri Geller and certain of the fictional characters depicted on "Star Trek."

"We wrote a couple of episodes about individuals who had such unique talents," he said. "As a matter of fact, our second pilot—and the one that sold the series—was on that subject. The character played by Gary Lockwood began to find out that he could, after having undergone a strange experience in space, accomplish things like moving a glass of water without touching it, and then he developed more and more power.

"We did the same thing in 'Charley X,' which is about a boy who had been raised on a strange planet. In both of those scripts, we drew a moral. We echoed a sort of warning that may have something to do with why such things appear slowly. In both of these stories, we had the people destroy themselves because they got too much power too fast. I think it would certainly be a dangerous situation if a child or an adult had this kind of power without having the kind of philosophical background and morality to balance the power as it becomes greater and greater. I think power does corrupt, and I think that even the innocence of a child is no protection against that.''

Roddenberry pointed out that there were a couple of instances in the episode where the Lockwood character started out using his abilities positively, but "he just became too powerful too fast. I was not being critical of such abilities. I was making a critical statement about the misuse of such abilities. I feel that such powers are neither negative or positive. I believe that they are just powers—just as some men use dynamite to build tunnels and other men use it to make war. I've seen very few instances of what could be called psychic phenomena, though I've admittedly seen a few things that could be called such occurrences.''

Had he ever seen a UFO? Roddenberry answered:

No, I have not, but at the same time, you can hardly work seriously in science fiction—or you can hardly be an educated person—and say that such things are impossible. I think to say that we are the only creatures in this galaxy is akin to sitting in fourteenth-century Florence and saying that the entire universe revolves around us. I think it would be the most mathematically incredible happening you could conceive that this is the only place in this great universe where these happenings that we call life occurred. Therefore, I think that it is likely that there are extraterrestrial civilizations ahead of us and behind us.

I think that any advanced life would be looking at us and saying, "Won't they be something when they grow up?" For that reason, I believe that if they do confer any powers or give us any help, they'll not do it in such a way that would deprive us of our free will.

There is a remarkable parallel in the growth of a race and the growth of a person. If you deprive a child of its free will, you're going to create an incompetent adult. I think these "others" would have to give us our free will with a little gentle shoving one way or the other. I think that anything that "they" might give us will be very much on the order of gentle prodding. I think that these powers, these abilities, may be appearing in exceptional people now; but I think it's likely that in the future these abilities will appear in all kinds of people.

Dr. Andrija Puharich has pointed out that there seems to be evidence in a wide variety of ancient texts that there have been visitations from other planetary civilizations occurring on earth. "Whoever these 'others' are," Puharich theorized, "they lay down instructions for humanity, but not with a heavy hand, for teaching should be a gentle thing. If you look over five thousand years of history, it seems to me that the presence of the UFO intelligence has been seen but scarcely felt. I'd say the influence has been like a father who is seldom around—but whose presence is still there."

Roddenberry expressed both an openness and a caution toward the accounts of UFO contactees, those people who claim to have interacted with the occupants of spacecraft and to have communicated with alien beings:

I think it is also possible that the power of thought allows them to create a place, not an imaginary place but a place that is as real to them as reality. I know that when I am writing very well, and I create a different planet, a different society, during the time that I am writing, it's as real to me and as solid as this tabletop. I have smelled the smell of a campfire with an odor from no wood you'd ever have on earth. There has been quite a reality there. I sometimes wonder how much farther I would have to go until, indeed, it became real.

I don't know how many worlds are going on all at once. All of us may be living in a different world on which we just sort of correspond. We're reaching each other through those dimensions. I think an exciting way to look at things is to consider that the ultimate power, the ultimate particle, the ultimate meaning is thought itself.

OLIVIA NEWTON-JOHN'S CLOSE ENCOUNTER

"I tend to agree with the movie *Close Encounters:* We are not alone," said Olivia Newton-John, telling about her life-changing UFO encounter.

When she was sixteen years old in her native Australia, Olivia and a friend were driving to a car rally on a Sunday afternoon. Suddenly, Olivia sensed something physical. "It was a needles and pins feeling— a prickling—rather like static electricity. I had the eerie sensation that something was nearby."

When she looked around, nothing seemed to be in sight. It was a long, lonely stretch of road, and there wasn't another car on it. Then as she gazed at the clear blue sky, she saw a strange-shaped object. "I was speechless! A brilliant, silver object was hurtling toward us, small at first but increasing in size. It looked triangular, but as I stared, it changed shape and became a ball with a glowing halo of different colors. It was able to change direction very suddenly and stop and hover, like no plane I'd ever seen. Sometimes it seemed quite still, like a bright star, then it would veer rapidly across the sky again."

Olivia and her friend were hoping to have other witnesses drive by them on the road, but they remained alone, watching the mysterious object for quite some time. They were so taken by the experience that the next day they did some checking to see if there had been any air balloons or aerial flights of any kind in that area; they found there had been none.

Olivia finds the subject of UFOs fascinating and reads whatever she can about the subject of extraterrestrial possibilities. Could this early UFO encounter have inspired her much later to star in the movie *Xanadu* (1980)? Olivia appeared as the muse Terpsichore, a Greek goddess who came to earth dancing and singing and roller-skating her way through a musical fantasy. This was, after all, an opportunity to portray an otherworldly being.

ENCOUNTERING THE E. T. PEACE CORPS

Lisa Hart is an actress with varied experience. In addition to appearing in such films as *In the Dead of Night* and *Another Time, Another Place,* she has been a cover girl for cosmetics and has been featured in commercials for soft drinks and cars.

"It was on Thanksgiving Day in 1987 while hiking in Joshua Tree that a friend and I not only saw a UFO but I believe that we experienced 'missing time,' " Lisa said. They first saw the object as a bright light in the sky and assumed that it must be an early star. Then for twenty minutes, in split-second jumps, the UFO swung like a pendulum.

"My friend and I saw lights that rotated clockwise on the object," Lisa said. "In the illumination caused by the blinking lights, we could see that the UFO was disc-shaped." She became convinced that intelligent beings were within the object, and she felt in tune with them. A spiritual counselor had predicted that she should expect UFO contact, so she felt absolutely no fear, only a kind of excitement.

"I had just begun to understand that the emotional vibrations that I was receiving from the UFO were what unconditional love felt like when the object disappeared." The two friends expressed disappointment, having hoped that they might experience a close encounter of the third kind if the craft should land. They sat in silence for several minutes before they noticed that certain of the stars in the night sky had begun to move.

"Six stars moved in the shape of a pyramid," she recalled. "My friend said, 'Lisa, they're in the shape of the crystal that you have in your pocket.' " Lisa acknowledged that this was so then held the crystal in her left hand and extended it toward the formation of UFOs.

"The crystal began to glow green," she said. "We felt light beings all around us. I know that they were involving us in some high-energy work. I am certain that we received some kind of initiation, some kind of graduation at that time."

Lisa and her friend lost all track of linear time. "When we returned to full conscious awareness of our environment, we found that we were freezing cold—and that two hours had passed!" She cannot say for certain if they were taken on board the craft, but she does have a memory of beholding a bright light that turned into a room filled with light. She also remembers looking out of a large glass window, seeing a number of men and women moving about in what seemed to be a happy party atmosphere in the brightly lighted room.

Upon deeper reflection, she feels quite certain that the people she glimpsed there in that mysterious room will be men and women with whom she will become connected in her future.

"I've always felt that we here on earth are being visited by the extraterrestrial counterpart of our own Peace Corps," Lisa said. "I feel privileged that I got to meet the 'E. T. Peace Corps' at firsthand."

A UFO ENCOUNTER SEEMS TO BE SHAPING HER CAREER

Carol Spilman wonders if a UFO encounter twelve years ago has anything to do with all the spacey roles she keeps getting. "When I appeared on an episode of 'The Golden Girls,' it had to do with UFOs," she said. "When the cast and crew of 'General Hospital' had their Halloween party, I'm the one dressed up like an alien. And not long ago, when I did an industrial film, I was to portray 'The Space Woman of the Future.' "

Carol, who has been featured in "Days of Our Lives," "One Day at a Time," and "Three's Company," was not at all reluctant to discuss her UFO encounter—in fact, she felt "compelled to share the experience."

It happened back in Carol's home state of Iowa, right after she graduated from high school in Clear Lake. She and her boyfriend were driving to an outdoor party when Carol noticed a number of bright lights in the distance, and asked what town was in that direction. (Coincidentally, Clear Lake is also the site of the famous plane crash on February 3, 1959, that took the lives of Buddy Holly, Ritchie Valens, and the Big Bopper, who all perished on "the day the music died.")

Her boyfriend answered that there was no town where she was pointing—only fields and farms.

"Then it's a school," she recalls she stubbornly insisted. "It's a country school, and there must be a ball game under the lights."

Carol's companion once again replied in the negative. There was no country school in that direction.

"Suddenly," she remembers, "there was this huge craft that took off and soared right over our car. It looked like the mother ship in *Close Encounters of the Third Kind.* Both of us were stunned, scared. I kept thinking over and over, 'I do not wish to participate!' I didn't want any kind of connection with it—mental or otherwise. The light coming from it was very bright. I stared at my feet and wished it to go away. And then, 'zip,' it was gone. Just like that. It was nowhere in sight, and we continued on to our party."

When they arrived at the gathering, none of their friends had seen anything unusual in the night sky. Carol mentioned the experience to a few people, but no one made a great deal about it.

Over the years, however, she has noticed that her psychic abilities have steadily increased, and a consultation with the spirit entity "Dr. Peebles," as channeled by Thomas Jacobson, provided a very interesting comment for the actress to mull over.

"Dr. Peebles said that I had been taken on board a UFO when I was younger," Carol said. "He said that aliens examined me then adjusted me to become more psychic as I matured."

She can now only wonder if *that's* why she feels so connected to UFO and outer space themes, and she continues to be very curious about what lies ahead for her in the future.

ELVIS PRESLEY—STARMAN

A woman we shall call "Peggy" to protect her anonymity became a close friend and confidante of Elvis Presley from the time that they first met on the set of *Girls, Girls, Girls* in 1962 until his death on August 16, 1977. Peggy and Elvis grew so close that she was one of the last people to whom he spoke in his final twenty-four hours on planet earth.

Peggy always kept their relationship platonic. She was happily married with children, and she still adhered to most of the strict religious tenets of her Pentecostal upbringing. It was her ability to discus religion that had intensified their friendship. She confirmed Presley's interest in spiritual matters and his extensive library of metaphysical books, but because of her knowledge of our special interest in the UFO enigma, she wished us to be aware of the following conversation that she shared with Elvis during a private party in Los Angeles.

Earlier in the evening, he had presented Peggy with a big teddy bear to give to her daughter; he seemed cheerful, but his mood began to grow increasingly dour as the night passed. The party that he was hosting had grown dull, and his guests were reluctant to say much for fear of irritating the King.

Peggy went outside to avoid witnessing a nasty flare-up of Presley's temperament and to sit alone in the dark to look at the lights of Los Angeles below the Bel-Air hills. She was surprised when Elvis walked quietly up behind her, pulled a lawn chair next to hers, and laced his fingers through her own, as was his habit whenever they spoke seriously.

A shooting star flashed across the night sky, and the two made a wish. Elvis told her that it wasn't very often that he was fortunate enough to find a girl who would sit and look at the stars with him. Someone who was interested in the stars, not just *the* star.

Then Elvis stated that his true home was from the stars, from "out of this world." He said that he was from the "Blue Star Planet" and that it had several moons.

People on earth, he said, would soon know about other races on other planets outside of their galaxy. He said that earthlings would begin to live longer once they learned the techniques of longevity from the outer space beings.

The aliens, Elvis said, would combine mysticism and science to produce a powerful healing medicine. They would be able to cure the diseases that earth science currently believed to be incurable.

Presley amazed Peggy by pointing out various stars and naming them, as if he had a telescope and had made a serious study of astronomy.

When she asked him how he knew so much about the cosmos, he grinned and answered that he had read a few things but mostly it was because he was "from up there," and he pointed toward the stars.

Peggy laughed, assuming that he was joking, and asked why, if he were from "up there," he did not have pointed ears and blue skin. Elvis replied that the basic difference between earthlings and aliens existed in their spirits, not the appearance of their physical bodies.

Peggy remembered that there had been something in Presley's eyes that made her believe that he truly did accept the reality of star travel and that he actually considered himself one of the star people.

Another aspect of their unusual conversation that evening still intrigues her: Elvis had joked about having come from a base on the ninth moon of Jupiter.

Later, Peggy looked up information about Jupiter and learned that it only had eight moons. However, in 1978, a year after Presley's death, it was announced that a ninth moon had been discovered in orbit around Jupiter.

Elvis had been correct about the number of moons orbiting Jupiter. Was he also correct in stating that he was aware of being a star person?

HOLLYWOOD ALIENS WALK AMONG US

Elvis Presley's belief that his soul essence came to this planet from somewhere else is not that unique. An increasing number of men and women—in Hollywood and throughout the world—speak of an inner awareness of their ancestral links to other worlds. Others recall memories of encounters with UFO beings in their childhood, saying that they have a *knowing* that their physical—or spiritual—ancestors came to earth from another planet or from another dimension.

The brilliant futurist Buckminster Fuller had no problem accepting the possible extraterrestrial origin of humankind. As he expressed it: "We will probably learn that Darwin was wrong and that man came to earth from another planet."

Other keen scientific minds have suggested the theory that our entire species may have been seeded here and nurtured by extraterrestrials, who even today may continue an active—but largely secretive—role in our evolution. Nobel Prize winner Dr. Francis Crick, the codiscoverer of the DNA molecule, was so struck by the uniformity of the genetic code on earth that he later startled his peers by declaring that our planet had been seeded by intelligent life from a distant world.

Sir Fred Hoyle, the internationally esteemed British astronomer and mathematician, has directly challenged the Darwinian concept of terrestrial evolution and has stated that he believes new physical evidence points "clearly and decisively to a cosmic origin of life on Earth."

Past-life reader and reincarnationist Dr. Patricia Rochelle Diegel has attuned herself to the past-life experiences of many Hollywood figures whom she is convinced had prior existences on other worlds or other universes. According to Patricia, when she told Gloria Swanson that she had experienced a prior life on another world, the legendary actress, whose career spanned from *Romance of an American Duchess* (1915) to *Airport 1975,* replied that she had always known that to be true. "Gloria could recall seventeen of her past lives, many of them on other planets," Patricia said. "She had a brilliant mind, you know. She had more than one hundred and fifty patents taken out in her name. She was always inventing something. She created an early form of the walkie-talkie for use on the movie set."

Once as Patricia sat next to producer-director Steven Spielberg, she picked up that he had been given his first "Earth Assignment" in the France of the 1500s. "In that life, his extraterrestrial body appeared to be human," she said, "but he was unable to eat earth food. He subsisted on 'prana,' a pure energy vibration. His inability to assimilate Earth food was somewhat awkward for him, for he was known then as the Count St. Germain, and he was in and out of all the courts of Europe."

She feels that Spielberg is currently in his third incarnation on earth and that he directs on assignment from extraterrestrial mentors. She went on to state her conviction that many of the special effects people who work for Spielberg are men and women with extraterrestrial awareness.

"I also feel that there are about half a dozen people on Spielberg's staff or among his acquaintances who are actual aliens who have fashioned hairpieces and other elements of disguise to appear human," she said.

What about George Lucas, the creator of the Star Wars Trilogy? Is he, too, an E. T. among us? "No," the reincarnationist responded, "but many people around him are of extraterrestrial origin. Most of the E. T.s in Hollywood usually work behind the scenes."

Among those Dr. Diegel believes have extraterrestrial awareness who work in front of the cameras are Tom Hanks, Alan Alda, Perry King, Martin Sheen, and Dennis Weaver. "Actor-author Tom Tryon's E. T. soul essence has been here longer than many of the others," she said. "Donald Sutherland is a more recent arrival."

Once when she was having dinner with Khigh Deigh, the sinister villain in *The Manchurian Candidate* (1962) and on such television series as "Hawaii Five-O," Patricia not only sensed his extraterrestrial origin but saw him sitting at the feet of Jesus. Although she is aware of the artifice of film, it suddenly struck her with wonder that Deigh, who is a Taoist priest and an obviously evolved person, could enact such monsters on the screen.

His answer was simple and direct: "Only the pure of heart can play villains and not be touched by their evil."

Deigh went on to refer to Vincent Price and Boris Karloff as two other movie monsters who retained purity of heart to rise above their screen villany.

"Sir Laurence Olivier had spent several lifetimes on other planets in a position of leadership and authority," Patricia Rochelle Diegel said. "He chose his present existence because he thought it was going to be a 'play life.' He was amazed at how hard he had to work as an actor.

"Robin Williams was able to project his E. T. memories into the alien character he played on 'Mork and Mindy.' I've heard it said that two-thirds of his lines on that show were ad-lib. This is his third incarnation on earth."

Perhaps it may well be as philosopher Eric Hoffer once mused: "I always felt that man is a stranger to this planet, hence our preoccupation with heaven, with the sky, with the stars, the gods—somewhere out there in outer space. It is a kind of homing impulse. We are drawn to where we come from."

8 • THE GREAT SILVER SCREEN IN THE SKY

The idea that we survive physical death, that some part of our being is immortal, profoundly affects the lives of those of us who harbor such a belief. The orthodox religions promise a life eternal, whose reality must be taken on faith; but thousands of men and women base their concept of a life beyond the grave on what they consider the evidence of survival that manifests through mediums, or channels, in the contemporary term.

If you approach the mediums and channelers of Hollywood with an open mind, you will soon see that the stereotype of the turbaned crystal-ball reader with the cheap bag of tricks is far from an accurate assessment. Whatever you may think of their messages from the spirits, you will have to acknowledge the professionalism and the overall intelligence of such communicators as Kenny Kingston, Kevin Ryerson, Thomas Jacobson, Jach Pursel, Betty Bethards, J. Z. Knight, Damien Simpson, and Clarisa Bernhardt.

Some researchers maintain that the only difference between a psychic-sensitive and a trance medium is that the psychic attributes his or her talents to some manifestation of ESP ability (such as clairvoyance, precognition, or telepathy), whereas the medium credits his or her powers to the interaction of discarnate entities. Certain parapsychologists have noted that the intelligence exhibited by the spirits seems always on a level with that of the channel through whom they manifest. These investigators admit that the information relayed often rises far above the channel's known objective knowledge, but they point out that the limits of the subjective mind are not yet known.

Critics of channeling point out that the spirits can often be controlled by the power of suggestion and can be made to respond to questions that have no basis in reality. These critical investigators state that they have been able to establish communication with an imaginary person as readily as a real one. Mediocre mediums have found themselves the object of ridicule when they have relayed a message from a living person or a fictitious entity.

The more sympathetic researcher soon discovers that the best manner in which to secure a demonstration of genuine spiritistic phenomena is to assure the medium of one's goodwill. When you have the confidence of the medium, you have accomplished an indispensable prerequisite to the production of genuine phenomena or high-quality channeling.

The idea of a spirit guide dates back to antiquity, and serious researchers have been asking the same question for hundreds of years: Is this alleged entity, who claims to speak through the medium, really a spirit, or is it the voice of the medium's subconscious?

The highly regarded British spiritualist newspaper *Psychic News* stated that it was the spirit of actress Carole Lombard who guided Lucille Ball into taking a chance on television and accepting the offer to star in "I Love Lucy." When the glamorous comedienne, who had died in an airplane crash in 1942, appeared to Lucy in 1951, it was considered very risky to leave the large screen for the small one. Because Lucille Ball accepted the spirit's urging to "Take a chance, honey," she made television history.

Perhaps the guide is yet another facet of psi phenomena, which may lie latent in each of us and come into play when we are threatened with danger, when we are ill, or when we are in some way facing a personal crisis. A number of parapsychologists have suggested that the spirit guide may be another as yet little known power of the mind that enables the medium's subjective level of consciousness to dramatize another personality, complete with a full range of personal characteristics and its very own voice.

The mediums and channels whom we shall meet in this chapter would probably concede that the action of the subjective mind is not entirely eliminated during trance and the arrival of the guide, but they will assert that their subconscious is taken over by a discarnate entity. An aspect of mediumistic channeling on which both physical researchers and channels will agree is that there is an intelligence that directs and controls them. Another area of agreement is that this intelligence is a human intelligence, characterized by the limitations, imperfections, and psychological drives of Homo sapiens. The area of dispute remains in whether that human intelligence issues from the living or from the dead.

An interesting point is that spirit communication still requires both a soul and a body—the soul of an alleged discarnate personality and the physical body of the channel. There seems to be an obvious parallel between so-called hypnotic sleep and the trance state of the channel. In hypnosis, the subject is controlled by the suggestions of the hypnotist. In the trance state, many researchers feel, the channel is controlled by autosuggestion. Just as a good subject for hypnosis can be made to assume any number of characterizations and can be made to believe firmly that he is the individual that he has been told he represents, so might the medium, through autosuggestion in the trance state, assume the guise of the spirit communicator who has come to speak to the sitters in the circle.

The Los Angeles area has been the center of the revival of channeling, and in an effort to "share guidance and wisdom from the wise and loving teachers of the spirit plane," Molli and Glenn Nickell founded the magazine *Spirit Speaks*.

In a statement defining their publication, the Nickells recognize that channeling is an "ancient form of communication, newly revived. The teachings we publish come to us through channels, formerly called trance mediums. These individuals have gained the ability to step aside from their normal state of consciousness to allow wise and loving spirit teachers to speak through them."

Molli told us that she liked publishing a spiritual magazine "right in the middle of the stew pot" that is Los Angeles. "This is a city of chaotic energy," she said. "It is a city that offers multiple learning opportunities. That's why the film industry is here, to say, 'Why not?' Every kind of experience is here, and those who are drawn to Hollywood or to Los Angeles have come to participate in rapid learning experiences."

She received a master's degree in film from the University of Southern California and Glenn became a corporate president at an early age; they lived well as "happy, overachieving, agnostic yuppies during the sixties and seventies." It was when their daughter Penny urged them to read the channeled works of Jane Roberts and they were eventually led to meet the spirit entity "Dr. Peebles" that their universe restructured itself dramatically.

"Hollywood tells us, 'I know I can be anything I want,' " Molli said, explaining why the world's motion picture center is also a spiritual center. "Incredible opportunities to expand and to understand about life are focused here. I believe that your soul draws you to the places where you can attain the most physical and spiritual experiences necessary to your learning. Hollywood has no responsibility to us. We have created Hollywood. The mass consciousness creates things. Things do not create mass consciousness. Hollywood is our mirror. It helps us understand ourselves."

She sees all products of the motion picture industry to be significant and to have their rightful place in helping us become more aware of who we are. "Even the 'slasher' films have their place. Freddy's nightmares, Rambo's crusades, all offer the audience a catharsis. They help us to release our anger. No film can force anyone to do anything that is not appropriate to them. I think that actors are courageous to expose themselves to us, to live out their experiences on the screen in order to help us grow and evolve."

Hollywood's dharma—its soul-sustaining code of conduct—is to share its marvelous gifts of communication with the world.

KENNY KINGSTON'S "SWEET SPIRITS" OF HOLLYWOOD

"Hello, sweet spirit" is Kenny Kingston's cheery greeting—regardless of which side of the grave you may reside in. He has served as the personal psychic to a veritable "Who's Who of Hollywood."

He was Marilyn Monroe's psychic when she was Mrs. Joe Di-Maggio, and he stated that for years after her passing, she appeared both privately and at many of the séances that he conducted, relaying information from the spirit world. It was one day in 1979 as he was driving to give a lecture for the Southern California Society for Psychical Research in Pacific Palisades that he discovered part of a very feminine fingernail on the floor of his car.

"It had been painted a burnt orange," he recounted in his 1984 book, *Kenny Kingston's Guide to Health and Happiness,* as told to Valerie Porter. "This was very puzzling since I'd had the car thoroughly cleaned and vacuumed the day before, with no female passengers since then."

The fingernail was discovered near a street named Capri, and Marilyn Monroe came immediately to his mind in connection with the fingernail.

"We had driven past that street together when I'd escorted her to the beach, and Marilyn would always say, 'Oh, I'd love to go to the Isle of Capri one day! I have such an affinity to it.' "

Kenny was convinced that he had received an apport—an object materialized from the Other Side—in the form of a fingernail from Marilyn Monroe.

A short time later, when he was making one of his frequent appearances on "The Mike Douglas Show," he carried the nail with him to show the popular talk-show host. As Kenny opened the envelope in which he had brought the nail, it literally jumped out onto the studio floor. There, before millions of viewers, were the cheery psychic and the genial host on their knees searching for Marilyn Monroe's fingernail.

Later, during meditation, Marilyn appeared to Kenny and explained that the business with the nail on "The Mike Douglas Show" was her way of getting his attention to inform him that she would be reborn as a boy in December 1980 on the Isle of Capri.

Kenny believes that his friend did reincarnate at that time. "Why a boy? She'd spent the greater part of her life as one of the world's most glamorous screen sex goddesses. She spent time after passing over studying philosophy to prepare her for a return as a male. She certainly was a real woman as Marilyn, and she wanted to get another perspective on life, this time as a man."

We asked Kenny who among the many stars he has known gave the most evidence of psychic ability?

"Mae West, without question," he said. "She was a natural psychic. She went to the spirit world for all of her answers. She had enormous depth of spirit. She could write screenplays in three or four days by dictating to stenographers while she lay in trance."

Knowing that Kenny and the late actor Clifton Webb were great friends, we asked for a progress report on that rambunctious spirit's ghostly activities.

"Beverly Hills will never be the same," Kenny said, laughing. "I've heard his spirit now stretches out from the house and into the street—and maybe across the street. Clifton bought the house from his very

good friend, the actor Gene Lockhart. Gene had wanted his daughter
June to attend school in that area, and one day when she was older,
Clifton, who had always loved the house, just wrote Gene a check for
the place.

"The Lockharts were also very much involved with the spirit world.
Gene wrote the popular song 'The World Is Waiting for the Sunrise'
while they lived in that house, and he also produced a great many
poems and other works. When I asked June why her father did not
publish such fine works, she replied that he could not. He had received
them from Joan of Arc, and he was too honest to put his name on
another's creativity."

Kenny explained how Webb had brought the worlds of Broadway
and Hollywood together in the house. "Everyone who was anyone in
Hollywood was a guest at one of Clifton's parties. Oh, how he loved
the place."

In 1966, three days before he passed over, Webb summoned Kenny
to his side and told him: "I'm not leaving this house—even at death!"

He told us that columnist Joyce Haber and her husband, producer
Doug Cramer, bought the house and some of Webb's personal effects,
such as his bedroom suite. "Now, you must understand that Clifton
was an inveterate chain smoker, while no one smoked in the Cramer
household. You can imagine their astonishment, therefore, when
Doug's mother, who was staying with them, would awaken in the
morning covered with cigarette ashes. She had, you see, been given
Clifton's bedroom suite. And the servants couldn't understand what
was happening to all the cats. They kept disappearing. Well, Clifton
hated cats, but he loved dogs."

Because so many of the servants had complained of seeing the ghostly
figure of a man, Joyce, on a hunch, brought home one of Webb's films
to see if they might recognize the late actor as the ghost. Not only did
the servants identify the restless spirit, but, according to Kenny:
"When the dogs saw Clifton's image on the screen, their hair stood
up on end and all three of them began to howl."

When Joyce and Doug divorced, Kenny said, a young couple, madly
in love, bought the home. "It wasn't long before they, too, had divorced, and now I hear couples in the houses around where Clifton
once lived are getting divorced. I told you: Beverly Hills will never be
the same!"

The psychic explained that he does not use astrology in his work nor does he read minds. He does utilize object reading and psychometry, and he does enter a light trance state, stating that he is fortunate in that he can turn his abilities on or off.

Kenny told of an interesting experience with the sweet spirits involving the multitalented Lily Tomlin. "Valerie [Porter] and I had been several weeks aboard the *Rotterdam* doing my nightclub routine for the cruise circuit. Anthony Newley, the singer-composer, urged us to see Lily Tomlin's one-woman show when we returned to New York."

They docked on a sunny April day and heeded their friend's advice, obtaining two tickets for Tomlin's show. To wish her luck, Kenny sent Lily a copy of his book. In reply, she invited them to join her backstage after the performance.

As they sat visiting, Lily suddenly asked Kenny, "Who was on stage with me tonight?"

"The first person I saw with you was my old friend Clifton Webb," Kenny said. "This was the very theater in which he had enjoyed so many personal triumphs. The second person you may not know, but it was Madame Maria Ouspenskaya."

Lily Tomlin's mouth dropped in astonishment. "This is incredible! Last night, I couldn't sleep and I turned on the television. I fell asleep watching Madame Maria Ouspenskaya in one of her old movies. Did she have any message for me?"

"She says," Kenny answered, "don't forget to use the Chloraseptic." Lily was once again startled. "When I awakened this morning, I sent my driver out to get some Chloraseptic!"

Kenny told us that Joan Crawford had been one of his clients. "She would often come for readings dressed in purple, as if trying to appear regal. She was very much into a study of the spirit world."

Christina Crawford had apparently expressed the same sentiments toward her former home to Kenny as she did to us, that the house should be burned to the ground. "Donald O'Connor bought the place from Crawford," Kenny said, "and he had a miserable time in the house. Everything went wrong for him. Anthony Newley acquired the house from O'Connor, and he suffered greatly there. He told me that he had tried to have the place exorcised. He felt under attack from the spirits of both Joan Crawford and Charlie Chaplin.

"It is too bad," Kenny said, sighing. "Joan's and Charlie's spirits are just not nice people."

PSYCHIC CLARISA BERNHARDT MEETS THE CROSSOVER CLUB FOR HOLLYWOOD SPIRITS

The spirit of Mae West, who died in November 1980 of complications following a stroke, has manifested to noted psychic Clarisa Bernhardt on several occasions. Mae, the earthy, buxom star of such films as *She Done Him Wrong* (1933) and *My Little Chickadee* (1940) was well-known for her interest in the supernatural.

"Mae doesn't like the term 'séance,' " Clarisa said. "She prefers to say that we speak to one another through 'interdimensional communication.' "

Clarisa Bernhardt is the only seer in contemporary times to predict an earthquake to the day, the location, the magnitude, and even to the *minute* of the event. The astonishing prediction was made on her radio show "Exploration" and referred exactly to the 1974 Thanksgiving Day quake in San Jose, California. The forecast was also acknowledged and documented with the local newspapers and the police departments; as a result, the U.S. Geological Survey in Denver set up a specific program that would be designed to investigate the potential of earthquake prediction. Of some two hundred participants in the program, Clarisa was the only one who demonstrated a significant consistency in her forecasts. Through her psi ability, she was able not only to beat out the other seers but the scientists and the computers as well.

Her talents are by no means limited to quake predictions. She has demonstrated an additional practical use of ESP by finding lost persons and by cooperating with law enforcement agencies as a psychic sleuth. She is regularly consulted by business executives who seek her assistance in making top-level decisions, and, in addition, she is an extremely gifted medium.

In 1982, two years after Mae West's death, Clarisa was asked to serve as the medium at a séance that was held in the lounge of Hollywood's Ravenswood Apartments, where the actress had lived for nearly fifty years. "Right away, I could feel a sense of joy coming from Mae's vibration,'' Clarisa said. ''I think the most important thing that came out of the séance was Mae telling us about the Crossover Club, a group of spirits who help new entities to adjust to life in that new dimension. She told us that there were a lot of people who were in show business who are in the club and that she would soon be qualified to assist and to greet some of those who will be joining her on the Other Side.''

Such spiritual information was of great benefit to a medium such as Clarisa, but the other sitters were more interested in seeking specific references to Mae West's life to convince them that they were, in fact, communicating with the late actress's spirit.

''Several of Mae's closest friends were there,'' Clarisa said. ''So were some reporters from the *National Enquirer.*''

The medium channeled information about several matters that convinced one of Mae's friends that the spirit essence of Mae was truly there.

''I received a communication about a problem with Mae's leg,'' Clarisa said, ''and he said later that she had broken her ankle back in the 1940s but that no one else had known about it.''

Mae's Secret Inspirational Writings

Mae's spirit also referred to some inspirational writings of hers that she now felt might be helpful to others. She described the work as having been written on ten to fifteen sheets of onionskin paper and placed in a thin brown cover. Mae's amazed friend confirmed that papers of such a nature did exist.

When Clarisa told the séance circle that Mae was expressing concern about a ring that had been lost, he once again immediately recognized the incident to which the entity made reference. ''He said that only Mae and he had known about the lost ring,'' Clarisa said. ''He stated that he took all these references as signs that Mae's spirit was actually present at the séance.''

The medium said that the spirit of Mae West had been so weak when she had left the earth plane that it had taken her a little while to get all her energy restored. At the séance, however, she had enjoyed a feeling of exhilaration, revealing that she had been trying to contact her friends in their dreams.

"One of Mae's friends told us that she had appeared in his dreams many times and very vividly. One of the authors said that he had also seen Mae in his dreams and that she appeared at her loveliest, looking young and vibrant."

Thoughts Are Things

The medium remembered Mae telling her friends that she was as close to them as their thoughts. "If you think of me, I'll be there."

Clarisa agreed with Mae's sentiments: "Thoughts are very powerful. Thoughts are things."

Mae West had also apologized for her conduct during her final days on earth. "She had not really been herself before she went," Clarisa said. "She said that if she had hurt anyone by the way she behaved, it was unintentional. She was sorry."

Although Mae thought that Ann Jillian had done an okay job portraying the actress in a television movie, she stated that she would like to see Loni Anderson play her in a feature film. "She said that she felt that Loni would reflect more of her true personality and that she would play her 'happy,' " Clarisa said.

After the séance was completed, the medium observed a strangely beautiful sight. A bag lady, with her hair coiffed in the elaborate manner in which Mae West had worn her silver mane, was struggling to free a bird that had become tangled in some string.

Later, as she sat eating at a restaurant, Mae came through to Clarisa again and said, "Through the humblest of efforts come the highest acts of love."

The medium felt certain that the spirit of the actress was admonishing them to act always with pure love toward others.

Clarisa laughed when she confided that Mae had appeared to her on another occasion and told her, "Honey, if you'd lose some weight, I could really operate through you."

She told us that she was amused but not tempted by the offer: "You know that I never let another entity take over my body. I am not that kind of channel. I never let a spirit possess me. They communicate to me, and I relay their words."

With a chuckle, Clarisa admitted that the entity did inspire her to lose fifty pounds. ''Mae went on to become a helper in the Crossover Club. She was there to meet Cary Grant when he crossed over in 1986.

"For some reason, on occasion I have been shown various stars when they arrived on the Other Side. For example, I saw that Grace Kelly was met by Bing Crosby. Later, I learned that there had been great affection between them.''

John Belushi Was Shocked by His Death

"I had a brief communication from John Belushi when he arrived in the spirit world in March 1982. He seemed to be as shocked by his 'accident' as were so many of his fans and friends. He told me that he was very sad about what had happened. He shrugged his shoulders and said, 'What can I say now? There is nothing that I can do.' Then his spirit just walked away from me,'' Clarisa said.

"I received the strong feeling from this communication that when John's spirit energy is renewed, he will come back into the astral plane—the plane that so closely parallels that of earth—and try to help young people who are having drug and alcohol problems. He will be there to assist them from the Other Side.''

Natalie Wood's Unhappy Spirit

"On that tragic November night in 1981 when Natalie Wood drowned, I could not help connecting the fact that on the same night a meteor had been visible blazing across the Northern California skies. I thought at once of Natalie and the movie *Meteor* (1979), in which she had starred with Sean Connery,'' the medium said.

"Natalie appeared to me some months later, and she was 'livid' about the possibility that Robert Wagner appeared to be considering marriage so soon after her death. Incidentally, very soon after that he announced that he would not be marrying a specific person with whom he had been linked in the newspapers.'' Wagner has since wed Jill St. John, a union of which the spirit of Natalie Wood has approved.

Meeting Marilyn Monroe on the Twentieth Anniversary of Her Death

In 1982, on the twentieth anniversary of Marilyn Monroe's death, Clarisa stood in the bedroom in which the star accomplished her extremely controversial crossover. As Clarisa watched, a small mass of swirling mist in a corner of the room became the face of Marilyn.

"In no way am I like Mae West," the entity commented, making reference to the recent séance that Clarisa had conducted. "She left at her time. I came *before* my time!"

Later, Clarisa walked in the garden that had offered such solace to Marilyn when she had been alive. "There were so many beautiful vibrations in that garden," the medium remarked.

Clarisa went to the bottom of the terraced garden then began to come back up the stone steps. "It was then that I received a most remarkable flash of one of Marilyn Monroe's past lives," Clarisa said. "She had been an Aztec maiden who had been sacrificed to the gods. Her spirit seemed to be telling me that she had been a sacrifice then— and in her most recent life on earth. It seemed so very important to Marilyn that her fans know that she did not commit suicide."

The spirit of Marilyn Monroe made a later appearance to Clarisa and told her, somewhat enigmatically, "If you are being mistreated in a relationship, it is not worth it to stay in it." Marilyn also seemed to be very upset over a book about her that had been recently published. "There were pictures that showed her after the autopsy," Clarisa said. "She felt that it was not necessary to reveal such photographs to the public. She wants people to remember her as she was at her peak. It gives her positive energy on the Other Side when people think highly of her."

Intense Emotion Keeps Pulling Elvis's Spirit Back to Earth

Clarisa mentioned that she is often asked if Elvis Presley is really dead.

"I have seen Elvis on the Other Side," she said. "He is no longer in the physical. However, it is my sincere feeling that the long-term, intense emotions about him by his millions of fans keep pulling his spirit body back to Earth. When people believe that they are seeing Elvis here and there, they are actually seeing his ghost.

"I have seen Elvis with Marilyn Monroe on the Other Side, and they have become good friends and a great help to each other.''

Clarisa went on to tell about a peculiar twist of destiny that occurred during her teen years.

"I was invited by a friend who had a radio show at a country-western station in Austin, Texas, to go on a blind date with a friend of his who was going to be in town for a few days.

"I told him that I didn't go on dates with people I had never met. I was too shy.

"He said that his friend was also very shy but very nice. He had just cut a record that was starting to do well. His name was Elvis Presley.''

Although Clarisa never met Elvis, she did have a vision of his death and she sent a letter warning him to take better care of himself. "I have no way of knowing for certain if he received my letter,'' she said, "but his spirit did appear to me within hours after his death.''

Grief for a Loved One Can Hold a Spirit to Earth

In 1978, Clarisa mourned the passing of her beloved husband, Russ. For thirty-five years, Russ, an actor, had become famous playing Scrooge in special presentations in the Los Angeles area. Although she knew that he had been called on a "new cosmic assignment," Clarisa suffered a great sense of loss.

"For the first three months after Russ's death, I went into a deep depression,'' she said. "No matter how much one knows, the loss of a loved one still hurts.''

Then one night, Russ appeared before her dressed in his Scrooge outfit, the kind of swirling London fog effect that he liked so much moving around him. "You must stop your grieving for me," Russ told her. "You don't know how much pain you are causing me!''

The spirit entity explained that it no longer had the protection of a physical body, and her grief was holding him too near the earth. "We are as solid in our dimension as you are in yours," he said. "When we are pulled into your dimension—the third dimension—we can no longer be solid and we become ghosts. It is fine that you miss me, Clarisa, but please do not overdo the grieving.''

She has since remarried and enjoys a happy union, moving between Hollywood and Canada, where her husband has a business.

"It is so important to keep your spiritual house in order," Clarisa advised. "The astral plane hangs heavy over Hollywood. There are too many people here who were unprepared to make their transition to a higher dimension. Part of my work—and that of the spiritual Crossover Club—is to encourage these confused entities to move on, to leave the earth plane, and to walk into the Light."

THE NIGHT THE SPIRIT OF MARILYN MONROE MATERIALIZED ON CALL

Bob Slatzer met Norma Jean Baker in the distant summer of 1946. As a correspondent for an eastern newspaper, he was writing some stories on major movie celebrities. Norma Jean was a young model trying to get work by making the rounds.

One day as they were each waiting to see prospective clients in the lobby of Twentieth Century–Fox Studios, they struck up a conversation and made a date for later that evening. Thus began a long relationship that led to their brief marriage in 1952.

Bob told us that Norma Jean, who was later transformed into the Hollywood Love Goddess known as Marilyn Monroe, became his closest friend, and he felt that they remained close until her death in 1962. Since her passing, many strange things have manifested in his life.

"I began to notice that particular odors would suddenly become apparent in my home, seemingly out of nowhere," he said.

The first time he remembered this occurring, the pungent smell of roses filled the air in the room. He looked all around but saw no flowers. He even opened his patio door, but no odor of roses drifted in. Bob knew the smell of roses. He used to grow roses as a hobby and had worked his way through college by working in a funeral parlor. This particular rose smell was funereal, different from a floral shop or a garden smell.

The phenomenon began to occur periodically, sometimes twice a week, sometimes once a month. If other people happened to be in his home, they wouldn't smell a thing. This occurred about sixteen or seventeen times from about 1963 until about 1981; then just as mysteriously as it came, the funereal scent of roses went away!

In 1973, Bob told us that he had participated in a ritual that had actually caused Marilyn Monroe's spirit form to materialize in front of witnesses.

He had met Anton La Vey and his wife at the home of a movie studio publicity man. During their conversation, he learned that La Vey was fascinated with Marilyn Monroe.

"We socialized for dinners and such over a period of about two years," Slatzer said, "then Anton contacted me and told me the following: About every eleven years astrologically, a cycle would repeat itself and the 'dark of moon' would come back on Saturday, August the 4th, just as in 1962 when Marilyn had died. La Vey needed some-one who knew Marilyn very well to help manifest her."

Bob agreed to La Vey's making all the arrangements and picking him up about 10:30 P.M. La Vey had received permission from the then-current owner of Marilyn's home to be there. Although she would be closing the gate, they were welcome to sit in the cul-de-sac. The location of the house was such that if an interloper were to intrude, there would be no place to run and hide without scaling a six- to seven-foot fence on either side. Their car was positioned against the gates, looking out, and there was no one else around.

Bob detailed his memory of that night:

I was sitting in the front seat on the passenger's side with Anton; his wife was in the backseat. From inside the car gazing at the night, it was like looking out into a tunnel, with a perfect line of vision, as each side of the street was dark.

Anton had a tape recorder with prerecorded songs from Marilyn's pictures. At about 11:45 P.M., he turned it on a little more than audible. He also had a very weak penlight that he held down low by the steering column, and he began reading something he had written. It was sort of like tongues or a chant or something. I didn't recognize it.

About 12:15 A.M., the night was still. Not one single blade of grass was moving. The leaves on the eucalyptus tree by the corner of the house were still. All of a sudden, a terrific wind came up! The tree seemed to have an isolated wind blowing on it. It looked as if it were in a hurricane for three or four minutes, yet nothing else on either side of the road was moving. It looked as though the wind was blowing toward us; but we didn't feel it in the car at all.

Then from out of nowhere (I didn't even turn my head or blink, and I have twenty-twenty vision)—this woman appeared! It was just like somebody set her there. She had on white slacks with a little black-and-white, splash-pattern top, little white loafers, and I could see a shock of blond hair. She started walking toward the car. I had goose bumps all over!

Then my second thoughts were from my journalist's mind. I wondered if this was a setup by Anton. I knew he had been in town for a couple of days, but I didn't think he'd do anything like that. He seemed too intense and serious about his work, and he didn't seem to be that kind of person.

So all we had was the light of the night, so to speak, and this figure began walking slowly toward the house—or it seemed toward our car since we were sitting in the driveway in front of the house. I asked Anton if he wanted to turn a light on. He sort of tapped me on the knee to keep quiet! I noticed that Anton was sweating profusely.

The figure came slowly toward us and stopped about thirty feet in front of the car. Anton had dimmed the music a little and finished his chant when she was about halfway to us. All of a sudden, she veered off to our left. There used to be a big tree there, and she just stood there, almost as if she were made of cardboard, with kind of a wooden look, but the figure was highly recognizable as Marilyn!

Then I really became a believer! She was so real! Anton's wife exclaimed something. I looked around at her. She had practically turned white and looked almost petrified! Anton—well, his breath was taken, I can tell you that!

Marilyn hesitated for a minute, her hands clasped. It didn't appear that she was looking directly at our car, but she seemed to be looking at an angle past us. It appeared to me as if she was looking past the gates, as if she wanted to enter the gates and go in but didn't want to pass the car.

Then she turned to her left and slowly started to walk down the middle of the boulevard. She was about halfway when I said to Anton, "Turn the lights on." He said no and appeared as if he was frozen and stuck in a fixed position!

I had my door open to the point where if I pushed it, it would open. Anton had the car doors and inside lights rigged so that they would not interfere when the doors were opened. I had the door ajar so in case I wanted to get out, the door would not make a disturbing noise when opened.

By now, Marilyn was about three-fourths of the way down the street, and without saying anything, I decided to get out. I was going to walk after her. I took off and walked as fast and as quietly as I could. When I was about one hundred and fifty feet away from her, she turned, and as she turned, walked to the middle of the street— and *vanished* into thin air! I saw this happen with my own eyes!

I noticed a little ditch where water was coming down from drainage ditches. The ditch on either side of the street was about two and a half feet wide. When I had hurriedly walked through the water, I noticed my footsteps left an imprint on the other side. The apparition, or Marilyn, had been taking short, small, measured footsteps on the other side of the road. There were *no* other footprints. If the "being" had stepped over or walked across the water, it would have made a very noticeably different movement from the small steps it had been taking. I'm not saying she walked on water, but if even her heels had touched the water or walked through it, there would have at least been a dripping of water.

Almost simultaneously upon my noticing that, Anton and his wife came up to me with a couple of flashlights, and their additional light further proved that my original examination and observation was true! Anton said that he was shaken by the whole experience. He begged off dinner, saying that he was completely drained and that he had no appetite. All he wanted was to go back to his hotel, take a shower, lie down, and go to sleep.

Bob Slatzer told us that he had repeated the story only to one person besides psychic-sensitive Clarisa Bernhardt—that was to the author Norman Mailer.

"He's interested in these types of things," Bob said. "To him, I said, 'Norman, I'm only telling you this because I know you are into things like this a little, and you are not a disbeliever.' I said, 'I'll tell it to you for what it is worth.' When I got through telling it to him, he said, 'I do not disbelieve it. I do believe these things—and that is quite a strange experience!' "

JAYNE MANSFIELD'S GHOST HAUNTS THE PINK PALACE

Popular singer Engelbert Humperdinck says that movies have always played an important part in his life, so it meant a great deal to him to purchase a house that had been previously owned by two film greats, Rudy Vallee and Jayne Mansfield.

"Jayne bought it when she was married to Mickey Hargitay," he said. "It is a three-story, six-bedroom, thirteen-bathroom mansion on Sunset Boulevard. I managed to buy it fifteen years ago for a few hundred thousand dollars. I've had it on and off the market for eight million. I'd like to sell it, but I keep changing my mind. It's a special place, and it means so much to me."

Engelbert says that Jayne Mansfield had painted the mansion "Pepto-Bismol pink" and that the neighbors were delighted when he toned the colors down a bit.

"The whole house—the Pink Palace—was really a monument to Jayne," he said. "From the heart-shaped swimming pool, with its matching heart-shaped Jacuzzi, through the waterfall, the statues and fountains—all overshadowed by fifty-five-foot-tall palm trees—to the copper-paneled ceiling of the den, the mansion is quintessential Mansfield.

When his family first moved in, the singer said that he saw her ghost on the stairs: "It was not long after her tragic death. Her presence filled the entire house in those first weeks. She had really left a part of herself behind in this house. I'm very intuitive, and I've seen ghosts before. This time, I was really aware of her presence.

"I walked into the hall, and I saw her clearly. She was on the stairs, walking down, wearing a flimsy dress. I was about to say, 'Hello, Jayne,' when I realized that she was dead. I didn't say anything. Then she faded out.

"I like to think that she was saying good-bye," Engelbert said. "I believe there is life after death."

The singer went on to speak of the place behind the barbecue area where Jayne used to keep her two lions and a tiger: "She would give them food through a hatch by the barbecue," which was inscribed with the words, "My Love Burns for You Forever." The bottom of the pool was painted with the declaration, "I Love You Jayne."

Although the pink walls and the inscriptions were repainted, Engelbert confessed that he maintained a private shrine to the onetime Hollywood sex goddess. ''In the billiards room, behind the paneling, where I have some of my gold and platinum records, there is a wall that was here when I bought the house. It's papered with a hundred magazine covers of Jayne. I didn't have the heart to take them down, so I had it repaneled and I put my trophies up near hers, but only I know hers are there.''

He told of another ghost that he had encountered some years ago when he and his wife Pat were vacationing at Settlers' Beach, Barbados. ''We had retired to bed. I woke up unexpectedly at 2:40 A.M. I know because I had on a diver's watch and the luminous hands told me exactly what time it was,'' he said. ''I saw a woman across the room. She was wearing a three-quarter-length skirt and seemed to be hobbling, swaying awkwardly from side to side. I watched her for about five minutes, knowing somehow that she wasn't really there, before I woke my wife. 'My God, it's a woman,' she said.

''Then a man appeared. He was right at the bottom of the bed. Both of the ghosts appeared to be very irritated with us, and the man was waving his arms at us to 'get out.' Then both of the ghosts faded away.''

The next morning, the singer and his wife inquired of the manager if there was anything odd about their suite: ''You know, ghosts or anything of the sort?''

The manager replied in the negative, saying no one had ever died in the room.

''As an afterthought,'' Engelbert said, ''the manager said that the owner of the house had died three months before, in America. 'Anything unusual about her?' I asked. 'Well,' he answered, 'she had two artificial hips and she swayed a lot when she walked. And she always wore three-quarter-length dresses.' ''

THE BEATLES' SEANCES WITH THE SPIRIT OF BRIAN EPSTEIN

When the outspoken John Lennon said that the Beatles were more popular than God, he did not intend the statement as a boast of his group's omnipotence. To the contrary, it was a pointed observation that the media and a relentless campaign of publicity hype could make the actions and the activities of a group of rock musicians from Liverpool, England, of greater concern to teenagers than their own personal spiritual quest.

By the time that Lennon, Paul McCartney, George Harrison, and Ringo Starr starred in *A Hard Day's Night* (1964), they already exerted an incredible influence on the musical tastes, fashion choices, hairstyles, and life-styles of young people all over the world. Director Richard Lester's imaginative interpretation of an average day in the life of the Beatles brought them even more fans and led to a second film, *Help!* (1965), which included the same zany mix of sight gags, offbeat humor, and new hit songs.

The essential point in Lennon's wry remark about their popularity supplanting the position of the Deity in the hearts and minds of the world's youth was not lost upon the group itself, and soon the wire services were buzzing with stories about the Fab Four meditating in India with guru Maharishi Mahesh Yogi. Insiders were well aware that the Beatles' private search for access to the inner world of the psyche had already led them to mind-expanding drugs. Transcendental Meditation with a yogi who giggled during his press conferences seemed vastly to be desired over LSD and the risky world of mind-altering chemicals.

Then, on August 27, 1967, while they were with the Maharishi, the Beatles' manager and longtime friend, Brian Epstein, died in London of an overdose of sleeping pills. Epstein had been the man who had launched the lads from Liverpool on their path to success. He was the force that had made Beatlemania a worldwide affliction. He had taught the Beatles almost all they would need to know in order to strike it big, and he was largely responsible for their huge financial success.

At about the same time that they were grieving the loss of their friend and mentor, the Beatles were becoming increasingly dissatisfied with the Maharishi, beginning to feel that the guru was turning his values upside down. His nationwide television tour of the United States with a pop music group in tow completely turned them off, for none of the Beatles believed that meditation could be taught—or practiced— in the atmosphere of a rock-and-roll concert. The guru himself had taught them the value of quietude and serenity.

George Receives the First Contact

Brian Epstein's first message from the spirit world came to George: "Not in words. It was more like a compelling feeling that came to me while I was relaxing in my home."

Harrison immediately informed the others of his experience, and they were eager to do something that might encourage Epstein's spirit to make further contact with them. It was decided that they would go to a medium with the express purpose of communicating with Epstein during a séance.

The Beatles all believed in life after death, and they could not accept that death could mean a cessation of their interaction with Brian Epstein. They agreed that his spirit would always be with them, and they felt certain that if he had found the bliss that he had been seeking, he would try his best to let them know. Their first attempt at spirit contact during a séance was a failure, so they resolved to take the time to locate a serious, dedicated medium who would not have difficulty accepting a world-famous singing group as clients.

Brian Epstein's Voice Manifests

In May 1968, the Beatles met at the home of a distinguished medium, arriving separately to avoid the ever-present possibility of being mobbed. The spirit medium had been advised of the reason for their visit, and he instructed them to place their hands down flat upon the circular table before them. He said a few words, which were mostly incoherent to them, then lapsed into silence as he moved into a trance state.

According to Paul McCartney, "From out of the silence, we could hear a voice. It was definitely Brian. The voice did not seem to be coming from across the room. It was more like it was welling up from within each of us."

As the Beatles could remember it later, Brian's message was as follows: "Hello, boys. I know you have all been waiting to hear from me, and I want you to know that I am happy. Are you still searching for happiness and seeking ways to give it to people? I am sure that you are. If you ever feel you need me, try to find me again."

When the spirit voice of Brian Epstein had finished speaking, Paul tried to ask questions about the mystery of death and the afterlife, but the entity did not answer. All four of them could feel that Brian had left. Encouraged by their success, George, John, Paul, and Ringo told the medium that they would like to return and hold another séance.

At the outset of the second session, the medium expressed doubt that they would be able to contact Epstein. After only a few minutes under trance, however, Brian's voice was greeting them. He said very little, only telling them that he was well and wishing the same for them. He then told the Beatles that he would speak again at a later date.

At the third séance, Brian was slightly more explicit but again seemed reluctant to convey very much. Although the skeptic might observe that the spirit of Epstein did not give the Beatles a great deal of substantial communication, it was enough for them. They were convinced that they had spoken with their departed friend.

Each felt that he could identify the sound of Brian's voice, as well as inflections and tonal patterns. They maintained a great respect for the abilities of the medium, and they refused to divulge his name. "We feel the Maharishi was damaged by all the publicity that came with his association with us," McCartney said. "If this medium should become well-known because of us, he may react like the guru. We want to prevent that from happening."

George Harrison, who would soon develop Krishna consciousness and write "My Sweet Lord," said that they had felt ". . . as close to Brian at the séances as we did when he was alive. I am sure he will tell us what we want to know when he is ready."

John Lennon remarked that Brian Epstein had always told them that he would attempt to contact them if he died first. "The day will come when he will tell us all what we want to know," he said.

Of the Beatles, it would be Lennon who would first enter the Great Mystery and rejoin their friend and manager. On December 8, 1980, he was struck down in front of his New York apartment by five shots from a crazed gunman; and was it only coincidence that the apartment building, the Dakota, was the same one in which Roman Polanski had filmed *Rosemary's Baby* in 1967?

JOHN LENNON SPEAKS FROM BEYOND THE GRAVE

Robin Givens, the former wife of heavyweight champ Mike Tyson and one of the stars of television's "Head of the Class," says that she is convinced that she is sharing her Hollywood home with the ghost of former tenant John Lennon, who stayed there when the Beatles were on the West Coast.

Robin reports that she has heard Lennon singing in the house late at night or sometimes talking quietly out by the swimming pool. She wouldn't think of calling out a ghostbuster like Nick Nocerino, however, saying she doesn't mind living with such a friendly spirit.

Linda ("Deer") Domnitz has also discovered the warmth of Lennon's friendly spirit. What is more, she has channeled more than a thousand pages of communication from the talented musician, many of which she has collected in her book, *The John Lennon Conversations*.

It was four days after Lennon had been struck down by an assassin's bullet that his spirit appeared before Linda and began to speak with her. She had been meditating with a colleague, and they both become very excited.

Although Linda was shocked that Lennon would manifest to her, she was not unfamiliar with the process of spirit communication. She had been able to communicate with her late husband, and she had conducted séances in her home for quite some time.

Linda's first reaction was to turn on the tape recorder. She heard the words from John Lennon in her head and then she repeated them aloud.

Lennon said that his death had been no coincidence or accident. He had accomplished what he had planned to accomplish, and now he was going to be a messenger of the truth connecting the earth plane with the spirit world for the mission of world peace and the salvation of the planet.

Linda was disappointed at the initial media response that she received from her channeling of Lennon, but she was encouraged when the well-known trance medium Kevin Ryerson confirmed that the communicating entity was, indeed, John Lennon. Ryerson went on to express his amazement at the clarity, power, and coherence with which Lennon was able to come through after such a short time of the leave-taking of his physical body.

Because John Lennon had told Linda that he wished to communicate through her on a regular basis, she began to gather friends to assemble for the channelings. As she became more comfortable with the routine, Lennon's words began to flow, sometimes for hours. "His presence was always very much felt in the room in the forms of temperature changes, drafts, twitchings, emotional releases, and actual sightings," Linda said. "He also started producing sound effects, such as during the channeling in Santa Cruz, California, on April 4, 1982.

"When I started the actual channeling, the first sentence, 'I am giving you all a big hug,' was punctuated by a huge crash on the roof. There were a few snickers, then John proceeded with, 'I repeat that I am here,' and immediately another resounding crash was heard. Everyone got the message, and there were no further interruptions."

The spirit of Lennon also gave personal messages to the sitters, which Linda claims where always "right on." According to her, the sessions had a very dramatic effect on people's lives. One could never be the same after such an intimate connection with John. "All of us working together can create the kind of utopian society that I have always envisioned," Lennon told those assembled on December 19, 1982. The spirit entity encouraged them to continue to emanate positive thoughts and vibrations.

On April 4, 1982, Lennon said that his efforts on behalf of humankind had never ceased: "I feel as strongly about helping the human race as I ever did before; and, in fact, more strongly than ever. I am unceasing in my efforts to promote world peace by any positive means necessary."

During one session, on July 3, 1982, Lennon told of his frustrated desire to cure the ills of society while on the earth plane. Now, however, he had allies in his crusade: "I never had the opportunity to work on such a grand scale as I am now through the united efforts of the spirit world, those in other galaxies—as well as our dear friends and animals on the Earth plane itself. Never before have so many of us [spirits] joined together with so many of you [humans] in beginning a crusade of true love and purpose for each and every other creature in the universe."

Lennon said through Linda Domnitz that he wanted people to understand that the Earth is one living entity of millions and millions of cells, which have a life and a life force and a vitality:

> We are in a symbiotic relationship with the Earth, as mother and child, and this is irreversible. We are connected to every single thing on the Earth, and everything on the Earth is connected to us.
>
> The Earth changes that the planet is presently experiencing are being felt within the very bodies by all of us here [in spirit], as well as by everyone on the planet. Understand that you are a mirror for Earth and that the Earth is a mirror for you and that what one of you undergoes is what the other undergoes, and vice versa.
>
> As the planet undergoes changes, you also undergo changes in your own personal lives. There is never a time when things just stand still.

ANDY GIBB STILL SINGS WITH THE BEE GEES

Andy Gibb became an instant teen idol in 1977 with his solo album, *Flowing Rivers*. The trouble was, in spite of the example set by the fame of his older brothers—Barry, Robin, and Maurice, the Bee Gees—Andy didn't really want to be a singer. Remarkably, all he really wanted was to join the Navy and become a pilot.

Tragically, Andy Gibb died in 1988 of a heart condition at the age of thirty. It is no secret that his death was hastened by drug and alcohol abuse and, according to some, by a classic broken heart over losing the love of actress Victoria Principal, one of the stars of the television series "Dallas."

A few weeks after Andy's death, Linda, the wife of Barry, was awakened by the touch of a kiss on her cheek and a "little bit of bristle." She opened her eyes, looked up, and there was Andy, standing there smiling. She later told her husband that she was not at all frightened because Andy looked so calm and peaceful. After a bit, he evaporated into thin air.

Maurice did not see Andy's spirit, but he did hear his voice. He had been barbecuing in the garden, a favorite spot of Andy's, when he heard his younger brother say: "How are you doing, buddy?" Maurice said that was a favorite expression of Andy's, especially when things were going well.

Things had not really been going well for the Bee Gees in recent years. When their score for the 1977 hit film *Saturday Night Fever* was translated into a soundtrack album, it sold nearly thirty million copies worldwide. For a brief but exciting two-year reign as kings of popular music, the Bee Gees and their music—"Staying Alive," "How Deep Is Your Love," and "Night Fever"—were omnipresent. Unfortunately, their costarring appearance with Peter Frampton in *Sgt. Pepper's Lonely Hearts Club Band* (1978) proved to be a box-office disaster. They had made a bad choice in attempting to act out an album that the Beatles had made famous. Although Barry, Maurice, and Robin were talented singers and composers in their own right, they had film personalities completely different from George, John, Paul, and Ringo.

Almost immediately following the unfortunate career move that smashed their potential as matinee idols, complex legal issues prevented the Bee Gees from issuing any new records for the next eight years. In 1989, as the Bee Gees set about shedding their *Saturday Night Fever* disco image, the ghost of Andy began to materialize during their live concert performances to inspire them to new heights of personal best.

"It is an incredible inspiration to us," Maurice said. "All of a sudden in the middle of a packed audience, there'll be Andy. He's there clapping, inspiring us to give a great performance. Sometimes, he even mouths the words to our songs. When I see him, tears well up in my eyes, and I sing like I've never sung before."

Maurice also suffered through a period of drug and alcohol abuse before his wife, Yvonne, convinced him to get professional treatment. He tried desperately to get Andy to realize that he was destroying himself. "But you can't do it for someone. You can only plant the seed."

Barry sadly theorizes that his brother's problem was not drugs or alcohol as much as it was lack of confidence. "He had lost faith. He had forgotten how to grab life." He knows that Andy is out there "somewhere." He cannot accept that one's life can be turned to dust and nothing more.

Barry Gibb's interest in UFOlogy, ghosts, and psychic phenomena is well-known. "I know the real Andy was never put into his coffin. I know his spirit has returned to let us know that he has found peace on the other side."

HOLLYWOOD SAINTS AMONG US

Larry Geller, who was Elvis Presley's hairdresser, personal guru, and close friend for fourteen years, reveals in *If I Can Dream: Elvis' Own Story* that the King wanted to become a monk and join a monastery after he had a visionary experience in a Southwestern desert.

The incident occurred in 1965, Geller said, as they were headed toward Los Angeles. Elvis was driving the bus when he suddenly stopped, awestruck by the shape of a cloud on the horizon. At first, the singer saw the face of Joseph Stalin in the swirling white mass, then the visage he perceived transformed itself to that of Jesus.

"I saw the Christ and the Antichrist," he sobbed, hugging Geller. "For the first time in my life, God and Christ are a living reality. Now I know. I'll never have to doubt again. God loves me"

We all know that Elvis never did forsake show business and enter the monastery, but today, thirteen years after his death on August 16, 1977, thousands of devout believers are worshiping Elvis as if he were a saint.

Dr. Raymond Moody, a professor at West Georgia College in Villa Rica, Georgia, has interviewed dozens of people who claim to have seen and to have spoken with Elvis after his physical death. In Dr. Moody's opinion, Elvis has become the center of a new religious movement.

"It's as if Elvis were a saint. People are praying to him, begging him to heal them or help them out of their troubles," Dr. Moody, the author of *Life After Elvis,* said. "People are having visions of Elvis, just like they have visions of Jesus or Joan of Arc or Saint Christopher. They travel to Graceland [Elvis's home in Memphis, Tennessee] just like pilgrims visit Lourdes."

What is more, claim many investigators, some people swear that they get positive results from praying to Elvis as their intercessor.

One nineteen-year-old girl said that Elvis was the angel who sang her back to life from a coma when doctors discovered that she had an inoperable brain tumor. Two years later, the Warrenville, Illinois, teenager was struck by a truck and sent into another coma. "Elvis's guiding hand came through once more," said her mother. "I played his records, and twenty-eight days later, she awoke. The doctors were amazed.''

Elvis Presley's longtime buddy, Charlie Hodge, remarked to journalist Valerie Jones that he was not at all surprised that people were worshiping Elvis: "When he was alive, he had so much love in him. He helped everyone in need that he possibly could; if he could figure out a way to come back, he'd do it.''

Princess Grace of Monaco Heals from Her Tomb

The late Princess Grace of Monaco, who was killed in an automobile accident in 1982, is another Hollywood ''saint'' who has been seen performing miracles from the Other Side. According to a high Vatican priest from Monaco, more than one hundred miraculous manifestations have been attributed to the former star of *To Catch a Thief* (1955), *The Country Girl* (1954; for which she won an Oscar), and *High Noon* (1952):

- A little French girl had her sight restored after she saw Princess Grace in a dream.
- An eleven-year-old girl was blessed with the sudden cure of her blindness as she placed flowers on Grace's tomb.
- Many people have stated that their prayers were answered after praying at her tomb.
- Actor David Niven is said to have confided to his butler that the spirit of Princess Grace comforted him and helped him through his own final days of pain and anguish.

''Who's to say?'' one religious observer commented over such phenomena. ''Perhaps an individual's religious experience can involve Hollywood figures as well as saints and more familiar spiritual entities.''

It does give us pause to wonder. Once again, when we consider the kind of love energy that some Hollywood stars generate among their loyal fans, who can deny that their spirit essence might not somehow interact with those on the Earth plane in a continuation of the healing power of love?

It would appear that Princess Grace had even more of that special energy than most. In the March 6, 1990, issue of the *National Enquirer,* reporter Jim Nelson disclosed that she had been tested at the world-famous Institute for Parapsychology in Durham, North Carolina, in 1980, two years before her fatal car crash in Monaco. Although para-normal expert Richard Noll stated that he could not provide any details of her tests, he commented: ''There is no question that she was an exceptionally gifted psychic.''

During the six hours in which she was tested, Princess Grace ad-mitted that she had always been interested in astrology and ESP, and she expressed her belief that her own psychic abilities had grown stronger throughout her life. She said that she always knew when fam-ily members were sick or injured, even when they were far away. She had a clear premonition that she would die in Monaco, and friends attested to the fact that she was ''very superstitious'' about the road on which she would die. She always said that she felt ''real danger'' every time she was on it.

She lived serenely with the premonition of her death. While at the institute, Princess Grace is reported to have said: ''I'm sure there's an afterlife, and I've been sure of it since I was a child. There's more to this world than meets the eye.''

KEVIN RYERSON—THE CHANNEL WHO TOOK SHIRLEY MACLAINE "OUT ON A LIMB"

Kevin Ryerson has certainly played an integral part in Hollywood's search for its soul, and he has had a profound impact on the lives of quite a few of its leading ladies, none the least of them being the Academy Award–winning actress, Shirley MacLaine.

In our interviews with the stars for this book, the phrases ''before Shirley'' and ''after Shirley'' were heard countless times. Many people said their experiences of the supernatural realm were kept to them-selves because they felt they would be looked upon as kooks or as being weird if they talked about these things. ''But,'' they would add, ''now that Shirley has paved the way . . . !''

That being so, we must also consider a strong force of influence behind Shirley, that is, Kevin Ryerson—or Tom McPherson or John or one of the others who speak through him. Shirley MacLaine documents the story of that influence in her 1983 book, *Out on a Limb*. Her best-seller was made into a five-hour dramatization for prime-time television in 1987, with Shirley and Kevin playing themselves. Since that remarkable international exposure, Kevin has continued to affect the lives of thousands upon thousands through his channelings, workshops, and lectures, as well as through countless television appearances and interviews world wide.

His involvement with the Hollywood scene was in and of itself foreshadowed by a supernatural event. "People often wonder what psychics, clairvoyants, or channels do when they themselves need advice," he said. "We practice what we preach. A good friend of mine, B. J. [Robert W. Jefferson], and I were doing some traveling together, and one day while we were sitting in San Diego, he looked up suddenly and said he had just had the oddest dream."

Kevin, the dream said, was going to meet a person of Irish descent, who had bright red hair, who was a dancer, who had a house in Malibu, and who was possibly involved in the motion picture industry. B. J. felt this person was going to write a very significant book that involved conversations and activities and would feature an interest that this person had in Kevin's work.

"This was in 1977," Kevin said. "Later on, after some mutual introductions, I met Shirley MacLaine, and the rest, as they say, is history."

B. J., originally from Kansas but now a resident of Phoenix, Arizona, was a fellow student with Kevin at the University of Life, founded by Dr. Richard Ireland. He continues to give life readings.

Shirley MacLaine is a person who is known as a keen social observer, politically and socially active. "She is very well-read, very demanding, but very professional," Kevin said. "Any student of her books will find that she was in a clear process of exploration. We had many, many conversations about parapsychology and about how these things would affect society at large; but, above all, a great deal of her interest was in her own personal growth. There is, of course, the obvious psychic high point about the entity Tom McPherson predicting her winning of the Oscar for her performance in *Terms of Endearment* [1983]!"

Something else that Shirley had a great curiosity in knowing about was what impact the developing interest in spirituality would have on the Hollywood community.

"The channeled response to her question," Kevin said, "was a spirit's prediction that Hollywood was going to experience a real return to much more introspective forms of motion picture making. Some of it would be in very subtle strokes, such as in *Field of Dreams* [1989], which is a very spiritual movie based on a popular American mythology. There would be attempts to understand even the intricacies of classic supernaturalism, such as in *Poltergeist* [1982] and *Poltergeist II* [1986]. There would be films of inspiration, such as *Resurrection* [1980], in which Ellen Burstyn portrayed a healer; and there would continue to be films that would explore the darker side, with such archetypal characters as *Batman* [1989; which in many ways is a morality tale]."

As a consultant to *Poltergeist II* ("Mostly in the scriptwriting phase and assistance in casting the film"), Kevin worked closely with Victor Grais and Freddie Fields, the producers, as well as with another clairvoyant. "We were working on the idea that it's the family's love for each other and the dignity of the family that would eventually prove to rescue them from these supernatural forces in what, quite frankly, is a well-told ghost story.

"We were trying to convey the idea that we only attract to ourselves those things that can test us and make us stronger. That was the message that came about in the father overcoming his own alcoholism through being strengthened by the spiritual counsel of his supernatural counselor, the Native American medicine priest. The miracle was in the love that the family had for one another told against the backdrop of incredible special effects. It truly was a very dramatic story."

Kevin continued his discussion of *Poltergeist II* by remarking that some of the performers, in particular Zelda Rubinstein, who played the psychic sensitive, are very clairvoyant. "Zelda has a tremendous rapport between herself and many of her animals. She seems to see and know their feelings, their pains. It was rather startling that many of the major actors and performers on the set, all in turn and very quickly, became diseased or left the body, including four of the major characters: the Native American gentleman [Will Sampson], the little girl [Heather O'Rourke], the original older sister [Dominique Dunne], and, of course, the very distinguished actor who played the villain [Julian Beck]. Statistically, this is *very significant* that that many major actresses and actors left the body."

To put this in perspective, Kevin said, a channeled message was requested asking why these things had occurred. In the information given, two things were called to attention: Two of the actors, Will Sampson and Julian Beck, were attracted to the script because they both had critical illnesses. They wanted to examine and to confront the issues of death and dying, the afterlife, and what the afterlife would be like. The spirit said that Heather O'Rourke and Dominique Dunne were attracted to the *Poltergeist* series because it would help people to begin to examine and to confront the issues of the afterlife. The spirit further stated that the two girls had karma in those areas.

"For the cast members," Kevin said, "those scenes were so real and their dreams were so intense after those performances that a lot of them found themselves unable to go on the set again for at least a couple of days because the experience was so powerful!"

There were also a few unusual things that occurred during Kevin's channeling scenes in the filming of the two-part television movie *Out on a Limb*. "On the set, I was being interviewed by Stan Margolis and Robert Butler, the director [actually, they were interviewing the spirit, and Tom McPherson was who they were speaking with through me . . . I was in a trance state]. Stan Margolis is a sensitive man who runs the crew like a family, yet he is disciplined, professional, and fair. Being a compassionate individual, Stan asked Tom McPherson in a very straightforward manner whether or not there was anything he could do for Tom on the set. He was also concerned as to whether or not any of their equipment, being electronic, would interfere with the spirit's communication. The spirit's answer was, 'Quite the contrary. What it is is, we'll be careful not to interfere with any of your electronic equipment'!"

Kevin found it interesting that the crew seemed tense; they felt they had only one opportunity to get the channeled information. "When they were dealing with just Shirley or just me, their concern was to get us to say our lines and everything would go along fine, with no tension. But then, suddenly, when the crew was confronted with the idea that they'd be speaking with 'supernatural personalities,' there would be this air of uncertainty . . . like, how do you interview a four-hundred-year-old Irishman—from the Other Side?"

It was not he, Kevin said, but Tom McPherson speaking through him while Kevin was in deep trance, who would put the cast and crew at ease. "Tom pointed out that in his day, the purpose of the Shakespearean stage was to inspire its audience toward higher values and higher knowledge and toward a better understanding of themselves and that in many ways, the purpose of Hollywood is the dream machine to instill similar values into people; therefore, the theatrical or the motion picture community, whether it was Greek, Shakespearean, or contemporary, always serves the same purpose.

"Immediately after Tom gave this little speech, he bowed out and the entity John came in," Kevin said, "and then something very strange occurred: During the entire period of time that John was speaking, there was a series of high-pitched, unusual noises that were going through the lines and onto the recording. When John would leave and Tom would come in and speak, the phenomenon would completely disappear. When John returned, the noises returned. So it appeared that we had an actual recording of an entity's pitch—or frequency—interfering with some of the electronic equipment! The entity John 'adjusted' his vibration, as he put it, so they didn't have to keep going through the adjustments with the equipment with the phenomenon repeating itself.''

Another incident that occurred while Kevin was filming *Out on a Limb* was an amazing confirmation of wisdom behind . . . and above . . . the set! It seems the crew was under tremendous strain wondering whether or not the entities would be able to repeat their lines. "Shirley was speaking with the spirit [as they were *reconstructing* the scene as it had actually occurred], and she came to a certain point in her lines where Tom McPherson all of a sudden went off script. Shirley was upset because she didn't know what her next cues were, but Tom was adamant that he was quoting the script correctly. What finally occurred to them was that about forty minutes earlier, *before* I came on the set, certain corrections had been made in the script . . . changes that I had no knowledge of consciously! When they went into quoting their lines from that particular section of the script, Shirley had forgotten about the changes and was working off the old script. Tom McPherson was apparently clairvoyantly quoting the changes that had been made!''

Hollywood crew members are generally pretty tough cookies. They have seen just about everything, so it would take something quite extraordinary to impress them.

"Over all," Kevin said, "they seemed less skeptical than when they first walked in. Even though working with a four-hundred-year-old

Irishman seemed to surprise them, some really seemed to open up to the experience . . . and the idea that maybe there *are* spiritual beings. As artists themselves, many of them recall things like past lives, and some have wondered where their talents came from. Perhaps some began to look at life in a new way and with greater depth.''

9 • HOLLYWOOD SEARCHES FOR ITS SOUL

Hollywood has been described as a vortex of energy, a place whose projective and reflective values mirror society's physical and nonphysical values or attitudes. Throughout this book, we have focused on the Hollywood stars and their interaction with the supernatural, delineating their remarkable range of experiences.

Many readers will be more familiar with our research into stars of quite another order, the stars of outer space. We are well-known for expressing our feelings and our belief that we are all star stuff, the earth may not be our true place of origin nor our final destiny and that among the stars, we may not be alone. One of the major themes in our ''star people'' research is that we may all have within us a deep molecular longing for our true home in the stars.

There is more of a common thread here than the word *star*, and that thread becomes a chord, perhaps the great OM, the universal vibration that binds us to everything. All life is interconnected, interrelated, and, most importantly, life continues—it goes on.

We have emphasized that to us the supernatural stories shared in this book have given us a great deal to ponder. Are there ghosts? Can spirits of the dead retain an attachment to a physical place? Does life continue in the form of reincarnation or in a heaven or a hell? Does the soul move on to another plane or planet or another place of learning and development—wherever that place might be?

The accounts here may not answer any of those great questions with any convenient dogma or belief structure. The *real* point is to ponder the questions and the seeming evidence that exists all around us that spells out *life continues,* the soul lives on—and most simply put, we each go to whatever that next level is and pick up where we left off.

It may sound simple, but it certainly melts a thousand and one spiritual dogmas down into a crucible to fashion a common golden thread that can be found in each of them. To us, the point is to pay attention to who and what we are here and now because if we don't like it, we have the power to change, to strive to be better. In doing so, we truly alter our here and now—and our destiny.

Although we just identified one common thread that runs through *star* and *supernatural,* there is another element that should be analyzed: Why stars, as in "Hollywood stars"? Surely, they are star stuff, but there must also be a different star stuff composed of the glitz and glamour that seem to fascinate us so. What is it that the stars of the silver screen, the television screen, the stage, or the rock concerts provide to our psyches? In many ways, that constitutes a supernatural question in itself. What are the inexplicable, paranormal phenomena that the Hollywood stars possess that make so many of us tongue-tied and dreamy? What is it that allows the Hollywood star to be so idolized, so worshiped? Stars captivate us, mesmerize us, and enchant us to the point of our wanting to know all that we can about their lives, their loves, their innermost secrets. We push and shove to get a glimpse of them. We pay for the privilege of having someone drive us by their homes. We want to know where they eat so we can see what they eat. We are unashamed of our invading their privacy to ask for an autograph. We adorn our walls with their pictures. Trends are set; fashions are dictated; their behavior is copied. Rightly or wrongly, many of us emulate our heroes.

Why?

In a recent scientific inquiry into American attitudes toward fame and famous people, conducted in late 1989 by the New York polling firm of Penn & Schoen and commissioned by *Spy* magazine, some astonishing things were revealed. For example, nearly all Americans have strong opinions about celebrities, so strong, as a matter of fact, that *millions* of Americans would undergo mutilation to become one of them! Not so surprising was that most Americans want beautiful blond women and tall, dark, and handsome men as their ideal celebrities and that people under fifty years of age have a higher regard for actors than older people.

With these findings and keeping our previous statement that all things are interrelated in mind, what do they have to do with our chapter about Hollywood searching for its soul? We will distill this question into two main themes, and we will focus mainly on the second. The first aspect has to do with *image.*

It was the legendary Louis B. Mayer who first decreed that "the public makes the stars." Indeed, there probably is not a star who has not acknowledged that truth when accepting an award; but who was it who said, "Stars are born and not made"? Another truth surfaces here: Many stars *are* made—literally.

Consider this: "The makeup man groaned about my face. 'An extraordinary face,' he finally announced. 'One side has absolutely nothing to do with the other. Miss Barrymore, which, if any, is supposed to be your best side?' I sat in a chair for an hour while I was repaired. My teeth were too crooked, they'd have to be capped. My forehead was too low, my chin too heavy, my mouth too small, my nose, why, the Great Profile's daughter had no profile!" wrote Diana Barrymore in *Too Much, Too Soon,* later to be a film in 1958.

Even Bing Crosby, against his desire and his will, gave in to allowing some camouflage rather than plastic surgery. For the screen, he donned a "scalp doily" (hairpiece) and allowed his ears to be temporarily glued back—as long as the spirit gum would hold out.

Joan Crawford once said, "I think the most important thing a woman can have, next to her talent, of course, is her hairdresser."

How many people know that Elvis Presley was a blond when he first arrived in Hollywood? He dyed his hair black, and later he had Priscilla do the same.

How does Victoria Principal keep her skin so young and beautiful? It's reported that she has volcanic ash imported all the way from Hawaii to pour into her "well-known mud baths—to the tune of ten thousand dollars for two hundred pounds."

Goldie Hawn was reported to have been so dismayed by how much older she looked than Mel Gibson when she saw early footage from their movie *Bird on a Wire* (1990) that she dashed to her plastic surgeon for a five-thousand-dollar eye job.

Cher said recently, "The reason I come off being sexy and attractive—I still can't bring myself to say pretty—is because I have had myself rebuilt. I had the hair under my arms taken care of, and I had an operation to firm up my breasts, and I spend about a thousand a week to have my toenails, fingernails, eyebrows, and hair put into top shape. I'm the female equivalent of a counterfeit twenty-dollar bill.

Half of what you see is a pretty good reproduction, and the rest is a fraud.''

Perfection. Can we ever achieve it physically? Yes, now we can with the marvels of plastic surgery. Sadly, once physical perfection is achieved and stardom is locked in, another problem comes with it. It's the age-old dilemma of fame, of ''what price glory?'' It is perhaps impossible for any of us to imagine what it would be like to be a Marilyn Monroe or an Elvis Presley, never to be able to go anywhere without being stared at, followed, stopped, touched, and so forth.

Let us clarify that we see nothing wrong with wanting to improve one's looks or in looking one's best. We are not even being critical of the amount of money spent on doing so; but we do see a pattern here: creating false images; manufactured idols putting on false fronts and reaping, perhaps, unfulfillment. To all things, *balance* is the key. So looking good, as Billy Crystal jokingly admonishes us—''It's more important to *look* good than to feel good!''—can be out of balance to an extreme. Because of the way we view stars—and for the stars themselves—that kind of thinking sets up the incredible tension of never being good enough, for them or for us. Low self-esteem and insecurity are the basic roots for stress, tension, and neuroses. It seems to be our human nature to compare, so with plastic reconstructive surgery now available for nearly everything for those who have the money, where might it end?

Whether it was ''The Donna Reed Show'' or ''Leave It to Beaver'' that made every housewife feel guilty unless her home was spotless and she had on a fashionable dress and had a gourmet meal in the oven when her husband walked in the door, or whether it was trying to look like Farrah Fawcett or Linda Evans when you wear a size twenty and have black hair, it was enough to drive every woman crazy . . . or to drink . . . or to drugs . . . or to death.

What we see happening now in Hollywood is a tremendous change in consciousness. With the problems of world hunger and environmental pollution being upon us—and being undeniably life threatening—the ''issues'' of tummy tucks or liposuction can hardly be all that important. Certainly, psychologically, self-image concerns are important as well, but we feel the good news is *honesty*. We applaud Cher, Phyllis Diller, Kenny Rogers, and all the other stars who are telling the truth about their improvements. Perhaps even more important are all the stars who are telling the truth about their addictions or former addictions and who are helping others to kick their habits. There are hundreds of stars—and their numbers are growing all the time—who are rolling up their sleeves, as well as reaching into their pockets, and helping enormously to improve the quality of life for the poor, the starving, the aged, the dying, and the ecology.

This is our second point: The Hollywood stars themselves are realizing that there is more to life than this stardom stuff. When the stage lights go out and the limo speeds by screaming fans, there is still the self to face—alone. Scores of actors and actresses are awakening inside to their own inner beauty and a greater Divine Plan of harmony and order.

Increasing numbers of stars are appreciating the position of power and leadership they hold, and they are using these attributes with *real power;* in addition to helping others, they are setting examples through honesty and involvement.

J. Z. KNIGHT—PREPARING HUMANKIND FOR A GREAT EVENT

J. Z. Knight channels "Ramtha" or "the Ram" for the purpose of presenting his message to humankind. The Ram says that he lived only one time on earth, thirty-five thousand years ago in Lemuria. Through the vehicle of J.Z., he claims that he did not die at that time but learned to harness the power of mind so that he could take his body with him into an unseen dimension of life. Ramtha states that he is now a part of an unseen brotherhood that loves humankind very much. He is, therefore, aiding and preparing humankind for a great event that has already been set in motion.

Superstars such as Shirley MacLaine, Linda Evans, and Richard Chamberlain have been in the audiences of the Ram, along with throngs of people around the country. Since 1978, thousands have studied the Ramtha videos, cassettes, and books. For a period of time, one could not pick up a weekly tabloid without finding an article about Ramtha in its pages.

When we asked J. Z. Knight about her own thoughts concerning the tremendous celebrity response to the teachings of Ramtha, she was most generous with her time and energy:

Certain people have reached a peak in their evolution. This has nothing to do with class distinction. Rich and poor, superstars and mediocrity alike feel that there must be more to life than this. The rich ask if there isn't more to life than material things. They also ask, "Who am I?" "What made me become famous?" and "Why am I doing this?" The poor ask if there isn't more to life than strife and suffering. The Ram so eloquently calls this point in peoples' lives the time of *fantastic realism.*

Ram says the journey has culminated that has identified self with the material world. The latter part of the journey changes, and the illusionary material no longer holds the same value. The self then turns inward into self-examination. The mystery itself becomes the focus.

There really aren't many mysteries anymore. In this age of communication and travel and the media, we have all been brought so close together. There really isn't much to discover about our binary-thinking world. The next step will have to be that the analogical mind takes things into a different perspective, and we find ourselves in an "unknown" mind, discovering what the ultimate journey is all about.

So when certain people are ready, there comes a light unto the world, a way, an instruction to guide those to what the journey is really about. Ramtha's word spread like wildfire with virtually no advertising. The very truths Ram was addressing were "potential truths," not knowledge, but people were ready to make that commitment to an unknown so they could gain knowledge about themselves.

Quite frankly, that's the reason Ramtha's teachings have endured against such persecution and hardship for so many years. His truth is consistent, and people have found themselves back in evolution rather than in stagnation—and from that evolves a radiant person.

It all began for J. Z. one day when she and her ex-husband were cutting out and putting together pyramids and experimenting with pyramid energy. She jokingly put a pyramid on her head, and as it slipped down over her eyes, Ramtha appeared physically in her kitchen before them.

In the beginning J. Z. said, she had misconceptions about how that transpired, giving a lot of power to the physical pyramid energy:

The energy of the pyramid did not induce that. I have grown to understand that it was a combination of the student being ready and the teacher appearing and my energy and willingness to take a step into the unknown.

I feel I may have created a state of readiness in my mind. Part of my mind said, "Girl, here you are doing something really bizarre." Another part of my mind said, "This is wonderful—you are starting to reach out and explore." I think by virtue of that process alone, the entity's consciousness was able to become visual to me at that time. If I had been one to scoff and not take the next step into the light or the unknown, I don't think that would have happened to me. It was my willingness to explore a possible region of potential that allowed that to happen—a leap of faith. So by my taking that one step, I brought on Ramtha.

Why did he choose me? I know some answers. It took two years of his working with me for me to get used to him. I can tell you that my persistent love of God maintained me. God has always existed for me, but not in a man-made altar or through the intellectual interpretation of a minister. I felt I had God on my side when I had no one else with me. I had that passion and a wonderful ability to move forward in my life in the midst of terrible pain. If things went bad, I changed them.

The love of God and the ability to move on seemed to be two "enablers" for me. The third was the courage to be able to do it. I think these three attributes—or virtues, if you will—led to my having this outrageous thing happen to me in my life. To have gone through the two-year study with Ramtha and the teachings, then to have the courage to change my life and to allow myself to be used as an instrument and to face a critical world and go on with the teachings led to a very beneficial personal growth and depth for me. I have been nailed to the cross of the media, and yet *nothing* will keep me from progressing because I know the truth.

J. Z. told us that Ramtha had given her teachings, but she made the point that teachings only become truth when you become one with them. "I had the knowledge of Ramtha's teachings and demonstrations for many years before I became 'it,' '' she said. ''For example, my son was allergic to everything but water. In a matter of less than a moment, he was cured by Ramtha's instruction.''

J. Z. confessed that she had a tremendous struggle to integrate these things into her life:

> It has taken me twelve years to integrate, mostly by experience, the things that Ramtha taught me. Now most of those things have become my knowledge base, but I had a definite struggle, especially a struggle with my image. I wanted to be beautiful! I thought I was ugly. Channeling this entity *was not beautiful!*
>
> I also had a time with my interpretation of God with what Ram was saying. Even though I didn't believe in the devil, I found myself wondering if there was such a thing. I found out there wasn't, that it only exists in the minds and hearts of those people who insist upon the devil being there.
>
> I had difficulty in allowing people to have their own truths or in turning the other cheek. I often wanted to come out and defend what the Ram was saying through me. The Southern girl in me wanted to punch someone's lights out if they called me names. That made me real angry at times *with Ramtha.* I had difficulty understanding.
>
> But time is a governing law. To the Ram, it's only relative in consciousness. I didn't understand consciousness, therefore, I disagreed about time. So when Ramtha would say certain things, and they would not happen when he said they would happen, that became my issue with him! Now I understand that based on God, creation within, and free will being through consciousness—and that time only exists in consciousness and is only relative to consciousness—some things happen and some things don't.

J. Z. said that Ramtha occurs in her life in three different ways. ''The first is when I leave the body. I have no conscious recollections of what transpires. He actually is a consciousness that works through the brain, the mind, the seven seals. He actually manipulates my body in order for that to occur. We both cannot occupy the same space, so I was afraid of letting go because that meant death, in a sense, to me. It took me two years to get over that and to finally experience that.

"Ramtha becomes channeled consciousness—not even a spirit. A spirit is different. As a consciousness that has hyperlucidity, Ramtha can be considered superconsciousness that affects itself through physical mass."

Secondly, J. Z. said, Ramtha appears separate from her. "He did this up until about three years ago, nearly every day, when I was having the most difficult time in my life. I was needing him constantly. I had no one that I could hold on to and talk to and try to understand things with. So there would be a *visual* appearance. Only recently, I have come to understand that the visual may be a hologram of his consciousness that was actually working through my brain to create that vision."

The third manner in which Ramtha can manifest is that he can answer when J. Z. asks a question. "I can actually hear the answer that is translated in my head. I hear that as a vocal voice. Ramtha has never imposed by taking over my body. Regardless of what anybody says, *I am not being possessed.* It is of my own free will. I don't think anyone can be possessed unless they allow it."

Many people have severely criticized J. Z. because of the high fees she charges:

> I had some difficulty for a time with Ramtha's saying that these teachings must be paid for. That went against everything I had thought was important. I used to think about how wealthy so many religious organizations were and how poor so many of their members were, and I'd be upset about that. So that made me a hypocrite.
>
> But Ramtha made a statement that has been constant: "People do not appreciate in binary thinking what they get for free. If they earn it, they will appreciate it."
>
> The only way we ever gain wisdom is when we interact and experience life. We pay the price of experiencing life in order to gain wisdom, the virtue of which is the prize of evolution. So the price we pay to attend the teachings is equal to the price we pay in life to gain knowledge and wisdom. It is equal and relative to personal experience, which always comes with a price.
>
> The teachings, in a sense, have been based on: "If you pay for this, you're going to appreciate this." It weeds out the insincere people who are simply looking for teachers and gurus. What it gives

people is an investment in their own education that affords them the experience to be able to integrate this into their lives.

I want to clarify that we are not a church. We are not a nonprofit organization. We pay business taxes and everything else a business does. We do have scholarships available. Sometimes, in fact, one-third of the audience attending is on grants.

It has been said in the tabloids and rumored about that Linda Evans cannot do a thing without consulting Ramtha.

If that were true, this organization would fall apart. Ramtha's teachings are not based on or directed to insincere people who want someone to tell them what to do. This organization survives on the basic truth that God is within you. If this fantastic reality exists within everyone, then everyone will have the answers, the light, the illumination, everything they need.

You can't say on one hand that God is within you and then on the other hand tell that person what to do. As far as Linda is concerned, she is one of the strongest women I have ever met in my life. She does not come off as Krystal [the part she plays on 'Dynasty']. She is a very strong-willed, very spiritual person who is highly intelligent. She is highly spiritual, in the sense that she has an extraordinary consciousness, coupled with a very strong will, and that means nobody tells this lady what to do!

We made the observation that it seemed as though Shirley MacLaine has blown both hot and cold regarding Ramtha's teachings.

What happened to Shirley was that in her fantastic search she came upon the Ram and loved him immediately. She spent a long time in his audience and in his tutelage studying. Many things she did not incorporate into her life because she did not give herself time to incorporate them, but they did become teachings—a context in which to set up a platform—in order for her to spread the word without further participation. The travesty that occurred there, as with many people, including myself, as I told you earlier, was the difficulty with many of the things the Ram said.

Then when all the outrageous press came out about me, when

they really got on me and were ready to nail me to the cross, so to speak, then, because Shirley is a public figure—a star—it would not do her any good to be associated with someone who all of the world is convinced is a fraud and a greedy demon. So in order to protect her image, she had to come out and take a stand against us. She had to say that she did not really know me or much about Ramtha and so on and so forth. That's all history at this point—the survival instinct.

Linda Evans, on the other hand, says quite openly that Ramtha has taught her how to find God within her. She says publicly that no one tells her what to do or think. She states that Ramtha implicitly says not to follow him.

And that is the truth. How are you going to follow a consciousness, anyway?

A DEEP PERSONAL COMMITMENT TO INNER GROWTH

Paul Andrews, the executive producer of Whole Life Promotions, has established the Whole Life Expos of Mind, Body, Spirit in Los Angeles as a popular showcase for the latest information on health, personal growth, new science, and metaphysical topics. A veritable who's who of popular speakers in the areas described above, together with hundreds of booths and exhibits, his expos bring crowds of forty to fifty thousand to convention centers in such major cities as Pasadena, Los Angeles, and New York.

"The expos are about consciousness," he said. "The physical balance is presented in the emphasis on holistic health. The workshops provide an opportunity for direct personal experiences. We try to present a focus for all aspects of the New Age and metaphysical communities."

We asked Paul about the many Hollywood stars who are very much in evidence at his expos. Were they there only because it is now stylish to be involved in metaphysical and environmental issues?

"The stars are there because of their deep personal commitment to inner growth," he said. "These people are very much involved in the consciousness movement. They are inner-directed people, and they are also dramatically concerned about the environment, global warming, the destruction of the rain forests, and so forth. There have always been Hollywood stars with strong interests in these areas. You know, as actors, they are more in touch with their right-brain selves. Their involvement adds a dimension to their lives that helps them transcend physical reality and explore nonphysical energies.''

Andrews observed that environmental concerns give the actors a more respectable platform to move into metaphysical topics, but he noted that many stars were openly interested in channeling, UFOs, metaphysical pursuits, and psychic phenomena.

He learned about the nonphysical realities firsthand in the mid-1970s when an automobile crash tossed him eighty feet from the scene of impact.

"I had a classic near-death experience," Paul said. "My physical body was thrown through the branches of a tree and lay crumpled on the ground, but the *real* me, the real Paul Andrews, was hovering somewhere above all the twisted metal and the battered bodies.''

One minute before, he had been the son of an oil company executive, a young man happily following the path of success in the business world with a nice home in the suburbs. In the blink of an eye and the squeal of tires before metal struck metal, he was undergoing an extraordinary out-of-body experience and expanding his consciousness to new dimensions of reality.

"Then," Paul said, "it seemed important to become reintegrated with my body, for I somehow knew that the vehicle was about to catch fire and someone had better pull my driver out of the wreckage or he would burn to death. I returned to my physical self, staggered to my feet, walked back to the car, and I managed to pull him free just before the vehicle exploded.''

Returning to the subject of Hollywood's search for its soul, we agreed with Paul when he stated that it is difficult to ignore celebrities when they choose to stand up for causes in which they believe.

"You cannot possibly overestimate the contribution that celebrities have made to the advancement of public awareness of the metaphysical/consciousness movement," he said. "Their participation and interest in this field has helped to catapult it into the international limelight. I would go so far as to state that the involvement of the Hollywood stars has been the single greatest catalyst propelling people into the inner-directed consciousness fields.''

STARS AND THEIR INNER CONSCIOUSNESS

Among those catalytic stars, according to Paul Andrews, are such men and women as the following:

Jeff Bridges: Bridges has an interest in aiding the environment, in seeking to limit world hunger, and in exploring the UFO enigma long before he accepted the starring role in *Starman* (1984). He remains active in matters of social stress, and he is keenly interested in the subject of UFOs.

Daryl Hall: The blond member of Hall and Oates, one of pop music's most dynamic duos, makes no secret of his interest in the paranormal.

Hall, born Hohl, is the descendant of Bavarian immigrants, stalwarts in the Methodist church. Several of the male members of his family were preachers.

Hall is so outspoken about his beliefs in a larger reality that some people who have met him are convinced that he is a magician—in the classic Hermes Trismegistus [a legendary author of works embodying magical, astrological, and alchemical doctrines] sense of the word. He speaks freely of dowsing and secret sources of exercising intense mental powers. As soon as energy or matter is released in the world, Hall philosophized, it loses its power. In other words, the song itself is sacred, but the act of writing it profanes the idea from whence it came.

Hall admits that way of thinking hearkens back to the ancient tenets of Gnostic theology, but he makes no apology for the journey.

To Daryl Hall, "flashes of inspiration" are the only pure things in the world.

"I think there's a basic underlying truth in all religions," he said. "If I have one belief, it is that you can influence reality through the will."

LaVar Burton: This young actor first gained international fame as Kunte Kinte in the television adaptation of novelist Alex Haley's monumental *Roots,* a fictional tracing of the history of the Afro-American in the United States.

In 1990, as one of the costars of television's "Star Trek: The Next Generation," he has moved from the past of his ethnic heritage to the future of the human species in outer space. It seems to suit Burton's mystical nature, his penchant for the out-of-the-ordinary— the character he plays on that series, Lieutenant Geordi La Forge, has been blind since birth and must wear a technological device called a Visual Input Sensory Optical Reflector (VISOR), which enables him to see.

In his teens, Burton became a seminary student, studying for the Catholic priesthood. Today, after recognizing the interconnected-ness of all things in his life, his attitudes are less traditional. Speaking of his interest in yoga and in crystals, he commented that he sees them as "tools to get me where I want to go."

His goal, he said, ". . . is to align myself with the spirit that connects me to all things, the spirit that I have in common with every other atom that exists."

Meditation is a part of LaVar Burton's journey, his process, but he hastened to add that it is not the whole thing: "Fire walking is a part of my process. Rebirthing is a part of my process. I follow the medicine path, and I attend sweat lodges, an ancient Native American ceremony of purification." Commenting on why crystals are important to this process, Burton said in the November/December 1989 issue of *Body, Mind & Spirit:* "I have always been aware of the concept that everything possesses inherent power. Everything. When crystals came into my awareness, they made a lot of sense. I want to push back the edge of the envelope to see what it means to be a human being and to explore everything that I can about this experiment called humanness. Ultimately, I think our strength as humans lies not in our intellects but in our emotions."

Lindsay Wagner: By her own testimony, Lindsay Wagner has appeared in more television movies than "anyone in history." She may not pick the "most fabulous parts," but the actress, known worldwide for the title role in "The Bionic Woman" series, says that she selects movies that she would want her children to see.

Offscreen, she is a strong supporter of efforts to understand and prevent child abuse and domestic violence. She is also an active worker on behalf of holistic health alternatives and such issues as learning disabilities. Lindsay would love to do a movie on reincarnation in the context of a love story and another that, if done properly, "would take everyone's belief structure and strip it away and get down to the essence of what is at the bottom of every religion and philosophy and really unify people."

Richard Hatch: Best known for his starring role in the television series "Battlestar Galactica," Hatch seeks to combine acting and metaphysics to assist actors and nonactors to become more deeply connected to their own creative potential. He is also active in many social concerns and in helping to save the rain forests.

Joanna Frank: This guest star of the popular series "L.A. Law" has told us of her deep desire to serve as a helper on the planet and to devote as much time as possible to the problems of hunger and the myriad issues of environmental concerns. She is also fascinated by the UFO mystery.

Ally Sheedy: It would be a great offense to dismiss this talented young star as a Brat Packer. Not only has she starred in such films as *War Games* (1983) and *The Breakfast Club* (1985), she dedicates her offcamera existence to living a healthy life that is balanced both physically and spiritually. She has worked for the mystic Brother Charles for many years, and she feels that his synchronicity tapes have changed her life.

Susan Strasberg: Although Susan has told us that she intends to become the "Jewish Shirley MacLaine," this talented actress and knowledgeable metaphysician/healer surely does not need to rest upon anyone's laurels other than her own. The daughter of the distinguished actors and teachers Lee and Paula Strasberg, she became the youngest star on Broadway in the title role in *The Diary of Anne Frank*. She has gone on to star in numerous motion pictures and television productions, a number of them with metaphysical themes.

A seeker and explorer of past lives, haunted houses, and spirit communication, Susan believes in pushing back the boundaries that hold us to preconceived concepts and thoughts. As she said, ''The universe may have things in store for us that are far beyond what we can imagine.''

Dennis Weaver: In 1983, Weaver, actress Valerie Harper, and a number of other concerned community leaders founded L.I.F.E. (Love Is Feeding Everyone), which daily provides food to more than four hundred people. Weaver has long been actively exploring everything from UFOs to the cessation of world hunger, and he passionately continues his work to make the planet a better place.

''The hearts of people must be changed if the world is going to be saved,'' he said. ''We've tried to bring peace, to change things, to create a morality by changing things outside of us. Laws won't change us. Treaties won't banish wars. We will continue to have crimes and wars until we begin to change *inside.*''

Stepfanie Kramer: A former model who costarred in the top-rated television series ''Hunter,'' Stepfanie has been involved in metaphysics since she was a child. The veils between worlds have always been ''rather thin'' for her, and she says that when she was growing up, there were always entities in the home that she would help to manifest.

Stepfanie esteems her Cherokee heritage, and she considers her spiritual life to be very important. She would very much like to produce a film that would emphasize problems unique to Native Americans. She is also a crystal enthusiast, utilizing them in meditation and as channels for healing, ''to complete and maintain a balance.'' If she lies down to meditate, she may place crystals in a particular pattern on her body so that they will align with the chakras and aid in bringing her physical self into balance.

SIRI DHARMA GALLIANO AND THE MIND-BODY LINK

What do Glenn Close, Christopher Reeve, Richard Gere, Daryl Hannah, Jessica Lange, and Susan Sarandon have in common?

They and dozens of other top Hollywood stars have all faced the punish-and-pamper regimen of superwoman Siri Dharma Galliano, a masseuse who has a brown belt in karate to assist her in enforcing her rules of discipline.

It would be simplistic to state that Siri shapes up the stars. Rather, she transforms them.

Gerald I. Isenberg, the producer of *The Clan of the Cave Bear* (1986), hails her as a "person of highest integrity, personal responsibility and intelligence." Siri was part of the crew for five months, between May and October 1984, in Canada, and she was responsible for training the cast and the crew for the rigors of the production, as well as serving as Daryl Hannah's personal assistant.

"I had to work with twenty-five cast members and transform them from actors to cave people," Siri said. "I used a lot of martial arts training to enable them to build up the necessary stamina to remain in a squatting position for ten hours at a time. I put them on juice fasts to help them shed weight. I made them take cold showers to get used to freezing temperatures. We were six weeks shooting on the glaciers of the Yukon."

Daryl Hannah, who had earlier portrayed a mermaid in *Splash* (1984), was a good choice for the part of the mystical cave woman. "She is very etheric," Siri said. "She was a tall and lanky young girl who retreated into a fantasy world of her own. To a great degree, as an adult, she still lives in that private world. She is very shy, and she loves to play roles in which she is an android [*Blade Runner,* 1982] or a ghost [*High Spirits,* 1988]."

One of Siri's greatest challenges was helping Jessica Lange become transformed from a real-life thirty-eight-year-old woman who had just delivered her third child to a movie-life twenty-two-year-old college senior.

"Jessica looked terrific in *Everybody's All-American* [1988], and it was her willingness to follow my program and her great self-discipline that helped to rejuvenate her," Siri said. "I had been her masseuse and her yoga teacher, so we had already established a good working relationship."

Siri placed Jessica on carrot-beet-apple-celery juice and a no-flesh, one-meal-a-day regimen. In addition, of course, there was plenty of exercising, yoga, and long walks. Jessica never wavered in her self-discipline. "Once they were shooting in a country club setting where the actors were being fed a ten-course meal," Siri said.

"I served Jessica a plate of steamed broccoli, and she didn't utter one word of complaint. By that time, she had undergone a change of consciousness. We were nine weeks in Louisiana, and Jessica looked nice and slender with a great body tone when she appeared before the cameras."

Siri admitted that she is a "benevolent despot" with her star clientele.

"I sweat them in the morning, then massage them at night. They'll do anything for that massage! I have to start hard, then soften up later. Punish and pamper."

Siri could not suppress a chuckle when we inquired about the regimen of Dennis Quaid, Jessica's costar in *Everybody's All-American.*

"To put it politely, Dennis has an excessive life-style. He had a jock trainer, lifting weights with him and so forth; but Dennis trained with beer and lobster dinners."

She was also bemused by the life-style of Jessica's "significant other," the playwright and actor Sam Shepard.

"They are complete opposites. They bring out each other's spark. Sam is the American cowboy. He smokes, drinks pots of coffee, eats bacon and eggs, and orders, 'Don't talk that yogurt crap with me.' "

Siri said that Glenn Close presented another example of an actor's self-discipline blending with her punish-and-pamper regimen. "Glenn started filming *Dangerous Liaisons* [1988] three weeks after she had her baby. You will notice that she is buxomy and somewhat matronly in that picture. We had more time to slim her down for *Immediate Family* [1989]."

What of the programs of some of the other members of her celebrity clientele?

SIRI DHARMA GALLIANO AND HER STARS

Christoper Reeve: "Some of the methods that he used to pump up for *Superman* [1978] have harmed his body. His tissues now have an unnatural feel to them. Christopher was originally a long, lean type. He is a really sweet being who is now living in a body that just doesn't match his personality."

*   *   *

LaVar Burton: "When he did *Roots Christmas* in 1988, I helped him with a fast to move from his present age of thirty-two to the young Kunte Kinte. He had to get back into that slavery consciousness all day, so at night I would have incense burning, a nice vegetarian meal, and a massage to help him return to his center. He is a very aware person who uses crystals, yoga, and both African and Native American techniques to stay in balance."

Richard Gere: "Richard truly walks his talk. He is glowing and radiant. He does t'ai chi, meditates, and there is no tension in his body. He is a gracious man of integrity."

Shelley Long: "Although she likes to be the center of attention, she is not the madcap character she often plays in the movies or on television. She meditates and truly wishes to serve as a vehicle of light. She desires to work for at-oneness, and she knows that it is God's will that she is on the path. She lends to causes and works on environmental issues."

Siri told us that her favorite fun was teaching yoga on the Starship *Enterprise* on the set of "Star Trek: The Next Generation." "In my opinion, the New Age fits right into the Space Age," she said. "I am certain that our descendants in the future will be acutely aware of the mind-body link."

LESLIE PARRISH-BACH—BUILDING A BRIDGE ACROSS FOREVER

With the publication of the runaway best-selling classic *Jonathan Livingston Seagull,* Richard Bach was propelled into fame and fortune. *Time* magazine featured him on its cover and called *Jonathan* ". . . perhaps the decade's top publishing miracle." In the ensuing years, other best-sellers followed as *Jonathan* was joined by *Illusions, There's No Such Place as Far Away,* and *The Bridge Across Forever.*

When Hollywood discovered Leslie Parrish, she was only nineteen. Her success as an actress was almost instantaneous as she starred in the loud and brassy musical, *Li'l Abner* (1959) and the powerful drama *The Manchurian Candidate* (1962) opposite Laurence Harvey and Frank

Sinatra. Gifted with both beauty and talent, Leslie became one of Hollywood's first women producers, and she also spent considerable time on political and social issues.

Leslie and Richard met while he was working on the screen production of *Jonathan Livingston Seagull* (1973). They fell in love, married, and have since collaborated on a book entitled *One,* which was released in 1988.

Our friend John Harricharan, the multitalented mystic, the author of *When You Can't Walk on Water, Take the Boat,* and a business consultant, not long ago asked Leslie what she considered the source of her intuitive and precognitive abilities.

"I think I'm finally beginning to allow, to recognize, an area of myself that I didn't like or want," she said. "My mother was very psychic when I was little. She knew many things before they happened. I got so frightened of that gift of hers, I surely didn't want to find it in myself. So I denied these insights for years and made a lot of bad choices because of that denial. Then I happened to meet this man, Richard Bach, who was very gifted in this way, too, and fascinated with psychic phenomena; and we talked about experiences that I'd had before I had ever heard about psychic experiments, such as spontaneous out-of-body experiences that I'd never mentioned to anyone until I met him.

"And he'd ask, 'How do you account for this, pragmatist?' And I didn't know. So we did some experimentation, and every time we did, we were amazed at the discoveries we made and how good we were at it."

Did Leslie think that anyone might be able to do these things if he or she practiced? "Absolutely. I've been a tough one to convince because I didn't welcome it. If it can get through to me, then it should certainly work for someone who is open to it. I think sometimes people try so hard to have psychic experiences that they use a conscious part of the mind when it seems the *unconscious* side is the part that excels at this. The things that happened to me seemed to come of their own accord—naturally. I'd say the best approach is to focus on something beautiful and open yourself to the possibilities."

The actress acknowledged that at the present time there was intense interest in the paranormal and spirituality. "It seems that humanity is ready to see another level of itself—a higher level," she said. "We feel that we're ready to open ourselves now to new emotional and psychic areas, and the result will be an emotional oneness. We see the birth of that today as walls of suspicion between peoples and nations are beginning to disappear, and we find love and friendship and joy in discovering one another at last.''

Harricharan wondered about Leslie's opinion of the current interest in channeling. ''Some aspects of channeling disturb us,'' she said. ''I feel that, in its best sense, we're using someone else to give us permission to affirm what we already know; and if that's what it takes to allow ourselves to recognize these perceptions or to pry them from the place we have hidden them, that's fine, but I think it is disappointing that some people become involved in search of spiritual insight and wind up, instead, involved in high finance. I think we should be wary of channels who urge us to buy more than a look at their ideas.''

What about crystals? Do they have a magic? Leslie replied that she and Richard had a beautiful crystal in their living room. ''It is from a dear friend, and we love it for its beauty and for the love of the friend who gave it to us; but aside from that, we don't see any magic in crystals other than the magic that we give to them ourselves.''

What does she think about astrology and other mystic arts? ''I was raised a Catholic, and I took from that system all that I felt was good, and I used it to grow,'' she said, ''but when it became a system for the limitation of my thought and my growth instead of a growth process, I left it and looked to other systems—astrology, various other religions, channels, all sorts of things.

''Now I feel that all of these systems—whether they are ancient religions or the methods that are developing in the New Age—are simply ways of focusing on our highest sense of right and allowing ourselves to see it. They give us permission to set time aside for inner exploration, to say, 'I'm going to assign an hour for church or twenty minutes for meditation or a weekend for a seminar.' We're using these methods to reach that part of us that knows more than we dream we know, and whatever it is—the cosmic dolphin or someone who claims to be the latest incarnation of God—if it elevates us, if it makes us see more clearly, if it makes us a kinder soul, if it makes us happier, then listen to it.''

The actress pointed out that sometimes disasters and misfortunes can become our teachers. ''I don't welcome these things, but if they come, there is something to be learned from them. Richard and I sometimes say, 'We knew better, but we did this anyway. Why did we do such a silly thing?' Then we find five years later that the 'silly thing' was a very small sample of what would have happened to us if we hadn't learned through that experience. It's as if we had this sample as an inoculation so we could develop antibodies. Five years later, we can say, 'We had a taste of that before, and we don't have to go through it again.' Thank goodness for that earlier 'disaster.' "

EARLYNE CHANEY—FROM STARLET TO SPIRITUAL LEADER

Early Cantrell, a young beauty from Texas, had a passion to succeed in the movies, and in 1942, she was well on her way. The distinguished actor Victor Jory had directed her in a little theater production of *The Philadelphia Story,* and he wrote letters of introduction for her so that she might conquer Hollywood by way of the Broadway stage.

She would have taken those letters to Broadway if her agent hadn't kept her so busy in the movies; and then, suddenly, there was the war effort, and Early felt it her duty to join the Women's Emergency Corps of Beverly Hills and to entertain the troops. It wasn't long before she was Honorary First Sergeant of Company C while participating in one war bond rally after another.

Next there were the movies in which she appeared with Shirley Temple, Edward G. Robinson, Merle Oberon, and Franchot Tone; others ranged from Boston Blackie detective thrillers to Jimmy Wakely Westerns to Shemp Howard comedies. She even had a handsome leading man offcamera in the person of Captain Marvin Moore of the Army Air Force.

Things could not have been going better for the young starlet. The captain's talk of marriage made her a little nervous, for as much as she loved him, she couldn't think of leaving her career. He would have to understand that Hollywood was her life, her breath, her very existence.

Then the war was over. She asked to go home to Texas to visit her family before she gave Marvin her final answer concerning his marriage plans. Early was twenty-eight, certainly old enough to get married if she wished. She just wanted to be absolutely certain.

On Halloween 1945, however, the terrible telegram negated everything. Captain Marvin Moore was killed that afternoon in an airplane crash. "The captain's death caused me such grief that I could not eat," Earlyne said. "I went nine days without food. I think on the subconscious level I wanted to starve myself to death and join him in a natural passing."

After she perceived the captain's spirit and began to communicate with his essence on the Other Side, the rising Hollywood starlet realized that her true mission in having come to earth was to share with others the answer of what happens after physical death.

"Acting had been my all-consuming desire," she said, "but then the Holy Spirit touched my soul and I was baptized in a different kind of realization. I could no longer continue with acting. I knew that I must fulfill my true mission on Earth. I left acting and began a serious study of metaphysics, yoga, and the philosophies of various spiritual teachers."

Her quest eventually brought her to Robert Chaney, the Spiritualist minister who in 1947 would become her life partner and in 1951 her partner in the founding of Astara, their "Mystical United Nations of the World Religions."

Although Astara, located in Upland, California, is oriented to mystical Christianity, it accepts and teaches all religions as beneficial to humankind. Other concepts and practices of the center include:

- A school of the Ancient Mysteries, offering a compendium of the esoteric teachings of all ages.
- A fraternity of all philosophies, coordinating many viewpoints of humankind and the interacting inner structures that unite us as one in the infinite.
- An institute of psychic research with special attention devoted to spiritual healing of physical, emotional, and mental aspects and to life before and after physical incarnation.

Earlyne said that she had always been aware of a Great Presence, even when she was very little. "When I would sit in our old barn on the sacks of feed, I would be aware of spiritual guidance. I was twelve when I saw the master for the first time. He said that someone's death would point the way that I should follow. He must have been preparing me even then for the captain's death."

She has also had visions of ancient Egypt haunt her since she was very young. Some years ago, when she visited the fabled land of mystery, she underwent a mystical experience in the Great Pyramid.

"Angelic voices sang out, 'Welcome back,' and I was taken through an initiation process by the Great Mother Isis, who became the Blessed Mother Mary," Earlyne said. "It was given to me at that time that I should conduct a rosary campaign for non-Roman Catholics."

She regularly leads mystical tours to the various global power places. In each one of these sacred areas, she plants a crystal, forming a holy grid work from one power spot to another. "Our prayers and meditations may thus begin to restore this old lump-of-coal planet into the diamond plant that she is supposed to be."

It was the Blessed Mother's influence that has been responsible for the resurgence of the spirit of peace in the world, she said. "She has crumbled the Berlin Wall. Remember the Fatima prophecy in which the Blessed Mother promised to convert Russia away from godless communism? Now we have Gorbachev visiting the Pope. Russia may create a new church that will combine the old with the new," she said. "We know that Soviet scientists have made many exciting advances in psychical research. They might combine 'psi' with the church and emerge with a New Age Christianity that lifts itself away from the old dogmas. It is very important in the days to come that we give God alone the credit and the glory. The Blessed Mother's prayers, blended with our prayers, are breaking down barrier after barrier. We must now see that organized religion strives for a higher level of consciousness."

What of the great catastrophes that some visionaries foresee in this time of great transition and change?

"Regretfully," Earlyne said, "most of the Earth changes, the great catastrophes, have already been set in motion, and they must be played out. Some can be negated with prayer, and Legions of Great Ones from the Other Side are working to assist us as we come to the end of a great cosmic age."

Is she one of those who envision Southern California falling into the Pacific Ocean during these end times? "Oh, no," she said. "This is too precious a place. Southern California is marked for greatness. There should have been a great pyramid built here, for it is as powerful a spiritual center as the Great Pyramid near Cairo."

Earlyne told us that although a great many motion pictures had been influenced by dark forces seeking to demean humankind, she was optimistic that producers and directors who channel the light will prevail. "Movies, such as those made by Steven Spielberg and George Lucas, will help to turn the tide against the Darkness. Hollywood and Southern California are the centers of a downpouring of spiritual energy of a delphic, precognitive nature, such as that in the ancient city of Delphos. Now how this energy, this spiritual essence, is used depends upon the receiver. It can be used for the highest forms of enlightenment or it can be debased and utilized to produce products of extreme negativity.

"I believe," Earlyne said, "that Southern California and Hollywood can accomplish a marvelous transformation of whatever evil and negativity they might have previously produced. They have the ability to transform the effects of darkness into things of great beauty, and when they do that, they will be under the protection of the hierarchy."

USING HOLLYWOOD'S MAGIC LANTERN TO PIERCE THE DARKNESS

Kevin Ryerson is not only one of the most well-known psychic channels in the world today, he is also a movie buff. He is especially pleased that a growing number of Hollywood stars, writers, directors, and producers seem to be serious about finding their cinematic souls.

Ryerson told us that the movie that he feels best represents what it is truly like to have psychic or spiritual gifts is *Resurrection* (1980) with Ellen Burstyn and Sam Shepard. Ellen, who was the courageous mother combating demon possession in *The Exorcist* (1973), this time brilliantly portrayed a woman who returns to life from a near-death experience and is gifted with incredible healing powers.

"*Resurrection* deals very accurately with a person who suddenly has a spontaneous gift," Ryerson said. "The film shows that we must deal with such people compassionately. The film also shows that our fundamental religious institutions have a very low tolerance of these kinds of things. In *Resurrection,* we see clearly that it is neither science nor religion that benefits the person but compassion, spiritual values, and friendship. I think that it is a very highly evolved movie."

Kevin also gave his approval to *Field of Dreams* (1989) with Kevin

Costner, Amy Madigan, and James Earl Jones. "Here is a person [Costner], an Iowa farmer, following his inner voice. The film shows us what interconnectedness we all have. It shows how personalities, even ones as controversial as Shoeless Joe Jackson, can be healed if we just learn to have more compassion and understanding for the actions of others. *Field of Dreams* demonstrates how past personalities can have both a psychological and a spiritual impact on us, and I think it also shows the subtle influences that psychic forces have on, and in, peoples' lives. It portrays the heroic quality of those forces."

Ryerson offers accolades for *Testament* (1983), with Jane Alexander, a motion picture that he feels very strongly impacted society in a positive way. The film grimly portrayed the struggle for survival in a small town after a nuclear holocaust.

"It is the only movie originally made for television that crossed over and became a major cinematic event," he said. "This film probably had the single greatest impact on nuclear disarmament of any message that has ever been created. Many sociologists say that the great demand for nuclear disarmament and the pressure that was put on Washington all came out of seeing that film. Think of it! All of it was written from one single comprehensive dream that the writer had. So that, if you will, is an example of a powerful film that came from a paranormal source. It was awesome in its subtleness, but it was relentless in its impact. Think of it! Every single word of dialogue, every single scene came from one person's dream. Now *that's* lucid dreaming!"

Yes, Hollywood can become an incredibly focused power for social change and the elevation of mass consciousness; but, as Ryerson observed, the "whirlwind pace and the pressure of keeping up an image all add to the fur-lined trap that ensnares so many stars who get lost and can't find their way back to what is real. If only the age-old truth 'For what is a man profited, if he shall gain the whole world, and lose his own soul!' [Matthew 16:26] was up on the Hollywood hill in neon!"

At the same time, Ryerson shared our enthusiasm about the many stars of Hollywood who have begun to use the platform of their stardom to accomplish more than personal glory.

"It is so wonderful," he said, "that a number of stars are being honest, telling the truth, talking about who they 'really' are. They are giving expression to the spiritual reality that this stage of life may be just one stop on the way to someplace better—or someplace worse—depending on how we handle our true 'role,' our real role—ourselves.''

Rising Above "Mommie Dearest"

Accepting the responsibility of playing our true role in life may sometimes require great courage. People were very angry with Christina Crawford when her book *Mommie Dearest* was published. Legions of film fans did not wish to hear that one of Hollywood's greatest stars could possibly have behaved in the manner described by her own daughter. Decades of moviegoers wanted to cherish their image of Joan Crawford as the glamorous woman who stood strong against all odds. None of them wanted an idol that had been scheming, manipulative, sexually permissive, irrational, and cruel to her children.

"I simply did not anticipate the negative reaction to my book," Christina said. "I thought people would be more understanding of the tragedy that had affected both my mother and myself." Eventually, she said, the tide turned, and *Mommie Dearest* was picked up by the media as a serious work that dealt with a serious problem, that of child abuse.

"The situation in the United States is so shocking," Christina said. "We now have two million children a year who are reported as abused. One out of every ten live births in the United States is affected by either drugs or alcohol. We are creating a different class of persons . . . persons whose childhood experiences have permanently damaged them."

Christina was disappointed with the film version of her book. "I felt the producers made a giant mistake by changing the point of view of the story. It was written from the point of view of a child who was vulnerable and helpless. I had hoped the film would be experiential and nonlinear, experiencing life as children do. I wanted it to tap into everyone's childhood experiences—whether or not they had ever had any kind of chaos or violence in their lives."

She told us that she had explored her possible karmic connection with her mother during a Bushido seminar conducted by Dick Sutphen. "It became clear to me that we went back a very, very long time, but it wasn't altogether the two of us. It was only partly that."

Christina said that when she went away to college, someone gave her a book on reincarnation. "It was the very first time that anything ever made sense out of the chaos of my life. That book actually saved my life. I didn't understand it thoroughly—and there weren't a lot of people in the fifties to talk to about such topics—but the organizing principle of the book literally saved my life. The theory of reincarnation made what had seemed to be senseless behavior fit into some sort of philosophical schema—so even if I didn't understand it, I understood it! The one thing that I especially apprehended was that I was going to get through this once and for all—because I don't *ever* want to go through this again! No second time around on this one!''

She said that the only thing that had kept her going as a child was her deep belief that some kind of spirit was guiding her. There was nothing else that would have induced her to continue living. She told us that several times as a teenager she had tried to commit suicide. ''I've had many brushes with death, both at my own hands, my mother's hands, and at the hands of the universe. It is quite clear to me that I am on some kind of a 'cleanup' life. I just have to keep the life spirit in me strong enough to keep it up.''

Christina did go into show business, at first in an effort to please her mother and then to fulfill herself. For two years, she starred in a leading role in the daytime series ''Secret Storm''; she appeared in a film directed by John Cassavetes and in another starring Elvis Presley when she was under contract with Twentieth Century–Fox. She also guested on numerous prime-time network television shows and did national television commercials.

Then, in 1981, she suffered a stroke that nearly killed her. ''I was completely paralyzed on the right side. I was unable to talk or read or write. It took many years for me to recover my health and my physical abilities, but this was an absolute major transition in my life. I am as certain as I am talking to you right now that I died. I was quite happy to have died. I was exhausted by my life and by the struggles and by the anger and the unending chaos.

''I was almost dead when they operated on me. I had already said good-bye to my husband and to a few people who were with me. So when I had this near-death experience—where I thought I had died—I was so happy to be finally released from all the pain of my life. I went to a place of peace, a place of love and caring. It was the exact opposite of the struggle, the chaos, and the violence of my life. This was what I had been looking for.

"Then somebody said something to me. I had this experience of an incredible fall—sort of like zooming through space. I opened my eyes, and I saw a masked face and somebody talking to me. I was put into intensive care, and I realized, somehow, that I was alive. Since I had been certain that I had died, I was completely disoriented for quite a long time. But I can assure you of this: I have never been the same since."

Because she could not talk or move and was completely cocooned in her body, Christina continued to feel absolutely no connection to the earth, to her body, to anything. She truly felt as if she were in limbo. "I had to reconnect myself," she said. "During that time I realized that there had to be only one concern in my life and that was to find the connection with spirit and to maintain it first and foremost at all costs."

When Christina got well, she served for three years as the commissioner of children's services for the County of Los Angeles. She served for seven years as president and chairperson of a major Los Angeles charity that seeks to assist abusive families and their children in getting proper treatment. She helped to raise more than a million dollars for family treatment centers.

In 1985, she founded Survivors Network, a nonprofit national organization that provides resource referral and research to adults who were abused as children. She is an honorary board member of the National Committee for Child Abuse Prevention and of Family Outreach of America.

Christina Crawford found her connection to Spirit, and she has focused that powerful energy into a force for good that is every day providing comfort and strength to those who had come to believe that for them there could only be pain and helplessness. She is helping victims to become victors.

Darkness has always brought us the supernatural, but as we have seen throughout the pages of this book, Hollywood's magic lantern and the indomitable spirit of those stars who care have an inexhaustible potential to pierce the darkness and bring us the light.

DIRECTORY OF MEDIUMS, CHANNELS, AND PSYCHICS

Many of the sensitives, channels, and psychical researchers mentioned in this book are available for private consultations. Others provide additional information for those who may be interested in their work.

Paul Andrews, Whole Life Productions, 432 Culver Boulevard, Playa Del Rey, CA 90293; 213-305-0064.

Dr. Maxine Asher, Ancient Mediterranean Research Association, P.O. Box 49421, Los Angeles, CA 90049.

Clarisa Bernhardt, c/o 203-365 Hargrave Street, Winnipeg, Manitoba R3B 2K3, Canada; Los Angeles answering service: 818-906-6767.

Edgar Cayce's channelings are referenced and distributed by the Association for Research and Enlightenment, Inc., P.O. Box 595, Virginia Beach, VA 23451.

Dr. Earlyne Chaney, Astara, P.O. Box 5003, Upland, CA 91785; 714-981-4941.

Dr. Patricia Rochelle Diegel, 2675 West Highway 89-A, Suite 333, Sedona, AZ 86336; 602-282-1316.

Angela Louise Gallo, 6641 Gloria Avenue, Van Nuys, CA 91406; 818-989-6042.

John Harricharan, 404-971-4526.

Dr. Stephen Kaplan, Parapsychology Institute of America, P.O. Box 252, Elmhurst, NY 11373; 718-894-6564.

Kenny Kingston, 4567 Willis, Suite 207, Sherman Oaks, CA 91403; 818-995-3003.

J. Z. Knight, 14507 Yelm Highway SE, Yelm, WA 98597.

Molli Nickell, Spirit Speaks, P.O. Box 84304, Los Angeles, CA 90073; 213-820-1260.

Frank R. ("Nick") Nocerino, Institute of Psychic and Hypnotic Sciences, P.O. Box 302, Pinole, CA 94564; 415-724-6603.

Ry Redd, Research Cooperative, P.O. Box 3130, Scottsdale, AZ 85271; 602-482-0907.

Kevin Ryerson, 1055 West College Avenue, Suite 320, Santa Rosa, CA 95401; 707-579-5572.

Dick Sutphen, Valley of the Sun Publishing, P.O. Box 38, Malibu, CA 90265; 818-889-1575.

Alan Vaughan, Mind Technology Systems, 3015 Glendale Boulevard, Suite 600, Los Angeles, CA 90039; 213-666-7243.

ABOUT THE AUTHORS

SHERRY HANSEN-STEIGER'S extensive background includes such varied pursuits as nursing, theology, counseling, and the media. A former counselor at the State University of New York on Long Island, and Smith Haven Ministries, Sherry is a licensed, ordained Protestant minister and a former staff member at the Lutheran School of Theology in Chicago.

In the 1960s, she cocreated and produced the highly acclaimed Celebrate Life multimedia awareness program, which was performed around the country for colleges, businesses, organizations, and churches. In the early 1970s, she founded one of the first schools for holistic education, as well as serving on the boards of directors for others. She has conducted stress management and family crisis counseling seminars and has been the keynote speaker for many national corporations and governmental groups, such as the Oklahoma Oil Marketing Association, the State Board of Education for New Jersey, the U.S. Naval Officers, and the Office of Family Education with the Department of Health, Education and Welfare.

Experienced in many aspects of the media as well, Sherry is a former magazine editor, advertising agency director, model, actress, and motion picture producer. As a model, she has appeared in such publications as *Family Circle, Redbook,* and *Woman's Day.* She has also written more than one thousand radio, television, and print ads and commercials, some of which she also directed. In 1979, Sherry appeared in the highly rated television movie *Amusement Park,* with Mike Connors, Louis Gossett, Jr., Beau Bridges, and Martin Landau. More recently she appeared in *Desert Rats,* directed by *The Wonder Years'* Ken Topolsky, and *The Highway Man,* starring Sam Jones.

Sherry's interest and knowledge of the UFO field greatly expanded when she served as Dr. J. Allen Hynek's personal manager and director of publicity until the time of his death in 1986. Her work and research are featured in Brad Steiger's *Exploring the Power Within, The Healing Power of Love, The UFO Abductors,* and *The Fellowship.* She is the author of *Seasons of the Soul* and coauthor of *The Teaching Power of Dreams*. Sherry's works in progress include *Starborn* and *The Shaman's Path to Inner Wisdom*, both coauthored with Brad.

Together, Brad and Sherry research, lecture, and conduct tours and workshops worldwide.

BRAD STEIGER is the author of more than one hundred books, ranging from biographies *(Valentino; Judy Garland; Jim Thorpe)* to the inspirational *(Revelation: The Divine Fire; The Healing Power of Love)* to the unexplained *(Mysteries of Time and Space; Atlantis Rising)*; from Native American belief structures *(Indian Medicine Power and Kahuna Magic)* to UFO research *(Gods of Aquarius, Project Bluebook, Strangers from the Skies)*.

Steiger is considered one of the world's leading authorities and a most respected author in the field of psychical research. Having taught literature and creative writing both on the secondary and college levels, some of the books that he has authored have been used as texts or supplementary reading in college courses and adult study groups. Steiger's biographical achievements were featured in *Outstanding Young Men of America, The Creative and Successful Personalities of the World,* Great Britain's international selection of *The Two Thousand Men of Achievement,* and *The Dictionary of International Biography.*

In addition to lecturing and conducting workshops for church groups, college and high school seminars, and a wide variety of organizations, Brad's syndicated newspaper column, ''The Strange World of Brad Steiger,'' had an international readership of more than five million. Science Research Associates adapted a number of his works for elementary schools across the United States.

In 1977, his *Valentino* was made into a motion picture by British director Ken Russell, starring Rudolf Nureyev and Michelle Phillips. In the next year, *Unknown Powers,* coscripted by Brad and narrated by Jack Palance, won the Film Advisory Board's Award of Excellence. His recent releases include two novels, *The Hypnotist* and *The Chindi.*